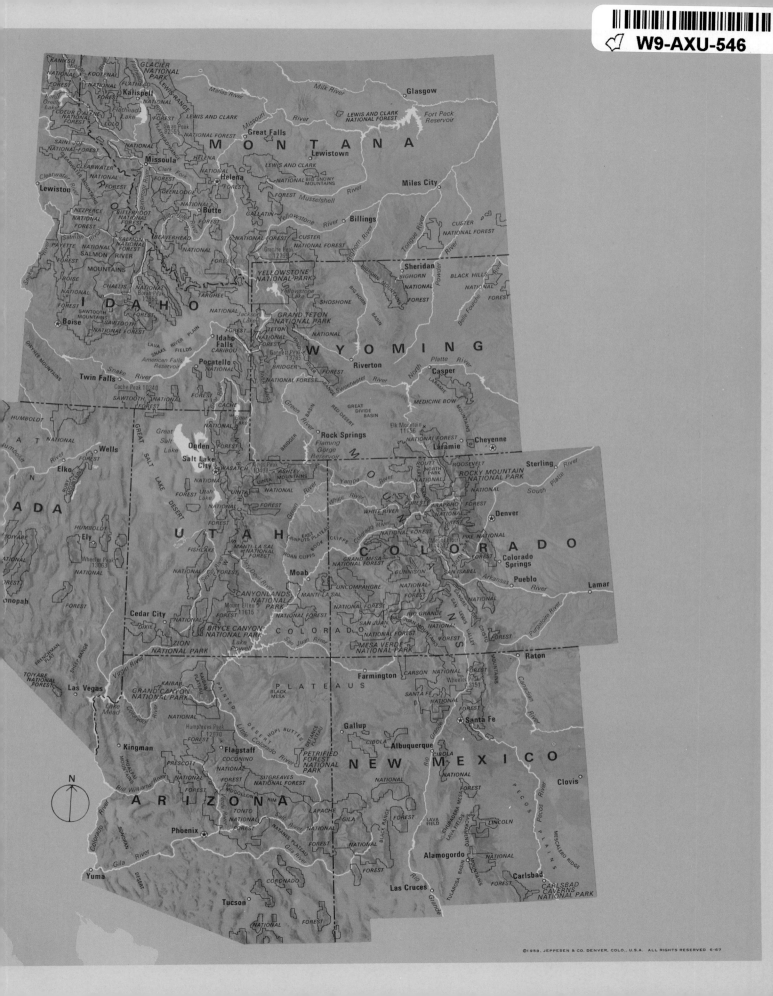

The Mountain States

TIME-LIFE Library of America

The Mountain States

Arizona Colorado Idaho
Montana Nevada New Mexico
Utah Wyoming

By Marshall Sprague
and the Editors of
TIME-LIFE BOOKS

TIME-LIFE BOOKS, New York

The Author: Marshall Sprague, an Ohioan by birth, graduated from Princeton in 1930 and thereafter worked as a newspaper reporter in Tientsin, China, and in Paris before joining *The New York Times* as a feature writer in 1936. In 1941 ill health sent him to the dry climate of Colorado Springs, Colorado, for what was to be a short stay; he has been an enthusiastic resident ever since. Mr. Sprague has found in the rich history of the mountain region a wealth of material for numerous magazine articles and books. Among his published works are *Money Mountain, The Story of Cripple Creek Gold; Massacre, The Tragedy at White River; The Great Gates, The Story of the Rocky Mountain Passes;* and *A Gallery of Dudes,* a book about some of the more colorful early visitors to the Mountain States.

The Consulting Editor: Oscar Handlin, Charles Warren Professor of American History at Harvard University and director of the university's Charles Warren Center for Studies in American History, is one of America's foremost social historians. His work on U.S. immigrants, *The Uprooted,* won the Pulitzer Prize in 1952.

Mountain States Consultant: Ray Allen Billington, Senior Research Associate at the Huntington Library in San Marino, California, is an outstanding authority on American history. His many books include *Westward Expansion, The Far Western Frontier, 1830-1860* and *America's Frontier Heritage.*

The Cover: Snow-capped even in late summer, the San Juan Range looms above a fertile valley in southwestern Colorado. The dominant peak, at right, is Mt. Sneffels.

TIME-LIFE BOOKS

Editor
Maitland A. Edey
Executive Editor
Jerry Korn
Text Director   **Art Director**
Martin Mann   Sheldon Cotler
Chief of Research
Beatrice T. Dobie
Picture Editor
Robert G. Mason
Assistant Text Directors:
Harold C. Field, Ogden Tanner
Assistant Art Director:
Arnold C. Holeywell
Assistant Chief of Research:
Martha Turner

Publisher
Rhett Austell
General Manager: Joseph C. Hazen Jr.
Planning Director: John P. Sousa III
Circulation Director: Joan D. Manley
Marketing Director: Carter Smith
Business Manager: John D. McSweeney
Publishing Board: Nicholas Benton,
Louis Bronzo, James Wendell Forbes

TIME-LIFE Library of America

Series Editor: Oliver E. Allen
Editorial Staff for *The Mountain States:*
Assistant Editor: Jay Brennan
Picture Editor: Sheila Osmundsen
Designer: John Newcomb
Assistant Designer: Jean Lindsay
Staff Writers: Peter Chaitin, Tony Chiu,
Jonathan Kastner, Frank Kendig,
Victor Waldrop, Peter Wood
Chief Researcher: Clara E. Nicolai
Text Research: Ruth Silva, Don Nelson, Evelyn Hauptman
Picture Research: Rhea Finkelstein, Toby Solovioff,
Marcia Gillespie, Margo Dryden
Art Assistant: Mervyn Clay

Editorial Production
Color Director: Robert L. Young
Assistant: James J. Cox
Copy Staff: Marian Gordon Goldman,
Patricia Miller, Florence Keith
Picture Department: Dolores A. Littles,
Marquita Jones
Traffic: Douglas B. Graham
Studio: Patricia Byrne, Jean Held

The text chapters of this book were written by Marshall Sprague, the picture essays by the editorial staff. Valuable aid was provided by these individuals and departments of Time Inc.: LIFE staff photographers Ralph Crane, Eliot Elisofon and Carl Mydans; the Chief of the LIFE Picture Library, Doris O'Neil; the Chief of the Bureau of Editorial Reference, Peter Draz; the Chief of the TIME-LIFE News Service, Richard M. Clurman; Correspondents Barron Beshoar and Charlotte Trego (Denver), Mayo Mohs (Los Angeles), Roy Gibson (Salt Lake City), Robert Campbell (Tucson) and William James (Great Falls).

Contents

Introduction

The Rocky Mountain West, I believe it has been said if in paraphrase, is a state of mind. I may have said so myself, drawing on some declaration dimly remembered.

In any case the statement is wrong. My West, as I call it out of an equation of affection with ownership, induces a state of mind.

The inducement is space. Even from burgeoning cities like Denver and Salt Lake, not to mention other and lesser and sometimes unfortunate flowerings, a man can get away. He can be by himself. He can be lonely.

But not lonely as in the great cities of the Eastern and Western shores and Great Lakes. There a man is pushed in on himself, made prisoner of steel and stone, cast adrift or islanded in human streams of no purpose. There, even though he may not be aware of it, he lives Thoreau's life of quiet desperation.

At best, after his day in the architectural canyons, he may commute and find fugitive relief with friends and family. He may have his own swimming pool, safely chlorinated as are those of his neighbors who call hello across the private fences. Possibly he has a rock garden or flower bed arranged to give dimension to his diminishment. In his immaculate retreat he breathes a little less of the maculate breath of progress and calls it fresh.

I have tasted this man's riches and am glad to have my own; and I take it on me to speak for others in my uncrowded West.

Space, the space I am speaking of, presupposes nature but not the nature of the atom cleaver or the astronaut. The nature I mean is the seen and unknown firmament, the stars like bonfires in the night, the unhappily beleaguered moon, the ground I stand on and the sky I look at and the life that inhabits earth and air.

Without these wonderments what is self? By what diet does it live or wish to? Where is full subsistence? I am glad, seeing clear, to recognize my old friend, the man in the moon, glad to smell a wild rose, to see grass waving to a rodent's flight, to hear the torn air of a bird's wing. Given the comradeship of space and nature, where's the man but does not feel uplifted, to use a preacherish but altogether right word here? A rugged mountain range, a sleeping mountain meadow, a plain that dishes up to the skyline, a desert that runs dizzy—by their size and permanence these make the viewer feel unimportant but important, too. Small though he is, he is a present part of his big world. He doesn't breathe, he drinks, the pristine air. Unafraid of typhoid or whatever, he bellies down and sucks from a stream that sheens a stone.

In this world the animals he sees become his kin, as indeed they are. It does not matter whether, instead of only gazing as I do, he goes after them with hook and shell. They are still of one blood, as man is man though he kills his own.

Some years ago I bought a place on the eastern apron of the Rocky Mountains in Montana. I call it small because its material worth is small, disproportionate to its eight hundred acres and two lakes, yet it is so valuable to me as to be beyond assessment.

I chose Montana because I knew it best. Here I grew up. Here I fished and hunted and worked summertimes on ranches or in the national forests. Here I identified flowers and trees and came to know the birds and beasts. Here, in space, I learned awe. Yet, but for those remembered times, another Rocky Mountain state would have served me as well, I think.

In my mountain cabin, as years and memories mingle and lines that I have written dodge in my head again, I sit and watch, alone but not alone. The mountain gopher, grown to incredible size as a consequence of my largess, is out early, his paws delicate on the melon rind presented to his greedy mouth. A chipmunk flirts out of the woodpile and runs for cover as a magpie lowers flaps. A raven, unconcerned with nevermore, wings down, and I wonder as he gobbles up my garbage whether ever before I knew what ravenous was or whence it came. Just as I wondered earlier, without wanting to establish the fact, whether snakes heard through their tongues. One appeared to, a bull snake, its tongue blocked by a half-swallowed mouse. It was unaware of me, though I approached within a foot. Then, abruptly, the engorgement completed, the tongue speared out, and at the little crackle of a blade of grass the snake fled.

The Clark's nutcrackers are making a racket in the trees around the lakes, and from the aspen depths come the repeated see-see-seeeesees of white-crowned sparrows and the lonesome calls of mated doves. On the knoll beyond my fence a grouse hen walks patrol for her unruly brood.

The great horned owl will fly his hunger quest tonight, and then or earlier a doe and fawn may make a call. Last year's black beggar bear seems to have given up my garbage in favor of more plenteous fare.

As I sit and heed, I am aware, without looking at it always, of the eternal thrust of Ear Mountain four miles away. It is softly shadowed now.

The place is all mine, and it belongs to the Rocky Mountain West. Elsewhere in this vast width and reach of common property, men are doing as I do. Always they watch, even if the immediate hope is for a good trout hole or a buck's antlers through the pines. They see and sense heights, depths, distances that they have feelings but no words for. The good loneliness soaks in.

Rhapsodies as well as generalizations are rightly suspect. Enter in the record, then, a generalization discordant with the rhapsody. We are a parochial people. Thousands of us are beyond daily reach of a daily newspaper. The dailies other thousands daily get, though often good, are mostly small and hence limited in coverage. Despite magazines, despite radio and despite television, which is not everywhere available, we have in our bones the not-unwelcome ache of isolation.

Parochials all, we are torn within our parish. Though sometimes troubled by the likelihood of losing basic values, thousands of pushers push for unneeded dams, for acres on acres of freeway regardless of cost or necessity, for industrialization—in a word, for development. Just as many thousands are convinced, along with me, that the only thing we have to fear is progress. As we are split here, so are we split politically. Right and left exist, with empty ground between, and both can prove infallibility by reference to common sense and other unbiased sources.

Insert in the record also that here and there and too often we have fouled our habitat. We have our pockets of pollution, our dirty air, our damaged and dead streams, our ravished resources. Lay part of the blame on the lingering spirit of the frontiersman who could not imagine the exhaustion of the riches he found. God had put the soil and the trees and minerals there to be plowed, felled and mined, and more of the same lay over the hill. Lay part of it to a belief in the physical right of the individual to do as he would with what he controlled, no matter the social cost. Later on that belief would individualize the corporation. But whatever our sins, much is left, and for much that is left we owe thanks to outsiders. No one makes a better conservationist than one from a region already ravaged.

It would be foolish to argue for the myth of the Garden and the Sturdy Yeoman. The myth, embraced for generations and still seductive, made much of the unsettled West a garden in which the venturesome and diligent would reap righteousness. From soil, soul. From grandeur, grandeur. From garden, a stout, deserving breed of man, proud of probity and self-sufficient. The Sturdy Yeoman: you find him yet sometimes in the equation of the nobility of mountains with the promotion of nobility in men. But the bright belief was and is a myth. No more than vitamins does nature nurture supermen.

Nevertheless, here in the Mountain West, space and nature shape us. Despite our differences, we are made a hopeful people, as the mountain men and the overland travelers and just yesterday's homesteaders were hopeful. As the gold-seeker and the mining magnates and the cattle kings were hopeful. Not always honest, mind you, not always capable or wise or successful, but almost always hopeful and hence astride of life. Call us exuberant. Call us carefree. We qualify at least by comparison.

In his short but inclusive and excellent book on the Mountain West, Marshall Sprague has caught the spirit I have at best touched on. He has information to support him, in such volume and detail as I have not. When he generalizes, he is wont to generalize from fact, whereas I speak mostly from impression.

Yet we hit the same note. The Rocky Mountain West exists for both of us—as it exists, perhaps not half-defined but surely felt, for thousands of our fellows.

—A. B. GUTHRIE JR.
Novelist

1

A Country
for Singing

Let us begin with the Joe Browns, typical Westerners from Salida, Colorado, or perhaps Thermopolis, Wyoming, or Prescott, Arizona, or Silver City, New Mexico, or Ely, Nevada. The Browns are driving home after visiting in the East—which they left some years back because they couldn't stand the crowds any longer, and the traffic and the humidity and the pressure of life and so on. They are glad to have the crowds behind them now and to be past such typical Midwestern sights as corn and redbirds as their car crosses the line into Colorado, where the Mountain States begin. It is too high and dry for much corn at 4,000 feet above sea level, and redbirds are rare west of the Kansas-Colorado border.

The air of late summer is tenderly crisp and cool but so thin and responsive to temperature changes that the Browns feel it warming up on their cheeks. The High Plains—soil from the Rockies washed eastward through eons of time—have been pretty flat over the last couple of hundred miles that the Browns have driven, but now the plains are starting to roll a little and bits of rimrock show here and

After a wearying climb, mountaineers ski down Skillet Glacier on the 12,594-foot-high Mount Moran in Wyoming's Teton Range. Though the Tetons attract many skiers, Moran is rarely attempted, for snow often blocks access to its base, and its slopes have no lifts.

there. The plains will meet the Front Range of the Rockies in another 150 miles, near Denver and Colorado Springs. The atmosphere has a stunning clarity and the sky is azure, whitening at the horizon. Joe Brown can see the white-concrete grain elevators of Burlington, Colorado, a dozen miles ahead, looking like giant cocktail shakers. A big magpie flops along beside the car, and a jack rabbit starts up and away with a coyote after it.

Joe stops the car, strips some silvery fuzz from a sage bush by the road and takes a whiff of the stuff. The sage that grows everywhere in the Mountain West has more than a delightful smell. It has the effect of a tonic, a promise of good health and youth eternal, a spurt of the optimism that gushes in the Rockies like the geysers of Yellowstone Park. Joe gazes at the gray-green emptiness to the west, where Longs Peak and Pikes Peak ought to be, and finds it friendly and reassuring. He hums a cowboy tune as though the mountains ahead made him feel like singing. Then he tells Mrs. Brown that it is good to be back in God's country.

Of course, everybody's country is God's country. But no other Americans seem quite so full of rapture for their place as the eight million inhabitants of the eight Mountain States. Both the natives and the newcomers tend to look down on the horrid rest of

The Mountain States' water deficit

The Mountain States *(outlined in white on the map below)* are the most arid region in the U.S. While the rest of the country (not counting Alaska and Hawaii) gets about 30 inches of precipitation a year, the Mountain States get only 14 inches. Only in a few portions of the region *(light brown areas)* does the average annual precipitation exceed water loss due to evaporation and the transpiration of plants, i.e., the moisture given off by leaves. Elsewhere there is a deficit. Though in many areas *(gold)* there is almost a balance, others have a daily deficit ranging from one to two million gallons per square mile *(tan)*; in a few places *(lavender)* the loss is even greater.

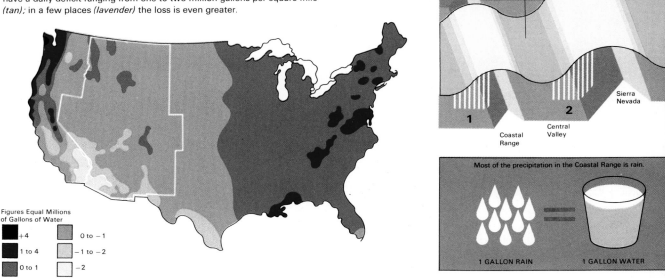

Figures Equal Millions
of Gallons of Water

+4   0 to −1
1 to 4   −1 to −2
0 to 1   −2

PACIFIC AIR MASS

1   2

Coastal Range   Central Valley   Sierra Nevada

Most of the precipitation in the Coastal Range is rain.

1 GALLON RAIN   1 GALLON WATER

the world with mild surprise at its survival. And Mountain States people are sensitive to criticism. If a tourist complains in the Billings (Montana) *Gazette* or the Twin Falls (Idaho) *Times-News* or the Durango (Colorado) *Herald* that the mountain roads are scary or that motel prices are outrageous or that the girls in the rodeo parades look silly in cowboy hats, the letters columns are full of rebuttals for several days.

Westerners who read history cannot forgive Lieutenant Zebulon Pike and Major Stephen Long, the explorers, or antiexpansionist Congressmen of the 1840s, for nasty remarks they made a century and more ago. Lieutenant Pike found no opportunities for developing the Mountain West. Major Long called the plains part of the region the "Great American Desert." The antiexpansionists seemed to regard the whole of it as a barren waste of prairie dogs, cactus and shifting sands, incapable of producing anything and therefore not worth retaining.

The May 1957 *Harper's* magazine contained an article by the historian Walter Prescott Webb entitled "The American West: A Perpetual Mirage." A map with the article showed the eight Mountain States and was labeled "Desert States the Heart of the West." Though Dr. Webb was merely elaborating on what Pike, Long and others had said,

the mountaineers rose as a body in passionate protest. Some of their rage may have derived from the fact that Dr. Webb was a Texan, and Texans are suspected of plotting to buy up the Rockies for a Texas colony.

But mostly the protesters went gunning for Dr. Webb because his article implied that their paradise was by no means the Garden of Eden they claimed it to be. A Denver *Post* editorial ("Us Desert Rats Is Doing Okay") warned him that "you better take off your glasses and your Ph.D. You've picked yourself a fight . . . You were determined to write something about the mountain states. So you decide to turn economist and geographer and impose on the editors of Harper's your own version of that hoary, old canard that the west is nothing but one vast desert, fit for neither man nor beast. Whatsthematter, doc? You got dyspepsia? Did you get taken in one of those Las Vegas crap games?"

Lately, water crises in the mountains have brought Dr. Webb's critics somewhat around to his point of view. They will admit in private, if not in Chamber of Commerce brochures, that their land is awfully dry in too many places. But it is still God's country, to them, a heck of a big country, a *big-sky* country, a high, wide and handsome country. The bigness is not debatable. The Mountain States

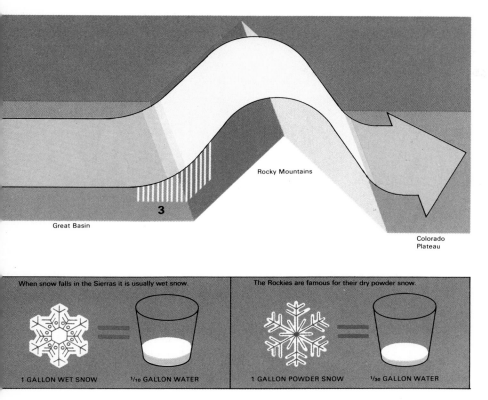

Great Basin

Rocky Mountains

3

Colorado Plateau

When snow falls in the Sierras it is usually wet snow.

1 GALLON WET SNOW   1/10 GALLON WATER

The Rockies are famous for their dry powder snow.

1 GALLON POWDER SNOW   1/30 GALLON WATER

The unusual characteristics of the precipitation falling on the Mountain States can be explained partly by what happens to moisture that comes to the area from the Pacific Ocean. Evaporated from the Pacific, this moisture is carried eastward by warm air masses. When this moisture-laden air reaches the western slopes of the 3,000-to-5,000-foot Coastal Range (1) it is forced upward. The air cools as it rises and heavy precipitation results. As the air drops over the Central Valley of California it is warmed slightly, then is shunted upward once more by the Sierra Nevada (2). Again the air cools and rain and wet snow fall on the western slopes. As shown at bottom center, one gallon of this wet snow produces far less water than rain does. The air masses, now drained of much of their moisture, then pass over the Great Basin where they are reheated. Finally, forced upward by the towering Rockies (3), the air cools again and light rain or, in winter, great quantities of dry, powdered snow fall. Though excellent for skiing, a gallon of this dry snow melts to form only 1/30 of a gallon of water.

occupy nearly 30 per cent of the area of the 48 states that lie between the Atlantic and the Pacific. The largest of the eight is Montana, with 147,138 square miles. Japan, a great nation, has only 140,680 square miles. The smallest of the Mountain States is Idaho, 83,577 square miles—more than twice as big as Scotland.

All together, the eight states cover 864,000 square miles. That makes them larger than the combined area of France, Spain, Italy, the Netherlands, Switzerland, Portugal, both Germanys, Belgium, Austria and Yugoslavia, plus Liechtenstein and Luxembourg. The size of a place is of course measured on a horizontal plane, as though mountains and valleys and canyons did not exist. Years ago, when Texas Governor Allan Shivers boasted that Colorado was less than half as big as Texas, Colorado's Governor, Dan Thornton, replied, "Take another look, partner. When you lay our mountains out flat with all their dips, spurs and angles, you come out with a country four times as big as yours."

Within this vast area, the Mountain West is as chaotically varied as the contents of a crossroads store. There is the southern part—high deserts in eastern New Mexico, where the wind sweeps unchecked for miles across the bunch grass, and low deserts in western Arizona, where the tall saguaro

cacti hold up their useless arms and lizards skitter about. This southern part extends 700 miles west from the peanut fields on the Pecos River in New Mexico past the orchards and red-pepper farms along the trickling Rio Grande to the semitropical winter resorts of Tucson and Phoenix and on down to the pecan groves of Yuma, Arizona, where residents feel chilly if the summer temperature drops much below 100° F. The high and low deserts are separated by very considerable ranges clothed with juniper and rich in a variety of minerals—the Sacramento Mountains, the Mimbres Mountains, the Mogollon Mountains and the Gila Mountains. These ranges run from the border of Mexico north to the painted Navajo country on the Colorado Plateau and to that overwhelming geologic phenomenon, the Grand Canyon of Arizona.

The central Mountain West—Colorado, Utah, Nevada and their fringes—stretches 1,000 miles from the plains of Colorado and southern Wyoming over the highest and widest Rockies, over Utah's red canyonlands, which look as Biblical as Pharaoh's Egypt, and on past the purple parallel ranges and desert troughs that form the Great Basin of western Utah and Nevada. This Great Basin, a painfully lonely vastness, begins at the Wasatch Mountains above Salt Lake City and runs west to the

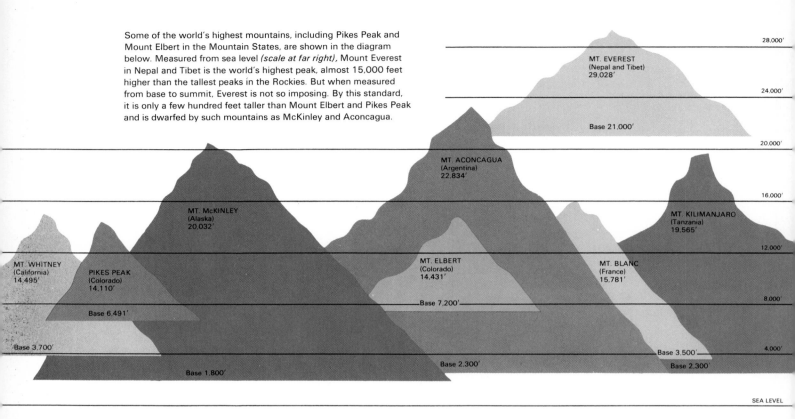

Some of the world's highest mountains, including Pikes Peak and Mount Elbert in the Mountain States, are shown in the diagram below. Measured from sea level *(scale at far right),* Mount Everest in Nepal and Tibet is the world's highest peak, almost 15,000 feet higher than the tallest peaks in the Rockies. But when measured from base to summit, Everest is not so imposing. By this standard, it is only a few hundred feet taller than Mount Elbert and Pikes Peak and is dwarfed by such mountains as McKinley and Aconcagua.

MT. EVEREST
(Nepal and Tibet)
29,028'
Base 21,000'

MT. ACONCAGUA
(Argentina)
22,834'

MT. McKINLEY
(Alaska)
20,032'

MT. KILIMANJARO
(Tanzania)
19,565'

MT. WHITNEY
(California)
14,495'

PIKES PEAK
(Colorado)
14,110'
Base 6,491'

MT. ELBERT
(Colorado)
14,431'
Base 7,200'

MT. BLANC
(France)
15,781'

Base 3,700'

Base 3,500'

Base 1,800'

Base 2,300'

Base 2,300'

28,000'
24,000'
20,000'
16,000'
12,000'
8,000'
4,000'
SEA LEVEL

California line beyond Reno. It is blocked there by the colossal barrier of the Sierra Nevada so that its streams have no way of reaching the Pacific. Some of them flow into Great Salt Lake and evaporate, leaving their salt in the lake to create its famous buoyancy (a bather would have to work hard to drown there). Several other Great Basin streams— the Humboldt River is the main one—just flow along until they sink in the alkali ground east of Reno. The sinking places, as might be guessed, are called "sinks."

Great Salt Lake covers less than 1,500 square miles these days. It is a remnant of Lake Bonneville, which used to spread over some 50,000 square miles before it began to leak away and evaporate 25,000 years ago. Another Great Basin lake, Pyramid, is a remnant of Lake Lahontan, which once covered 8,400 square miles of the Great Basin.

Colorado, the roof of the central Mountain West, has an average altitude of 6,800 feet above sea level, and that is the least of the facts the residents like to startle visitors with. Did you know that the state has every one of the 54 peaks in the entire Rockies system that soar to 14,000 feet and more and a total of 1,143 mountains that reach 10,000 feet and more? Below the peaks lie large pastoral parks and small emerald valleys in which streams are always

boiling along. The peaks have the special majesty of both height and breadth, numbering among them the Uintas of northwest Colorado and eastern Utah, the Grenadiers and Needles and San Miguels of southwest Colorado, the Elk and Sawatch Ranges above Leadville, and the great, rounded summits west of Denver and to the northwest in Rocky Mountain National Park. The lacy crests of the Sangre de Cristos sweep up from the dreamy grasslands of northern New Mexico. There are attractive lesser ranges in Colorado—the Never Summers and Mummys above North Park, the Mosquitoes and Tarryalls in South Park, and the Wet Mountains above Pueblo.

The northern Mountain States extend 650 miles from the golden prairies of eastern Montana and Wyoming to the mile-deep Hells Canyon of the Snake River, where Idaho meets Oregon. The northern terrain is complex. The Big Horn and Wind River Mountains soar out of the Wyoming plain. Their massive beauty is so great that it is almost a shock to come upon the Tetons mirrored in Jackson Lake and find them more beautiful still. In central Idaho, above the vast arc of the Snake River Valley, the Salmon River Mountains rear craggy and snow-peaked. Most of this theatrical wilderness can be reached only on foot or horseback or by rubber raft down the boiling River of No Return, also known as the Salmon.

In Montana the average altitude is only 3,400 feet above sea level. The Rockies become lower and lower as they approach Canada. But Montana's forested ranges are spacious, peaceful to live with and numerous—they include the Absarokas and Crazys west of Billings, the Belts and Bearpaws in the central north, and the Bitterroots, Beaverheads, Sapphires and Rubys in the west, as well as two dozen more. It rains a lot in the country west of the Continental Divide, and the rain collects in superb natural lakes like Flathead and Swan in Montana and Coeur d'Alene and Pend Oreille in Idaho, all of them sparkling blue. There are thick forests of larch and white pine and Douglas fir, and plenty of elk splashing around in the marshes.

In all the American Rockies, southern and central and northern, it can get extremely noisy and tense during storms—earsplitting thunder echoing to kingdom come, trees crashing when lightning strikes, and hail whacking down hard. A person's skin tingles and his hair stands on end because of all the electricity in the air. The higher the cooler, of course. It is likely to frost any summer night above 8,000 feet. One discovers a curious thing about mountain plants. High altitude corresponds to high latitude as far as their life zones are concerned. A traveler riding to the 14,110-foot summit of Pikes Peak on the cog train that climbs the mountain from 6,000-foot-high Manitou Springs, Colorado, passes through several zones, finally to reach the Alpine zone, where little plant life survives. On the way he sees the same plants that he would see in the same succession of life zones if he traveled north along the Rockies toward the Arctic Circle.

The Mountain States present an epic story of terrestrial change over the last billion years or so. Geologists tell us that all the Mountain West was inundated by shallow inland seas time and time again. The seas would lay down thick layers of sediment, bearing oyster shells and other marine objects, which people today pick up as fossils, wondering how they ever got there. Then the earth's crust would heave up, the seas would go away for a while, and volcanoes would spew out lava. In recent times, say 60 million years ago, the Rockies began to rise up and stay up. They were carved into distinctive shapes by wind and weather and slides of ice and stone. There was a lot of splitting and faulting, folding and doming.

Meanwhile, the rains carried soil down from the summits to form foothill valleys. Rains and rivers washed more soil all the way to Kansas and Nebraska and the Dakotas to build the Great Plains. As the Rockies rose, parts of them had a way of shedding their overlay of sedimentary rock. The overlay slid down the slopes to hit bottom and make quaint, multicolored picnic grounds of tilted sandstone and limestone such as the Garden of the Gods near Colorado Springs and the natural amphitheater of Red Rocks Park near Denver. When the mountains shed their overlay they exposed the deeper rock of which they were composed. That set the stage for miners of modern times, because an area of exposed rock is a likely place to find gold and other precious metals. In the Mountain States the expression, "There's gold in them thar hills," is just the truth, that's all.

The Continental Divide—noble phrase—is a twisting height of land that meanders northward through New Mexico, Colorado and Wyoming, ambles around Montana and passes into Canada amid the striated glories of Glacier National Park. A stretch of the divide forms a particularly enchanting part of the Montana-Idaho border. Travelers treat the divide with respect and perform little ceremonial rites when they cross it, such as standing on their heads or having their pictures taken sitting on the top of the highway marker.

Rain falling on the eastern slope of the divide becomes creeks and then rivers that flow eastward, eventually to empty into the Gulf of Mexico. Westside streams form rivers running to the Gulf of California and to the Pacific. This east-west division of waters is the rule, but there are exceptions. In Glacier National Park a few streams like the St. Mary's River and the Belly River flow from the divide and wind up neither in the Gulf of Mexico nor in the Pacific but in Hudson Bay.

The divide itself has moments of nonconformity. Near Rawlins, Wyoming, it becomes two divides that circle around the edge of a saucer of red desert called the Great Basin of Wyoming. This basin, 100 miles across, drains in on itself like the larger Great Basin of Utah and Nevada. The two Continental Divides join up as one again 10 miles south of that historic gate to Oregon and California, South Pass, and continue north through Wind River Range and Yellowstone Park. In the park, near Old Faithful and the gassy, muttering West Thumb mudholes known as paint pots, the divide makes a tortuous turn so that the eastern slope faces northwest for some miles.

In 1940 something like four million people were living in these delectable hills. Soon after, a huge migration began from all parts of the nation and

Sage and sagebrush

Rocky Mountain sage and the big sagebrush that is so often romanticized in songs of the Old West are totally different plants, though both flourish in the Mountain States. Sage, an erect, multibranched herb with blue flowers, grows to a height of only three to 12 inches. Found at altitudes between 4,000 and 7,000 feet, sage, once thought by some people to have medicinal properties, was used as a home remedy for malaria and rheumatic fever. (The sage used as a cooking herb is a different species.) Sagebrush is a much larger, shaggy shrub, sometimes growing big enough to hide a horse. Distinguished by its tripointed silvery leaf, sagebrush is brewed into a bitter tea and is also used by some Mountain States' residents as a tonic, an eyewash, an antiseptic and a remedy for colds. Its seeds were once ground into meal by the Cahuilla Indians. Possibly the most abundant shrub in western North America, the sagebrush is still used as forage for sheep and goats.

ROCKY MOUNTAIN SAGE (Salvia reflexa)   BIG SAGEBRUSH (Artemesia tridentata)

the world. The population of the Mountain States neared eight million a quarter century later and was increasing at the rate of 160,000 a year. Nevada had the largest percentage growth in the 25 years—from 110,000 to almost half a million. Arizona had more than tripled its numbers by 1965—half a million to 1,640,000. Colorado's 1,123,000 rose to an estimated two million. New Mexico and Utah doubled their populations to a million each.

This immigration was sparked during and after World War II by the westward movement of immense amounts of public and private capital. During the war, the federal government set up training camps and civilian bureaus and defense industries and bombing ranges all over the mountains and deserts. Additional amounts of federal and state money have been spent since the war on interstate highways and reclamation projects and improvements in the national forests and parks—and all of this has brought more people.

Denver has acquired so many government bureaus that it is practically an annex of Washington; its defense plants make Titan missiles and nuclear products too mysterious to talk about. At Cheyenne, Warren Air Force Base and the Union Pacific Railroad's properties have burgeoned. The Atomic Energy Commission built its large National Reactor Testing Station near Idaho Falls and put an operations center at Albuquerque, prompting the city to call itself "the heart of the Nuclear-Space Age" as it spreads along the Rio Grande below the Sandia Mountains. Phoenix has accumulated electronics and meat- and fruit-packing plants. U.S. Steel moved into the Salt Lake City area in 1946 when it bought the federal government's wartime Geneva plant near Provo. The Strategic Air Command established an ICBM base at Great Falls, Montana, in addition to its Malstrom Air Force Base there. Oil- and food-processing plants in Billings, Montana, expand incessantly. Colorado Springs has the Army's Fort Carson, the $200 million Air Force Academy, and a $100 million bombproof cave in Cheyenne Mountain that holds the three-story combat operations center of the North American Air Defense Command.

The immigrants who have come with this expansion have been motivated by every sort of circumstance. Some came west (or east from the Pacific) because their employers sent them, and found that they never wanted to go back home again. Some fell in love with the country during military service. Members of the 10th Mountain Division, for example, learned skiing and survival on the Continental Divide at Camp Hale in Colorado; after their

14

Italian campaign in World War II, many 10th Mountain veterans hurried back to the Rockies to become leaders in the ski industry.

Millions came west primarily to better their social and economic lot, but they yearned to get away from it all, too—away from their relatives or their own psychoses or their debts or the smog or the dampness or the old social rut or to rid themselves of commuting a couple of hours each day. Many had health problems in their families that they hoped would clear up in the mountain air—asthma, hay fever, arthritis, tuberculosis or plain old-fashioned rheumatism. Some are refugees from ethnic tensions, like the ex-New Yorker in Montana who not long ago remarked, "Out here you don't hear a lot of nasty racial cracks. This is how I want my kids to grow up."

The mere thought of all those 864,000 square miles of space has moved people to pull out of their overcrowded communities. Plenty of room out west to feel free in, to walk the dog in, even to have a horse. And the Mountain States are not just big as all get out. They are sparsely settled. Colorado, the most populous of them, has only 17 people per square mile. Wyoming has fewer than four. Pennsylvania, by comparison, has 252. Furthermore, much of the space in the Mountain States belongs to the United States government—it is everybody's, in effect. The state of Nevada is 85 per cent federal property; Utah is 66 per cent; Wyoming, 48 per cent. The eight-state percentage comes to almost 50 per cent federally owned. That makes almost half a million square miles removed from the blighting aspects of civilized society. The national parks are but small parts of this magnificent estate of the common man. Most of the federal territory is composed of national forests blanketing the Rockies, and open grazing lands in the prairies adjoining the mountains. Half a million square miles with scarcely a "No Trespassing" sign!

The newcomers have settled down with the natives. Many have taken to string ties and big hats, to sending Christmas cards back where they came from with cowboys and Indians and miners worked into the Christmas theme. Or maybe the cards just have a sprig of sage pinned to them as a token of optimism. There is no single type of newcomer. In Denver there are Dacron-suited types talking stocks and real estate on Seventeenth Street and scientists from the Martin plant south of the city and packing-house workers in the Globeville section, all enjoying the dignity and style and comfort of that largest of Mountain States communities. The new arrivals have settled in the Mormon Mecca, Salt Lake, perhaps the tidiest of American cities, and one of the most beautiful. They have swarmed to Phoenix to help plant more palms and shopping centers and havens for senior citizens, urged on by the huge metal thunderbird that revolves atop the Valley National Bank, symbolizing success and the bank's deposits of a billion dollars. They have turned up in Albuquerque, New Mexico, as brightly new a town as Phoenix, though they are a bit nonplused by the contrast between its sleek modernity and the easygoing old countryside around it. They have bought Spanish-style adobe homes on Canyon Road in Santa Fe, an old settlement perpetually fragrant with the odor of piñon smoke from fireplace chimneys, and they have festooned their doorways with red peppers and gourds. Fifteen thousand of them—mostly nuclear physicists and members of their families—have settled near Santa Fe at Los Alamos, which may have the highest I.Q. per capita in the nation. In 1942 Los Alamos consisted only of a boys' boarding school, population 50 students and teachers.

You find them ranching on the Big Hole out of Wisdom, Montana, and mining out of Moab, Utah, and working with Indians at Window Rock, Arizona, and Fort Washakie, Wyoming, and Hardin, Montana. They run motels in Estes Park, Colorado, and tend bar in exchange for free skiing in Aspen and Vail and Sun Valley. They are salesmen in quiet Montana river towns like Missoula and Bozeman, and saddle makers in noisy Montana towns like Miles City, where nothing is so beautiful as a Hereford bull, unless it is one of Charlie Russell's cowboy paintings. They have retired in resorts flavored Western like Jackson and Cody, Wyoming; resorts flavored Mexican like Tucson, Arizona; resorts flavored partly Long Island and partly Hollywood like Scottsdale, near Phoenix; resorts flavored like nothing ever seen before on this planet—Las Vegas, Nevada, mainly.

They associate with Finns and Norwegians and Italians in Great Falls, Montana, or with Basque sheepherders in Winnemucca, Nevada, or with Japanese onion growers in the San Luis Valley of Colorado. Some have found their hearts' desire in the scenery and peace of Gunnison, Colorado, or in the fishing paradise of Sandpoint, Idaho, or in Toquerville, Utah, where residents grow pomegranates and tell visitors about the town's fine old duplex ("cohab") homes where a Mormon husband used to be able to keep two wives, or more if he wanted them.

Most of the boundaries of the Mountain States are simply lines that were selected without much deliberation, and yet there are sharp distinctions between the states. Arizona is made up of harsh, hot deserts and cool, green mountains. Navajo Indians dominate the northeast quarter. The state's conservatives have enshrined ex-Senator Barry Goldwater of Scottsdale as a resistance hero as legendary as the Apache leaders Cochise and Geronimo. But chiefly Arizona is remarkable for the phenomenon of metropolitan Phoenix, a realtor's dream expanding at a fantastic pace. The area's sights include a Phoenix outpost of Saks Fifth Avenue among the fountains and olive trees of the Biltmore Fashion Park, and the exotic Grady Gammage Auditorium that the late Frank Lloyd Wright designed for Arizona State University at nearby Tempe. Phoenicians, as the *Arizona Republic* calls the local residents, are every kind of people from everywhere. Some of those wintering in homes around the Arizona Biltmore Hotel look like well-heeled New Yorkers. The gorgeous girls who decorate the tables around motel swimming pools along Van Buren Street seem to be fresh from some Hollywood movie set.

Nevada is a bleak, rolling plateau inhabited by ranchers and miners and missile testers, until one comes to Reno, a pleasant town where one need not shoot craps on Virginia Street if one prefers to study the arts instead in the new University of Nevada library. Of course, Las Vegas is in Nevada, too, and there is no question what one does in Las Vegas. One gambles. The clubs offer top-notch floor shows and acts, but gambling is the lure, the city's reason for being. North of Nevada is Idaho, as innocent as sweet sixteen. Its citizens are mainly well-to-do potato farmers in the south and lumbermen up north. The charming state capitol at Boise seems more like a county courthouse. When the governor steps out on the lawn to stretch his legs, his constituents walk by saying things to him like, "Hi, Gov. How's the wife and kids?"

Newcomers to Wyoming find an immense, windy region of ranches and ranges and oil fields. On the west is Evanston, where Utah's non-Mormons go on Friday nights to get the drinks they cannot buy in Utah. On the east is Cheyenne, a dusty supply center that constantly hears the racket of Union Pacific freight trains moving east and west and south. There are saddle shops galore in Wyoming but hardly any bookshops.

Montana is a spacious country of grand mountains and vast salubrious plains. The restaurants serve a side dish of pancakes for breakfast whether it is wanted or not. Montanans in cowboy garb really are cowboys and wear Stetsons for protection from the sun, not for effect. The state's largest cities are Billings on the Yellowstone and Great Falls on the Missouri. Billings is brisk and ambitious and full of reverence for the Anaconda Company and Montana Power, the state's economic giants and also its traditional political bosses. Great Falls is noted for its idealists who complain that the state's 400 one- or two-teacher grade schools are not educating Montana children very well. They charge in addition that the state university is deteriorating because the legislature will not see to it that faculty salaries are raised.

Colorado is the wealthiest of the eight states. It is probably the best-balanced economically, with resorts and manufacturing plants, mines and farms, and huge federal establishments. The lively supply centers of Durango and Grand Junction on the western slope are growing rapidly, but most Coloradans live on the east side of the Continental Divide in the plain along the Front Range between Fort Collins in the north and the steel center of Pueblo in the south. The University of Colorado at Boulder ranks high among U.S. state universities. Denver and Colorado Springs are cosmopolitan cities that aspire to the cultural, culinary and social pretensions of San Francisco. Old ruling families in these two cities still handle some of the region's largest businesses, but they have been sharing power of late with young managers sent out from New York or the West Coast to run branches of national firms.

New Mexico has such a soft, gentle, Spanish-Mexican flavor that it does not seem to be in the United States at all. In the hills north of Santa Fe there are Spanish-Mexican villages where English is rarely spoken. Newcomers to arty Santa Fe and Taos and even to "the heart of the Nuclear-Space Age," Albuquerque, succumb easily to this *mañana* way of life and soon find themselves wearing sandals, stuffing themselves with spicy enchiladas and reading up on Spanish colonial history. Mixed in with this pseudo-Spanish world is the culture of the Pueblo Indians, whose ancestral cliff dwellings can still be seen.

Nobody can spend a day anywhere in Utah without feeling the power of the Church of Jesus Christ of Latter-day Saints. At least half the population of Salt Lake City is Mormon. The state elsewhere is 70 per cent Mormon. Though the power of the theocracy is subtle, it is all-controlling. It shows in the order and prosperity and sweet sanity of everything, in the wide, much-washed streets, in the well-staffed stores and handsome homes clustered around every Mormon Temple or chapel. Many Saints are blond and have a sort of proud Viking look, perhaps because so many of their ancestors came to Utah from Scandinavia. Newcomers find that they get along quite well with the Mormons, but it is not good business to be too curious about their affairs.

In the process of settling down with the natives, newcomers everywhere in the region have discovered something about the mountains that they did not perceive at first, something the natives knew all along. Man, it seems, sickens and dies from a feeling of helplessness. But he thrives on challenge, on triumph over his environment. That aforementioned *Harper's* article by Walter Prescott Webb implied, at least to the editorial writer of the Denver *Post*, that the Mountain West is "nothing but one vast desert, fit for neither man nor beast." Practically speaking, this is all too true. These mountains and deserts really are fit for neither man nor beast, as any resident will admit if you pin him down to it.

And therein lies the point and the paradox. The Western environment brings joy to people precisely because it offers difficulties to be overcome and the opportunity to triumph over the difficulties. Somebody looks at a 14,000-foot peak and is determined to do what the peak seems bent on preventing him from doing. He wants to climb it partly because of the optimism we have mentioned—the optimism and the heady sense of freedom produced by the bracing climate and the wide-open space. He wants to climb it also to prove his physical and moral strength—and to see what is on the other side. If it is an easy climb, he can always make it harder, risking his neck by challenging the east face of Longs Peak, for instance. In his book *Of Men and Mountains*, Justice William O. Douglas put it very well. "When [the climber] wins, there comes an exquisite moment, a feeling that anything is possible. There comes a sense of austerity, a feeling of peace. All the tensions are gone."

The newcomers look around and realize that it is as much of a challenge to live in the mountains as to climb them, and that mountaineers are inspired to meet the challenge. Everything is difficult at a mile or two above sea level. There is not enough water for growing food, and so the Colorado-Big Thompson Project in Colorado has been built—and the Salt River Project in Arizona and Lake Powell in Utah and the Palisades Reservoir in Idaho. Many of the necessities of living have to be hauled up from sea level, and so men meet the challenge of gravity with easier highway grades and projects like the pending Straight Creek Vehicular Tunnel under Colorado's Loveland Pass. Land gets more expensive everywhere, and so farmers find out how to grow 34-bushel-an-acre wheat, as they do in Idaho's Magic Valley around Twin Falls. Ranchers make their beef cattle grow faster and fatter by introducing new strains.

It never seems to occur to most mountaineers to knuckle under to their difficult environment. They build golf courses at a terrible cost on wastelands where not even gophers can survive. They go in for motorboats and for water skiing even when they have to haul the boats hundreds of miles to find a dab of lake big enough to turn around in and warm enough not to congeal a water skier. Many of them build houses of the same kind that they would build in Hannibal, Missouri, with steep roofs to shed rain that seldom comes and with Victorian gingerbread for pack rats to nest in and with large lawns. It has been said that it takes more water and labor and thought to keep Denver's lawns green than it takes to run Denver's industry.

High altitude often makes noses bleed. Men and women who imbibe feel their liquor more. The normal human pulse rate of 72 beats a minute may rise to 100 beats in higher parts of the Mountain States. Unacclimated opera stars pant through their arias like steam locomotives during the summer festival at Central City, Colorado (8,500 feet). There are two basic causes of the problems encountered by human beings at high altitudes. One is that high air contains less oxygen than sea-level air; the other is that human lungs are designed to operate at sea-level atmospheric pressures and must work harder to supply the bloodstream with the required amounts of oxygen at the lower pressures of high altitudes. To compensate, a person's blood has to have time to build up an additional number of oxygen-carrying red corpuscles. Doctors in Denver have found that it takes a month for blood to adjust fully to the city's mile-high altitude. It might take a year for the blood to get in shape for a comfortable existence on top of Pikes Peak at 14,110 feet. Some newcomers in the Rockies suffer from "mountain sickness" for several days. This feeling is "equivalent to the worst hang-over you ever had," says one Denver-based Army scientist.

Altitude is a severe challenge to cooks. Water does not get very hot up there because it boils at a lower point than the customary 212° F. As a result, beans and potatoes take longer to cook, and it takes six or seven minutes of boiling to bring off a five-minute egg. The uncertainties of barometric pressure make popovers a bad risk. In automobiles the combustion process is less efficient because of the reduced amount of oxygen available, and engine power can be cut by as much as 20 per cent. Pilots of airplanes have still more problems. Air at the lower pressure of high altitudes has far less lifting power than sea-level air, and at 10,000 feet planes need twice as much runway to get off the ground as they need at sea level. The problem gets worse in the summer. Warm air does not have as much lifting power as cool air; a pilot who puts his plane down nicely on the Oxbow Dam strip in steepwalled Hells Canyon of the Snake River on a cool summer morning may be unable to get it out in the steamy afternoon.

Altitude has some good effects, of course. As early as the 1830s Captain William Drummond Stewart observed that buffalo meat kept indefinitely if cut in strips and hung in the high Wyoming air. Stewart was present when the noted missionary Dr. Marcus Whitman removed an arrowhead from the back of Jim Bridger, the great mountain man. The arrowhead had been in Jim's back for three years, and Whitman wondered why it had caused no infection. "Meat don't spoil in the Rockies," Jim is said to have replied.

The refined English spinster Isabella Bird, aged 42, confessed to her sister in the 1870s that she never knew what life was about until she climbed Longs Peak from Estes Park, Colorado, and found herself able, at 12,000 feet, to have entirely unspinsterish feelings toward her one-eyed guide, Mountain Jim Nugent. In 1875 Mrs. George Webb produced the first white baby to be born in the San Juan Mountains of Colorado—under a fir tree on a snowbank near the top of Stony Pass (12,594 feet). Mrs. Webb nicknamed her daughter "The Lily of the San Juan" and was able to get along to Silverton in a day or two.

The thin, clear air makes for the vivid colors that artists in the mountains rave about. Wonderful parhelions—mock suns or sundogs—often circle the horizon and light up the plains of Wyoming. The northern lights in Montana and the sunsets of the Snake River Plain in Idaho are indescribably lovely. The stars anywhere above the Rockies have a brightness that seems to increase with the dawn. Comets blaze brighter, and if a man-made rocket happens to trundle across the sky, it appears to be just above one's shoulder.

The climate of the Mountain States is mixed, to put it mildly. At best it is superb. The desert of Arizona, for instance, is so sunny in winter, so dry, so delightful, that Elizabeth Arden chose to set up near Phoenix her famous Main Chance Farm for readjusting the weight of otherwise alluring females. The fall season, blazing with the gold and orange foliage of aspens, lifts the heart everywhere in the

Rockies. And winters are surprisingly moderate in most places. It is not unusual for families to picnic on a sunny January day in the parks of Pocatello, Idaho, or in those of Fort Collins, Colorado. Snowfall is generally light, and the snow melts rapidly, except in the highest mountains where the skiing is —the Elks above Aspen, the Tetons above Jackson, the Wasatch Range above Salt Lake City, the Sawtooths above Sun Valley.

At its best, superb. At its worst, the weather is so terrible that Westerners never tire of boasting about the challenge it presents. Residents of Phoenix flee to the mountains from mid-April to mid-October if they can afford it. Otherwise they estivate in airconditioned homes while outside temperatures run above 110° F. for days on end. At the opposite pole, inhabitants of Fraser, Colorado, freeze a good deal of the time and are proud of it. They fight to guard their town's status as the nation's coldest—opposing particularly the claims of Big Piney, Wyoming. If Big Piney reports a reading of 40° below, Fraserites have another look at the thermometer and turn in a splendid 41°.

Idaho's specialties in climatic disaster are storms of hailstones larger than golf balls and devastating forest fires caused by the frightful lightning common in the Salmon River Mountains. At the U.S. Air Force Academy in Colorado it has been considered necessary to put a sort of electric blanket 160 feet wide by 300 feet long (16½ miles of cable) under the grass of the football field of Falcon Stadium so that the grass will keep growing to the end of the football season instead of turning brown with the September freeze. Coloradans boast of the ice that can form without warning at any season on Monument Hill and close down the superhighway between Denver and Colorado Springs. They boast also of summer snows breaking down their elms and lilacs, and of the cloudburst of June 16, 1965, when 12 inches of rain suddenly fell near Denver and caused some $300 million worth of property damage in the city.

Such are the Mountain States—splendid, spacious, charming, varied, dramatic and hard to put up with when an ugly mood is on them. These mountains and their qualities were what Joe Brown was thinking about as he crossed the Colorado line and sniffed a handful of sage on his way home. And he knew that the old spirit of the frontier was still in them, that the challenge was still there and that he was not helpless in this environment. He could do something about it.

That is why he found it good to be back in God's country, and why he hummed a cowboy tune.

Ross "Rusty" Musselman lugs a raccoon pelt out of the Abajo Mountains in southeastern Utah. A vigorous example of a vanishing breed, Musselman accepted the challenge of the high country on its own terms and has wrestled it to a draw. Besides trapping, he has herded cattle, raised horses, run a trading post and worked as a wagon skinner. "I came out here from New Jersey with my father when I was twelve, and I slept on the ground for thirty years," he says. In 1965 Ross Musselman became sheriff of 10,000-square-mile San Juan County. "Tracking a criminal is a lot like tracking an animal. You just have to know what to look for."

Men against the mountains

The first white men to encounter the Rocky Mountains saw only a terrible wall of rock and weather blocking their way to the Pacific. Later, a tough and stubborn few suffered blizzards, torrents and rockslides, fought Indians, shot game and collected furs to wrest a hard living from the high plains, peaks and valleys. These were the fabled mountain men. Vestiges of that life remain—the trapper at the right is one example —but new kinds of men are taking over. Most of those who enter the mountains today are specialists. They come to learn how the earth was formed, to mine ore, to instruct skiers or to supervise the public land areas. But whatever their background and whatever their purpose, each in his own way has been profoundly affected by the high country. Within its primeval grandeur each man sees a powerful reason to be alive.

BASQUE SHEEPHERDER

Claudio Abanzabalegui drives a band of 2,500 Columbia sheep toward higher pasture in Idaho's Sawtooth Mountains. For more than half a century men from the mountainous Basque country of northern Spain have been coming to the desolate hills of central Idaho, center of America's sheep-raising industry, to work as contract shepherds. Abanzabalegui is a shy man in his mid-30s who first arrived in the U.S. in 1958 on a three-year contract and later returned to become a permanent resident. Now he spends the months of April through September almost entirely alone. "This is big country," says Abanzabalegui. "I was lonesome at first. But I like my work. I herd sheep. They must graze and fatten and I must protect them from bears and cougar." After the sheep have reached high summer pasture, Abanzabalegui, who travels with a truck as well as several horses and dogs, sets up camp. He rises in the morning at first light to start the sheep to new grass, returns to camp for lunch, then takes the sheep to water and to high ground before dark, and again returns to camp for dinner. After about eight days he moves his camp to a new site. "This is a good life and a good country," he says.

MOUNTAIN RANCHER

Norman Palm throws a calf for branding on his Home Ranch, which covers 400 square miles in the Medicine Bow Mountains in Wyoming. Tending the 20,000 sheep and 6,000 head of cattle that graze on his spread is a big job. Palm is up each day before dawn—"If you don't get up before the sun, you're running all day to catch up"—and sometimes works in blizzards at temperatures as low as 30 below. But he likes his work and loves the mountains. "I've never gone a day when something interesting or exciting hasn't occurred," he says. "I've never been at the top of one hill when there wasn't a higher one in sight, or crossed a canyon where there wasn't a deeper one ahead."

ASTRONOMER

Dr. Helmut Abt stands on a railed balcony at the base of the huge dome that houses the 84-inch telescope of the Kitt Peak National Observatory in Arizona. Dr. Abt is professionally fond of the Arizona climate; the clear, dry air is excellent for astronomical observations. But he also loves it personally, especially for the variety offered by the state's deserts and mountains. As he notes, "You can change the climate simply by changing your elevation."

Dr. Abt first fell in love with Arizona when, in 1955, he came with a team investigating locations for a new national observatory.

He helped explore more than 150 mountain ranges and developed a keen interest in mountain climbing. After the 6,875-foot-high Kitt Peak site had been selected and the ultramodern observatory built, Dr. Abt returned to take charge of its 84-inch scope, the fifth largest in the world. Like most of the observatory staff, he lives in Tucson, 56 miles away. He owns a Jeep that he uses to "bum around the Southwest hiking canyons." An avid and gifted amateur archeologist, he has encountered on a single hiking trip as many as 100 Indian cliff dwellings, some with as many as 40 rooms.

MINING ENGINEER

At the Leonard Mine near Butte, Montana, Nelson Jones *(below)* motions to an assistant after sighting his transit. Jones is the assistant chief mining engineer for the Anaconda Company, the largest copper producer in the world. A native son of the mineral-rich area surrounding Butte, through which the ridge of the Continental Divide twists and turns like a dragon's tail, he has never tired of his home country. "Sometimes when you are out in the mountains on survey work or visiting the ghost towns, you feel that if things could only talk, what a lot they would have to say. You see an old cemetery and look at the faded grave markers and you wonder. The children used to die so early."

RESEARCH GEOLOGIST

J. David Love, supervisor of the Wyoming office of the U.S. Geological Survey, uses a rock outcropping for a desk while taking notes high up in the Teton Range. Love was born in Wyoming on a ranch. "When I was a boy we saw few people," he says. "About the only ones we did see were cowboys and geologists. We were already cowboys, so that had no appeal. But these geologists brought a new world. They would show us fossils they found, right where we had walked and not seen them." Love later studied geology at Yale. "I have come into these mountains to study the earth's history. Some of these rocks date back two and a half billion years. That's a big slice of history."

WHITEWATER GUIDE

Ted Hatch, a six-foot, 200-pound, good-natured redhead, guides a 12-foot neoprene raft through the rough water of Green River in Dinosaur National Monument. The son of Bus Hatch, who pioneered the sport more than 40 years ago, Ted started riding "whitewater" when he was nine. He now runs Hatch River Expeditions, which guides groups of 10 to 20 people down some of the wildest water in the West. After securing a degree in education from the University of Utah, Hatch taught school for six years. "Then one day," he says, "I decided a desk job was too much." He is now back on the water where, as he puts it, "I enjoy the high canyons and the scenery from the bottom up."

SKI INSTRUCTOR

Eddie Morris, shown sailing through a turn in deep powder snow at Alta, Utah, is just five feet five inches tall and weighs only 135. But he is regarded as the best deep-powder instructor in the country. As assistant director of the Alf Engen Ski School in Alta, Morris has taught countless disciples the fine points of handling the deep, light snow that is so plentiful high up in the Rockies. "It's hard to explain the exhilaration of skiing," says Morris. "I guess it's the movement and the freedom." Movement describes Eddie Morris—as does freedom. "I like to get off the beaten path, onto the back of the mountain. That's more of a challenge—more of a contact with nature."

PARK RANGER

Bert McLaren, checking snow conditions during a spring storm high up on Trail Ridge Road in Rocky Mountain National Park, uses a walkie-talkie to advise rangers at the park entrance to close the road. McLaren and another ranger are responsible for virtually everything within the control of man that transpires on the west side of the park—some 86,652 acres of mountain wilderness in northern Colorado. The son of a park ranger, he grew up in the area and now lives with his wife, Shirley, and two children near Grand Town, six miles from the ranger station. McLaren somehow manages to integrate home life and leisure with a 24-hour-a-day, seven-day-a-week job. A short-wave receiving set in his home is continuously "open," and he may be called out at any hour of the day or night to check a forest fire report, search for a lost camper or follow the progress of a blizzard. Of his work he says, "It isn't a job, you know, it's a way of life. My work is all fun, even the hard, disagreeable parts. One prerequisite is liking people. They have so many ways of getting into trouble in the wilderness, and I gain satisfaction from helping them—and sharing this country with them."

2

The Scramble
for Settlement

It took four centuries for men imbued with the old frontier spirit to discover the Mountain West and to make eight states out of it. Spanish conquistadors got there first, partly as a result of an accident. After wrecking their ship on the Texas coast and being held by Indians for six years, the indestructible adventurer Álvar Núñez Cabeza de Vaca and three companions—stark naked, the story goes, because their clothes had shredded away—wandered in 1535-1536 through what is now southern New Mexico. The wandering occurred 71 years before the English founded Jamestown in Virginia.

Eventually Cabeza de Vaca reached the haven of Mexico City, which had been taken by the Spaniards in 1521, and reported Indian tales of great northern cities that contained quantities of gold. This account evolved into a story about seven cities of solid gold, the Seven Cities of Cíbola. In 1540 a Spanish grandee, Captain General Don Francisco Vásquez de Coronado, led an expedition from Mexico into Arizona and New Mexico to find them. Cíbola turned out to be the dwellings of Zuni Indians,

built of adobe and rock instead of gold. Coronado's luck was no better when he continued east all the way to Kansas to check a rumor of gold in an area called Quivira and found only windy space.

Interest in this frontier of New Spain died down, but it revived after a wealthy rancher named Antonio de Espejo took a party into the territory in 1583 and reported that it was rich in minerals and grazing lands. Acting on this report, Don Juan de Oñate, the son of a wealthy Spanish mining man, in 1598 led a group of colonists north from Mexico to found San Juan, New Mexico, on a fertile site on the Rio Grande near some Pueblo Indian villages. The social history of the Mountain West began as of that date, and Spain could claim to own the whole of it—wherever it was. Even experts were vague about Western geography and would remain so for the next two centuries. In 1609 another group of colonists, under Don Pedro de Peralta, arrived and set up a village not far from the first beneath the Sangre de Cristo Mountains and called it La Villa Real de la Santa Fé de San Francisco. And so Santa Fe (holy faith) started a career that would make it, successively, a Spanish, Mexican and, finally, a Mountain States capital.

It is hard to believe that a section of the future United States was coming into being in so remote

Winding beneath lofty, snow-capped Ouray Peak, a Denver and Rio Grande freight train makes its way in the 1880s through the mountains of Colorado. The Denver and Rio Grande, founded in 1871, laid rails to almost every mining area in the Mountain States.

a place so long ago. In that same 17th Century, William Shakespeare was writing *Macbeth* and *King Lear*, Cardinal Richelieu was running France, and the Habsburgs were exercising their dwindling influence over European affairs. In 1700, while Louis XIV and his ladies were having an elegant time at Versailles, the Jesuit Father Eusebio Francisco Kino built his San Xavier del Bac Mission near a village of Indian brush shelters called "Stjukshon" (now Tucson, Arizona). The United States declared its independence from England in 1776 as the Franciscan Fray Silvestre Vélez de Escalante and a party of companions hiked from Santa Fe around the south and west sides of the San Juan Mountains of Colorado and on northwest toward Great Salt Lake in Utah. They had hoped to blaze a trail that would tie New Mexico to Spain's newest province, California, a route that would have water for the horses and would avoid the heat of Father Kino's Arizona. But winter was coming on and they could not make it. They returned to Santa Fe by way of a ford deep in the awesome canyon of the Colorado River at a point in southern Utah.

Escalante's trek into Utah and Governor Juan Bautista de Anza's swing from Santa Fe north to Pikes Peak in 1779 to subdue the Comanche were the high-water marks of Spanish exploration in the Mountain West. The kings of Spain never supported their New Mexican and Arizonan outposts with any enthusiasm, since the region's few colonists failed to find gold for them. Besides, the kings were occupied with European problems.

As the 19th Century began, Spain's empire in the Rockies started to slip away. The last of it went in 1821 when Mexico separated itself from the mother country. By then, the United States had acquired, as part of the Louisiana Purchase, about a third of today's Mountain States—the eastern slope of the Continental Divide in present-day Colorado, Wyoming and Montana. In 1818 the United States and Great Britain both laid claims to the Oregon country, an area that included what are now Oregon and Wyoming, as well as Idaho and western Montana. Three years later the new nation of Mexico took over the Spanish claim to what was left— roughly present-day New Mexico, Arizona, Utah, Nevada and western Colorado.

The United States' acquisition of this vast domain began in an almost comically casual way. President Thomas Jefferson had hardly been able to believe it when he found in 1803 that he could buy the 828,000 square miles then known as Louisiana from Napoleon, who had only recently taken it from Spain. Jefferson accepted France's price of $15 million for the territory, sight unseen and size unknown. It consisted of the western watershed of the Mississippi, and neither Jefferson nor anyone else knew where the western boundary of the watershed was. Nobody knew what was within this far-flung domain, either.

Though Jefferson himself never got west of the Allegheny Mountains of Virginia, and could not know what he had acquired, he still ranks as one of the very greatest of the Western pioneers. His mind had the optimism and the curiosity to imagine what was on the other side, the joy of meeting challenges that we have mentioned as being characteristic of mountain people even today. His thinking was on a global scale. His mind leaped at the possibility that his small nation could spread all the way to the Pacific.

In typically Western style, the President took action to achieve this goal. In 1803 he sent 40-odd explorers to have a look at the Louisiana Territory and to continue on to the Pacific. They were led by one of his staff aides, Captain Meriwether Lewis, and Lewis' boyhood friend, Lieutenant William Clark. A generous Congress put them on a budget of $2,500. Leaving St. Louis in 1804, they went by way of the Missouri River through the Dakotas and Montana and on to the Columbia River watershed in Idaho and Washington, reaching the Pacific in the fall of 1805. Their best guide was the incomparable Sacajawea, a young Shoshone Indian girl who carried her baby boy on her back a good part of the way. The 6,000-mile round trip was made with the loss of only one man—Sergeant Charles Floyd, who died on the outward journey of what the expedition's official log described as a "Biliose Cholrick."

Meanwhile, the U.S. Army sent Lieutenant Zebulon Pike and a smaller party to explore the central Mountain West. They traveled past the soaring Colorado mountain that subsequently came to be called Pikes Peak in the lieutenant's honor and went almost to the source of the Arkansas in the highest Rockies. Pike and his men nearly starved to death in the Sangre de Cristo Mountains of Colorado before they were picked up by Spanish soldiers on the charge of taking military possession of Spanish territory. They were hauled off to Santa Fe, then to prison in Chihuahua. Released during the summer of 1807, they eventually got home safely.

These epic expeditions proved to the world that the Rocky Mountains that the early Spanish priests and adventurers had reported on really did exist. The American explorers also located the Continental Divide that formed the western boundary of the

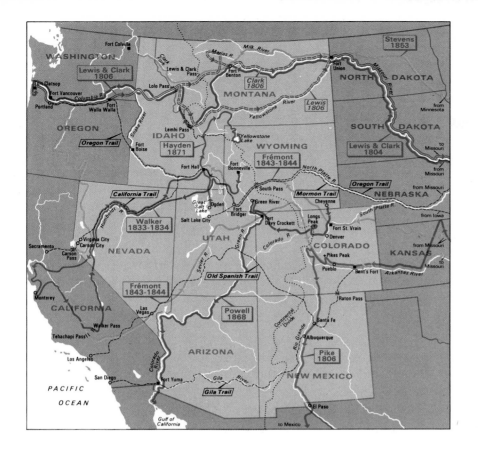

The routes traveled by some of the men sent out by the federal government to explore the Mountain States are shown on the map at left. One of the earliest explorers, Lieutenant Zebulon Pike, led an expedition from St. Louis through much of Colorado, New Mexico and into Mexico in 1806 and 1807. About this time the famous Lewis and Clark expedition made the first overland trek across the continent, reaching the mouth of the Columbia River in 1805. In 1833 Joseph Reddeford Walker, a Virginia-born fur trapper, crossed the Utah salt flats and blazed what was later to be called the California Trail. Some 10 years after Walker's journey, John Charles Frémont set out to travel the entire Oregon Trail and on his return covered much of California. Trying to find a route for a transcontinental railroad, Isaac Ingalls Stevens explored the upper part of the Mountain States in 1853. By the late 1860s, men of science also began to inspect the Mountain States. Two explorer-scientists, John Wesley Powell and Ferdinand Hayden, contributed greatly to the study of the geology and natural history of the region.

Louisiana Purchase. But broad knowledge about the region was not acquired until after the War of 1812 with England, and the impetus was, of all things, men's fashion. Not long after the war, tall hats made from the fine felt of beaver fur became popular among the men of Paris, London and New York. Brigades of trappers began pushing into the Rockies to find beaver to provide the fur. There were only several hundred of these mountain men at any one time—most of them young Americans, French Canadians, Spaniards, Scots and Englishmen. Their business was the quintessence of adventure. It was dangerous. It took courage. But it promised the ultimate in freedom.

Since beaver stay along wooded waterways, the trappers were lured up every mountain stream to its source in some alpine meadow—and then followed the water flowing down the other side. The streams were trapped out quickly, and this kept the little brigades moving to new streams, new watersheds, new ranges. There were advance men like John Colter, who saw geysers in Yellowstone country in 1808, and Andrew Henry, who wintered below the Tetons in Idaho two years later. During the 1820s, Ewing Young's party trekked from Taos, New Mexico, to California. Great Salt Lake was visited in 1824 by Jim Bridger and was also seen by Etienne Provost, the Bible-reading Jedediah Smith and Peter Skene Ogden. Smith and Joe Walker also led parties through the Great Basin of Nevada.

In 1824 trappers dispatched by the St. Louis promoter William Ashley reached the Green River in Wyoming by crossing the south end of the Wind River Range at South Pass, which, because it offered the only uninterrupted passage through the central Rockies, was to assume a major role in the development of the West. Antoine Robidou operated in the Gunnison River country of Colorado and in northeastern Utah. In the early 1830s Captain Benjamin Louis de Eulalie de Bonneville, a Paris-born West Pointer, worked into the Wind River Range and Idaho's Salmon River Mountains.

As they ranged the country, these men learned about Western climate and survival. And they came to know all kinds of Indians—dangerous ones like the Blackfoot, Sioux and Arikara tribesmen who raided and pillaged throughout the northern sections of the region, friendly ones like the Pawnee. They knew the Indians because they traded with them, fought them, gambled with them, got drunk with them and courted their women. Kit Carson married Alice, an Arapahoe; Milton Sublette married a Crow, Mountain Lamb; Joe Meek married Virginia, a Nez Percé; Jim Bridger married a Snake;

William Bent married Owl Woman, a Cheyenne.

The beaver boom lasted less than 20 years. But in that short time this handful of knights in greasy buckskins won the mountain empire that the Spaniards had failed to win in three centuries. The work of the trappers, and the related work of traders on the Santa Fe Trail between Missouri and New Mexico, did not seem to amount to much at the time. But a flood of expansionist activity during the next decade made their knowledge of supreme importance to the United States, and Jim Bridger and the others emerged as national folk heroes.

The expansionist flood commenced to roll before the American urge to span the continent became labeled by the term "manifest destiny." Just as the beaver trade was ending, Americans began to look to the West and to covet it. Farmers and missionaries by the thousands went to the fertile valleys of Oregon in the early 1840s by the South Pass route through Wyoming and Idaho. Other emigrants went to California to settle and to dream of ways to bring that fruitful outpost of Mexico into the Union. To help the emigrants, and to plot expansion on the sly, Congress sent Lieutenant John Charles Frémont and a body of men all over the Mountain West to check the trapper trails. Frémont, his own way eased by expert guides, returned with enthusiastic reports of easily traveled trails and fertile valleys.

Americans were ready to believe—and act on—advice even more optimistic than Frémont's. The fact that much of the land they were pushing into did not belong to the United States failed to deter them. They meant to make it American. And in the cataclysmic year of 1846 they did. In June of that year the United States became sole owner of the Oregon country south of the 49th parallel when Great Britain relinquished its joint occupancy over the area. The Republic of Texas, which American settlers had wrenched from Mexico, had just been annexed in 1845 as the 28th state. When Mexico raised objections to the annexation, Congress declared war in the spring of 1846. During that summer, 1,700 American soldiers traveled the Santa Fe Trail through what is now eastern Colorado and on over Raton Pass into the Mexican frontier province of New Mexico. They seized the province without firing a shot. A hundred men then hurried on west through the Arizona desert to help complete the conquest of California early in January 1847.

The last battles of the Mexican War were fought in Mexico. The war ended with a peace treaty signed on February 2, 1848, near Mexico City. By the terms of the treaty Mexico relinquished its claims to Texas and in addition handed over to the

U.S. not only its huge part of the Mountain West but California as well. That seemed to fulfill the dream of a nation stretching 3,000 miles from the Atlantic to the Pacific. But there was another equally significant outcome, though few people could guess its import just then. A week before the treaty was signed, an obscure mechanic, James Marshall, spotted gold in California's American River.

The emigration of the 1840s was simply outclassed by the mass movement of gold seekers to the region of Marshall's discovery. Nothing quite like it had ever occurred before. Tens of thousands of migrants flocked to California from the ends of the earth, some by sea, but most by the old South Pass route through Wyoming and the southern desert route across New Mexico and Arizona.

The rush began in 1848 and continued for 11 hectic years until the easy-to-find gold in California petered out. But the migrations went on, inspired by new gold discoveries in 1858 and 1859 around Denver and in the Colorado Rockies, by the wealth of Nevada's silver-and-gold Comstock Lode after 1859, and by the find of rich diggings around the gold camps of Bannack City and Virginia City and Last Chance Gulch, far away in Montana. Not even the Civil War caused a lull. The rushes continued throughout the war and went on afterward until every remote inch of the Mountain West stood revealed. The later rushes included the great Colorado silver boom of the 1870s and 1880s at Leadville and Aspen, the Nevada silver excitement in the 1900s, and the emergence of copper as still another bonanza in Montana, Utah, Arizona and Nevada soon after the turn of the century.

The riches of the mine fields were not the only lure of the mountains. Some people went west to look over the new real estate the nation had taken from Mexico. But the greatest stimulus seems to have been spiritual, proceeding out of the sweet sense of freedom implicit in American democracy. The gold fields symbolized freedom. The gold belonged to any man with gumption enough to get himself out there. He could pick up a fortune in some gulch and keep it all for himself—and the prospect of that kind of freedom *gave* a man gumption. If the ideal of democracy was getting a bit tarnished back in the effete old East, the raw new West was eager to freshen it.

The gold rushes destroyed the mystery of the wilderness, broke up the open spaces into mining areas and headed those areas toward statehood. To speed the conversion of the wilderness frontier into politically organized states, a remarkably prescient law was already on the books—the Northwest

Scouts of the frontier

Legendary among the heroes of the Old West are these frontier scouts who, usually working alone, learned the dangers of the wilderness.

1. Jim Bridger, celebrated as both a guide and a storyteller, opened Fort Bridger in southern Wyoming, where he sold supplies to explorers and settlers traveling the Oregon Trail.

2. James Baker, who guided the Army in an expedition against the Mormons, took to the Indian way of life, often wearing Indian dress. He married six times—each time to an Indian.

3. Jim Beckwourth turned from trapping to spend eight years among the Crow before becoming an Army scout. Later, on a mission to pacify the Indians, he mysteriously disappeared.

4. Christopher "Kit" Carson was already a famous scout when he became an Indian agent. Later, as an Army officer he led successful campaigns against Indian uprisings.

Ordinance of 1787. This instrument had been designed so that areas in the "territory northwest of the river Ohio" could achieve statehood before the pioneers there had begun to suffer from feelings of colonial inferiority.

The ordinance provided the basis for the political organization of frontier regions where the inhabitants yearned for stable, democratic government. First, the region might be designated a territory, with a governor named by Congress. When such a territory, or part of a territory, had 60,000 free inhabitants, it could be admitted to the Union as a state on an equal footing with all other states. On occasion the 60,000 requirement was not enforced.

The Mountain West part of the Louisiana Purchase was still unorganized in 1848 when Congress made the Oregon country a territory. Against the wishes of the South, slavery was banned in the territory, and for many decades the slavery issue was a black cloud hanging over Western affairs. In 1850 the California gold seekers were in such a hurry for statehood that they bypassed the territorial phase and got California into the Union as a slave-free state. Congress decided to create a New Mexico Territory at the same time, extending it west from Texas and on through present-day Arizona to the California line. To accomplish this, Congress paid

Texas $10 million to give up its claim to an enormous tract of land. When Texas had been admitted to the Union, it had put its western boundary inside New Mexico on the east bank of the Rio Grande and had also claimed a strip of faraway land stuck on top of this piece of Texas like a stovepipe. The strip ran some 300 miles north through present-day Colorado. It included some of Colorado's most rugged mountains—today's skiing terrains of Crested Butte, Aspen, Vail and Steamboat Springs.

New Mexico had considered itself linked to the East since the opening of the Santa Fe Trail in 1821-1822. Officials in the new territorial capital, Sante Fe, continued this eastward orientation. They had little interest in New Mexico's western section, whose residents in 1856 petitioned Congress for permission to set up a government of their own. That took time because of Congressional jockeying over slavery. Finally, in 1863, after the issuance of the Emancipation Proclamation, Arizona Territory was formed of the western half of New Mexico Territory.

Utah's long struggle for political recognition began in the spring of 1847 when 148 members of the polygamous Church of Jesus Christ of Latter-day Saints headed west on an extraordinary mission. They were seeking a sanctuary in the Rockies where the main body of 12,000 Saints (Mormons) would be safe from persecution, which had driven them first from Missouri and then from Illinois. As summer approached, Brigham Young, the head of the Church, led his vanguard across present-day Wyoming and Utah, and on July 24, 1847, reached Emigration Canyon. Young gazed down on the valley that was to be filled one day by the sprawling and lovely Salt Lake City and, according to legend, spoke words later to become famous: "This is the place." Before a year was out, some 1,500 more Saints had reached "the place," streets had been laid out, dwellings built, irrigation ditches dug and a Temple site chosen.

About 11,000 Mormons had settled in and near Salt Lake City by 1849, when Brigham Young petitioned Congress to make a state out of his curious theocracy. He had given it the attractive name of "Deseret" (honey bee)—a word in the Book of Mormon, which the Church's founder, Joseph Smith, had published in 1830 as a sort of Mormon supplement to the Bible. Young's Deseret comprised about half of the Mountain West—stretching all the way from what are now western Colorado and New Mexico into California, with chunks of Wyoming, Idaho and Oregon thrown in. Congress refused to accept the pretty name and denied statehood to the area mainly because the Mormon Church sanctioned polygamy. Instead, a smaller area was designated Utah Territory (after the local Ute Indians). Utah Territory consisted of what are now Utah, western Colorado and most of Nevada, plus a sliver of Wyoming.

In 1861 the Mormons lost a considerable part of their Utah Territory to Nevada and Colorado, and it was whittled down still more in 1862, 1866 and 1868. Young pleaded unsuccessfully for statehood right up to his death in 1877, when his family consisted of 27 wives and 56 children. Mormon polygamy was the stumbling block; the practice scandalized most Americans and kept Congress in a state of nervous exasperation. It was not easy to explain precisely what was wrong with polygamy and a ticklish problem to legislate against it since the Constitution did not forbid a man to have as many wives as he wanted. And if his religion sanctioned the having, Constitutional guarantees of religious liberty seemed to prevent Congressional interference.

Antipolygamy laws were passed anyhow—and upheld by the Supreme Court. The issue of Utah's statehood dragged on for years while polygamous Mormons turned out splendid children by the thousands and were harassed as common criminals by the U.S. government. That was the period when husbands frustrated investigators trying to catch them wiving plurally by making their single-family homes look as if they housed two independent families. They simply fitted the houses with twin entrance doors, making them into "cohab" duplexes that are still on view in Utah. At last, in October 1890, the Mormon Church officially abandoned polygamy and urged Church members to obey the antipolygamy laws. President Benjamin Harrison issued a proclamation granting amnesty to husbands who gave up their extra wives and the territory of Utah became in 1896 the state of Utah—as respectable as any of the other 45.

The path toward statehood was not quite so tortuous for all of the Mountain States, although they too had to spend time in the territorial stage. Another of these territories had come into existence in 1853, when Congress carved Washington Territory out of Oregon Territory. It consisted of today's Washington, western Montana and northern Idaho. Eight years later President James Buchanan signed Colorado (the name means "red-colored" in Spanish) in as a territory on February 28, 1861. And only two days after that, Buchanan announced the creation of Nevada ("snow-covered") Territory, out of which was to come the first state to be formed in the Mountain West.

Slavery and the Civil War were factors in Nevada's swift passage to statehood. The territory was considerably short of the 60,000 inhabitants that were theoretically needed. But President Abraham Lincoln badly wanted two new Senators to help vote for the 13th Amendment and formally abolish slavery. Nevada could provide them, and after some maneuvering, it was proclaimed a state on October 31, 1864, only three years after achieving territorial status.

Meanwhile, Coloradans kept asking Congress to grant them statehood, but largely because several of their proposed state constitutions barred Negroes from the vote, their petitions were rejected. Colorado finally acquired statehood in 1876, exactly a century after the Declaration of Independence, and became known as the "Centennial State."

Idaho also encountered difficulties on the road toward statehood. Its present odd shape, with the northern panhandle cut off from the south by the deep Snake and Salmon River canyons, traces back to competing gold rushes of the early 1860s. One bonanza area was along Orofino Creek in the north, centering around the supply town of Lewiston. The other, which surrounded camps called Idaho City and Boise, was in the Boise River Valley to the south. The miners combined forces to make sure of getting a territory. What they got, the Idaho Territory of 1863, turned out to be a monstrosity larger than present-day Texas, being composed of eastern parts of Washington Territory and western parts of Dakota Territory. Its capital was located briefly at Lewiston and then, in 1864, was moved south to Boise. Idaho folklore abounds in pathetic tales of territorial governors who were never able to take office because of their inability to find the capital in that vastness of valleys and mountains.

The monstrous Idaho Territory of 1863 inevitably had a short life. Within a year the Montana gold seekers of Alder Gulch and Grasshopper Creek induced Congress to form Montana Territory out of a huge northern piece of Idaho Territory. Still another chunk was lopped off in 1868 to make Wyoming Territory. Montana achieved statehood in 1889. Idaho and Wyoming came in the following year. The roster of the eight Mountain States was completed in 1912 when the territories of Arizona and New Mexico presented constitutions acceptable to Congress and were admitted to statehood at last —four centuries after the first Spaniards arrived.

During the Civil War, the United States had abandoned its rambunctious infant in the West to fight for its own survival in the East. The mountaineers took care of themselves. They allowed the Confederacy to capture Santa Fe and hold New Mexico for a month. But when General Henry H. Sibley's Texans began moving north to seize Denver and its gold mines, Colorado's Governor William Gilpin sprang into what might be called typically Western action—enthusiastic, impromptu, unauthorized and, seemingly, ill-advised. He called out a tatterdemalion miners' army of his own, gathered supplies and guns from Denver stores and mining camps, and sent his men scurrying south over Raton Pass. Joined by a detachment of U.S. Army troops from Fort Union, New Mexico, Gilpin's "Pet Lambs of Colorado" whipped Sibley's regulars in La Glorieta Pass near Santa Fe on March 28, 1862. That ended the Civil War in the Mountain West.

The Indian wars were, however, just beginning. They would continue for 30 years until the compulsions of manifest destiny had stripped every member of the nomadic tribes of his land, his pride, his creative impulse, his dignity and every other conceivable thing that made his life worth living. The mining rushes of the 1850s and 1860s and the linkup of the Union Pacific and Central Pacific railroads in 1869, connecting Omaha with San

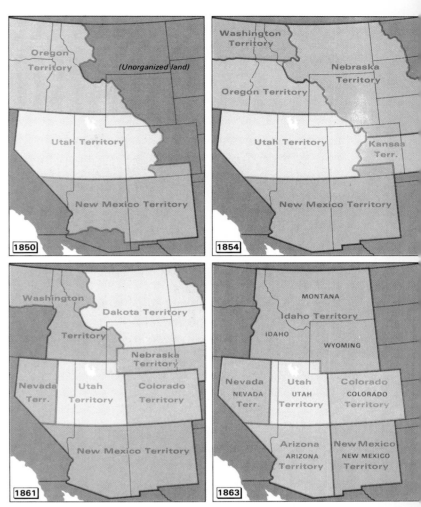

Political boundaries in the Mountain States area went through almost constant change during the 1850s and early 1860s. Territories were established and then either dissolved or subdivided. One of the major causes of this continual shifting was the nation's disagreement over slavery. The Northern politicians wanted slavery prohibited in the new territories so that they would eventually become free states; the Southerners wanted slavery permitted so that the new states would be antiabolitionist. Trying to satisfy both camps, Congress passed bills such as the Compromise of 1850 and the Kansas-Nebraska Act of 1854, which resulted in the juggling of Western territories shown at top. Other factors also influenced the shifting of territorial boundaries. In 1854 the territory of Utah, for example, included all of what is now Nevada and Utah, and much of Colorado. Primarily to stop the spread of Mormonism, a religion that then sanctioned polygamy, Utah Territory was whittled down between 1854 and 1861 and again between 1861 and 1863, until it reached the approximate size of the state. By 1863 (lower right) the territorial boundaries were more or less stabilized, and over the next several decades the various states came into being as shown.

Francisco, were enormously helpful in building the West but they sped up the Indian crisis. The presence of increasing numbers of white men brought great pressure upon the Indians; in addition, the white men caused a significant—and to the Indians, nearly fatal—change in the ecology of the region. They began the systematic slaughter of buffalo, whose hides make fine carriage robes and whose pickled tongues became something of an Eastern staple. Moreover, in a misguided effort to "civilize" the tribes, the federal government encouraged the killing of buffalo. But buffalo were everything to the High Plains tribes—food, clothing, shelter, ornament, fuel. After years of shameful slaughter ("Buffalo Bill" Cody claimed to have killed 4,280 of the huge creatures all by himself in one brief period of his career), the big herds were gone and the situation of countless Indians became desperate.

And so the 1860s, 1870s and 1880s brought battles and massacres from Montana to Arizona. Sometimes the Indians killed the whites, as on the lazy Montana afternoon of June 25, 1876, when the Sioux killed Colonel George Armstrong Custer's young men in the Battle of the Little Big Horn. Sometimes the whites killed the Indians, as in 1864 when Denver volunteers slipped up on a camp of sleeping Cheyenne and Arapaho tribesmen at Sand Creek

in Colorado and blazed away. Sometimes all horrors were combined, as in 1877 when Chief Joseph and 600 Nez Percé men, women and children tried to escape to Canada by way of Idaho and Montana through a gantlet of several U.S. armies. After four months of flight the Nez Percés were caught by troops under Colonel Nelson A. Miles about 30 miles short of the Canadian border. They numbered only 418 by then and were sent to a reservation in Indian Territory.

Whoever killed whom or chased whom, it all amounted to a tragic failure in the conduct of human affairs. And it brought a sense of guilt that is with Americans still. Perhaps that is why they have made heroes out of so many Indian leaders and have named so many landmarks and towns and counties and streams and goodness knows what all for them—for Cochise and Geronimo, Red Cloud and Chief Joseph and Charlot and Washakie. Even the ladies have been honored, including Chief Ouray's wife, Chipeta, and Pitamakan, "the Joan of Arc of the Blackfeet," whose claim to immortality is based on her skill as a military leader. Colorado has Chipeta Mountain near Salida and the town of Chipita (*sic*) Park. Montana has Pitamakan Pass in Glacier National Park.

Gold and railroads had brought Americans to the

Mountain West, and something else had helped: the large amount of available land. The public domain was huge—half a billion acres. One might think that this land would have had to be surveyed, broken down into quadrangles, counties, townships and sections, and recorded on paper in an office somewhere before people or companies could acquire it or use it. Not in the Mountain West. Starting in the Denver area in 1858, towns were mapped, streets and roads built, lots sold, mining claims staked, timber harvested, and ranches and farms laid out on the public domain without surveys. And when the cowboys of the 1870s drove their herds from Texas north across the plains to Wyoming and Montana, they just drove as they pleased. Many of them settled on ranches, but it did not occur to them for years to buy the land. Instead they put all their money in cattle, horses and ranch buildings. Why put money in land that they could use for nothing?

As soon as the U.S. Department of the Interior got itself organized to cope with the situation, it placed General Land Offices in towns throughout the Mountain West. Under the Pre-emption Act of 1841, a measure that was originally intended to produce revenue for the government, serious settlers could pre-empt 160 acres of land for as little as

$1.25 an acre, notify the land office and be sure of getting title to it when surveys were made—someday. In 1862 President Abraham Lincoln shocked many people by signing the first Homestead Act and arranging to *give* land to pioneers—a something-for-nothing plan that had been bitterly opposed by Southern Democrats, who rightly saw it as a threat to slavery. Lincoln's purpose was to promote Western settlement, to increase land values and to speed up the process of getting public lands into private hands. By the terms of this first Homestead Act, a settler would receive free a tract of 160 acres if he lived on it or cultivated it for five years. A tract could also be purchased for $1.25 an acre after only six months if certain improvements were made. As things developed, many homesteads fell into the hands of speculators, and all kinds of frauds were worked by people who claimed to be homesteaders but used the land free without living on it or actually making improvements. A man would swear, for example, that he had built a 12-by-14 house on the property without revealing that the measurements were in inches rather than in feet. Still, the program worked out fairly well. Some 250 million acres of Western land were disposed of under the several homestead laws enacted after 1862.

Title to the homesteads could not be officially

secured until the land had been surveyed. For years settlers simply squatted on their acreages waiting for surveys to be made. And surveyors did show up finally. We have seen that men like Lewis and Clark, Pike and Frémont all brought something to people's knowledge of the Mountain West. But it was the post-Civil War government geological surveyors who revealed its overwhelming grandeur and gave it practical dimensions. One of the most extensive of the government surveys was conducted by a geologist and physician, Dr. Ferdinand Vandiveer Hayden, who had an unquenchable thirst for nature's secrets and a child's joy in the wonder of the outdoors.

Hayden and his young subordinates surveyed the geyser-and-paint-pot corner of Wyoming in 1871 to prepare for the creation of Yellowstone National Park a year later. From 1873 to 1876 the Hayden men mapped thousands of square miles of the Colorado Rockies, including Pikes Peak, the Mount of the Holy Cross, Mesa Verde's cliff dwellings and the whole stunning spread of the San Juans. Today's maps are splattered with the names of Hayden geographers—Gannett Peak in Wyoming after Henry Gannett, Marvine Lake in Colorado for Archibald Marvine, Mount Wilson in the San Miguels for Ada D. Wilson. Hayden himself is memorialized on Colorado maps by the town of Hayden, Hayden Lake, two Hayden Mountains and three Hayden Peaks.

Hayden mapped the mountains well, but a greater contribution was made by Major John Wesley Powell. Powell's government survey area included the canyonlands of Utah and northern Arizona from the Uinta Mountains south to the area of the Grand Canyon. The major was an indomitable explorer; he had lost an arm as a result of a wound sustained at Shiloh but he nonetheless led a party of men in 1869, and another in 1871-1872, through the perilous gorges of the Green and Colorado Rivers.

Epochal as these journeys were, Powell's real achievement was not what he found but what he wrote. His prophetic *Report on the Lands of the Arid Regions*, which the federal government published in 1878, described in scientific terms the Mountain West and the realities of its aridity, its altitude and its climate. The report explained what men had to do to convert obstacles of geography into advantages. Among other things, Powell said that the values represented by the mountains— values in water, in crops, in livestock, in timber, and in health and recreation—were national assets of potential benefit to every citizen. They had to be preserved and enhanced for posterity by careful conservation methods and regional cooperation.

Powell's report was deeply resented at first. Westerners were convinced that his pleas for conservation threatened their freedoms and the sanctity of their paradise. But by the late 1880s they were becoming disturbed by the overgrazing that was occurring on the public domain, by the destruction of timber resources and by a succession of crop failures caused by drought. In 1891 some of them approved when Congress passed the Forest Reserve Act and President Benjamin Harrison put 13 million acres into federal reserves to protect the Western watersheds. President Theodore Roosevelt earned his great reputation as a conservationist by increasing the reserve by more than 148 million acres of forest lands and 80 million acres of mineral lands, much of it in the Mountain West.

It was Roosevelt also who helped Congressman Francis G. Newlands of Nevada and other Western Congressmen to pass the Reclamation Act in 1902, putting the federal government into the business of building dams in the West for irrigation. The popularity of the act showed how much Westerners had changed in two decades, how far they had moved toward their present odd duality of attitude—rugged individualism and willingness to engage in communal effort, stout defense of states' rights and eager acceptance of federal aid.

And still this new West today loves its past, fights for old freedoms and clings to its old ways. A Spanish girl in Taos or Santa Fe swirling by in a long skirt with flowers in her black hair looks about the same as a Spanish girl looked in the 1820s on the way to the fandango with a trapper on each arm. Skiers and climbers and hunters swarm over the Colorado highlands as adventurously as did the prospectors of Leadville and Cripple Creek and the San Juans. The high rollers who shoot craps for big stakes in Nevada have not changed since Comstock Lode days. In Las Vegas and Reno they still endlessly throw the dice—and look to California for suckers. In Wyoming the cowboy is still king, despite all the big money in oil.

Of course a good part of these mountains belongs to all Americans, not just Western Americans, because of the national parks and forests, the national grazing districts and wildlife refuges and the missile test sites. Any mountaineer will admit *that*. And he knows that the politicians in Washington spend a large share of the money they get out of him in taxes improving his shining land. Mighty nice of the Washington boys, eh, podner? And, come next election, let's show the old frontier spirit and throw the rascals out!

High in the Grand Tetons of Wyoming in 1872 explorer-photographer William H. Jackson prepares wet plates for his camera.

Bringing the West back East

To most mid-19th Century Americans the lands of the mountain region seemed remote and valueless. But by the end of the century the popular image of this expanse of painted deserts, soaring peaks and deep gorges had become one of romance and opportunity. In large measure this change was effected by a few photographers who took thousands of twin-image shots that, when placed in a home viewing device called a "stereoscope," seemed to leap into three-dimensional scenes. These startling views created interest in the West both in Congress and in millions of parlors. For the "stay-at-homes" they were a window on the frontier; for the adventurous they were a spur to migration.

A now-familiar sight in Yellowstone Park, Lower Falls was unknown to most Americans until this photograph appeared in the 1870s.

Pictures that helped create a national park

In the years following the Civil War a number of scientific expeditions explored the great American wilderness of the mountain region to collect detailed information on natural resources, geography and Indian tribes. Often photographers accompanied these survey teams to record the areas under study. These pictures reproduced here, showing parts of what is now Yellowstone National Park, were taken by William H. Jackson. They so impressed members of Congress that the lawmakers abandoned their initial opposition to the idea of a park and voted, in 1872, to establish the now-famous nature preserve.

Mounds of sulfur, spewed up by Old Faithful in Yellowstone Park, surround the quiescent mineral pools of the geyser as two smaller geysers *(background)* set off impressive displays of their power.

Recording the ways of the Indians

Though bad blood between red man and white was flowing bitterly through the Southwest during the third quarter of the 19th Century, survey-team photographers still found it possible to capture on plates the bitter yet proud Indians and their tribal rites. In some instances these pictures remain the sole photographic record of the customs of the tribes. Soon a number of the tribes would disappear altogether, their grazing and hunting lands taken over by the relentlessly expanding whites. Other tribes attempted to adopt some of the white man's ways and in so doing lost much that was unique in their own cultures. Still others have maintained the rites of their ancestors, but so wary have they become of the white man and his way that they often refuse to permit pictures to be taken. Even during the 1870s most Indians of the Southwest were camera shy; despite this, photographers were able to bring back a priceless record of their culture.

Zuni Indians dance in their pueblo square a re-enactment of an attack by the Navajo. The "Navajo" wear white men's garb.

A youthful Navajo brave and his mother pose for Timothy O'Sullivan in 1873, shortly after the tribe had been defeated by U.S. troops.

Chief Ouray (center) of the Utes poses with other chiefs. His liking for scout Kit Carson extended to many whites, including photographer Jackson.

Life and work on the Western frontier

When the post-Civil War survey teams entered the Mountain States region they found an already flourishing frontier society made up of ranchers, Indian traders, hunters and miners. With its rich gold and silver mines the West had a reputation as an El Dorado peopled by daredevils and ruffians; the survey-team cameramen showed that ordinary men, too, could prosper in the West. Their pictures played a significant part in spurring migration—not only of rough-and-ready adventurers but also of many thousands of homesteaders who in due course would bring peace and law to the region.

A begrimed worker mines the silver-rich Comstock Lode in Nevada. The picture, the first ever shot in a mine, was made by the light of flaring magnesium.

Rifles and pistols close at hand, several members of an 1872 surveying team warm themselves by the fireside at a rustic ranch house in Wyoming territory.

New tourist attractions to entice the rich

So well had the explorer-photographers done their work that it was not long before wealthy sportsmen, adventure-seekers and tourists began to make their way West in large numbers just to see with their own eyes what they had already viewed through their stereoscopes at home. Arriving by the trainload in specially outfitted and usually luxurious cars, gentlemen hunters—called dudes by the earlier settlers—disembarked and dressed themselves in cowboy hats, leather chaps, hand-tooled boots and bandannas for a spell of game shooting. By the late 1880s even well-to-do ladies from the East Coast were journeying to the Rockies to marvel at and absorb the wonders of nature. For by then a trip to the West had become an exciting yet safe and rewarding experience, rivaling in its attractions the traditional grand tour of Europe.

Dressed as if for a shopping trip, a group of proper Eastern ladies and their children tour the sulfur terraces of Yellowstone National Park.

Four dudes from back East strike virile poses beside mounds of antlers after a highly successful hunting expedition.

Straining up a tortuous trail, carriage horses wend their way up Pikes Peak in the late 1880s. Though the trip to the top took about five hours, tourists were rewarded with an awesome view.

3

Water: More Precious than Gold

Major John Wesley Powell, the greatest of the explorers of the Mountain West, wrote almost a century ago, "All the great values of this territory have ultimately to be measured to you in acre-feet." An acre-foot is 325,851 gallons of water: the amount of precipitation—rain, snow, hail or sleet—that must fall to cover an acre of ground to a depth of one foot. Powell meant, of course, that the region is too dry in too many places and therefore puts a premium on water supply. Its annual precipitation is less than half the national average.

People in humid regions may think of water as the dullest of liquids—two parts hydrogen and one part oxygen. To mountaineers, water is immeasurably thrilling, a spiritual as well as a material essence, a mystic omnipotence that is indispensable to life and the pursuit of happiness. When it rains, mountaineers are full of hope and good will. When it does not, they are stingy, gloomy and mean. The storm center of Western politics hovers over the issue of who gets how much water. Nothing else involves so much controversy, or so many federal,

regional, state, district, county and municipal agencies, boards, authorities, commissions and clubs, or such a tonnage of recorded rights, compacts, decrees, reports and angry letters to the editor.

Western water has been called "liquid gold," but it is far more valuable than gold. In an average year 600 million acre-feet of water falls on the Mountain States, though only a small portion—roughly 130 million acre-feet annually—is available for use by man. Most of the water quickly evaporates in this arid and semiarid country. In addition, some of the water that nurtures the forests and grassy prairies floats away from the vegetation in a process called transpiration. And still more is lost as it seeps deep into the earth. Each acre-foot that remains for use costs the average rancher or farmer approximately two dollars when it is delivered through irrigation ditches, and sets back urban dwellers and Western industries as much as $50 for the same quantity. So estimated, this would bring the cost of the 130 million acre-feet to two billion dollars in one year. By contrast, the Mountain States have produced only $2.8 billion worth of gold in 100 years.

The 130 million acre-foot treasure of the Mountain West is the runoff of springs, creeks and rivers being carried down toward the seas by the force of gravity from heights of land, the Continental

Winding through the lower reaches of Arizona's Grand Canyon, the Colorado River gently curves past bluffs of stratified rock that were carved by the river itself. Here the Colorado is stately and placid, but farther upstream it is a series of treacherous rapids.

The Continental Divide

The map at right traces the route of the Continental Divide *(heavy line)*, the ridge of the Rockies that separates rivers flowing toward the Gulf of Mexico from those flowing toward the Pacific. It also shows the courses of the rivers in the six major drainage basins. Northeast of the divide is the Upper Missouri Basin; its main river, the Missouri, flows 2,700 miles before joining the Mississippi for another 1,200-mile trip to the Gulf of Mexico. Due east is the Upper Arkansas Basin, which feeds the Arkansas and other rivers that also flow into the Mississippi. To the southeast is the Upper Rio Grande and Western Gulf Basin, which drains directly into the Gulf of Mexico. Northwest of the divide, the Upper Columbia Basin sends its waters to the Columbia River *(off the map to the left)*, which eventually reaches the Pacific. Due west is the Great Basin, the only one that has no outlet to the sea. Caught between mountains on all sides, the rivers here flow into landlocked lakes or simply evaporate in the desert. Most important as a source of water to the generally arid area is the southwestern Colorado Basin, whose main stream, the Colorado, with its tributaries, drains all of Arizona and parts of five other Mountain States before flowing into the Gulf of California.

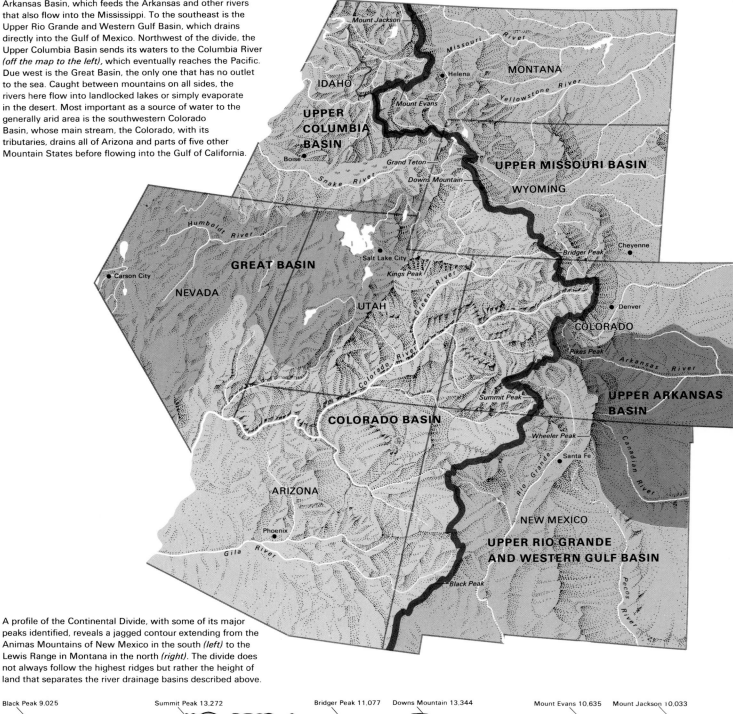

A profile of the Continental Divide, with some of its major peaks identified, reveals a jagged contour extending from the Animas Mountains of New Mexico in the south *(left)* to the Lewis Range in Montana in the north *(right)*. The divide does not always follow the highest ridges but rather the height of land that separates the river drainage basins described above.

Black Peak 9,025   Summit Peak 13,272   Bridger Peak 11,077   Downs Mountain 13,344   Mount Evans 10,635   Mount Jackson 10,033

Divide in particular. Along the divide, at altitudes of 9,000 feet and up, rain and snow fall in considerable quantities—the annual precipitation can be greater than the national average. Precipitation is heavy at these elevations because clouds of warm vapor from the Pacific hang on to their moisture as they scud across the lower deserts and prairies of the West and then drop it when it condenses in the high, cold air above the divide. So we have a basic condition. Most of the usable runoff is collected in high, rugged country far from the centers of population that need it the most.

All of the West's great waterways begin in especially wet parts of these thin, humid belts along the divide. One of the belts surrounds Glacier National Park, where the heavy precipitation creates important Montana and Idaho rivers like the Flathead and the Kootenai. Wyoming's Yellowstone National Park is soggy too. Many rivers—the Yellowstone, Madison, Snake, Shoshone, Wind and Green—start in the park, or within 50 miles or so of it, in groves of lodgepole pine near the divide.

There is a lot of rain and snow in the ranges of central Colorado, where the Rockies raise their highest summits and the big ski resorts flourish. The Arkansas, South Platte, Gunnison, Roaring Fork and Blue Rivers start as rills in alpine meadows amid 14,000-foot peaks. South of the Sawatch Range, between Stony Pass and Wolf Creek Pass, the Continental Divide receives winter and spring snows to a depth of 100 inches; drifts have reached 20 feet. Some years ago a Wolf Creek Pass snowslide swept a 40-ton truck from U.S. 160 and buried it so deep in a ravine that it was not dug out until May. In this great curl of the divide, the Rio Grande, the San Juan, the Animas and a dozen other waterways begin as trickles of melting snow.

All the divide's streams combine to form five main ocean-bound river systems—five main watersheds—plus the handful of Great Basin rivers that drain into and evaporate from Great Salt Lake and Nevada's lakes and sinks. If the eight million people of the Mountain West had the good sense to distribute themselves evenly, and if each river system received an equal share of the 130 million acre-feet of annual runoff, and *if* there were no thirsty megalopolis of Los Angeles, which takes a great deal of its water from one of these systems—the Colorado—and in so doing agitates everybody, the whole water situation would be sweetness and light in the Mountain States.

Such is not the case, and to a painful degree. First of all, the population of the region is scattered haphazardly and spottily over the land. But more important, the water yield is extremely uneven, and what water is available is not necessarily handy to the population centers. Two of the five ocean-bound watersheds—the Rio Grande and the Arkansas River systems, which serve New Mexico and Colorado—gather only tiny amounts of water from their drainage areas—roughly four million acre-feet. Even less water drains from the alkaline soils of the Great Basin of Utah and Nevada, much of which receives virtually no precipitation.

While these three southern drainage areas—together covering some 300,000 square miles—collect only seven million acre-feet of water annually, three northern rivers in Idaho and Montana—the Snake, the Kootenai and the Clark Fork—carry the enormous total of 74 million acre-feet as they leave the Mountain States to join the great Columbia River in the Pacific Northwest. Idaho's Snake River alone carries 40 million acre-feet to the Columbia from a western-slope watershed of 109,000 square miles.

Meanwhile, on the eastern slope of this water-blessed northern area, the Missouri River system gathers almost 20 million acre-feet each year from the Rockies of Montana and Wyoming. The Missouri system includes the flow of the Yellowstone and its tributaries—the Powder, Tongue, Little Big Horn and other rivers of the High Plains that people heard so much about during the Indian wars. The Missouri has the largest watershed and is the longest of the rivers that drain from the Rockies, extending 2,700 miles from the source of its highest Montana tributary, Red Rock River, to the Mississippi. But the western-slope Snake River carries by far the most water of all the Mountain States' rivers—30 per cent of the entire runoff.

The Missouri and the Snake are fine work-horse rivers. But the prima donna among the lot, the most varied in repertoire, the most admired, fought over and berated, and the most eccentric and historically exciting, is the Colorado. Its modest flow is out of all proportion to the river's fame and the amount of responsibility piled upon it. The flow has averaged only about 15 million acre-feet over the years, as measured near the upper end of Grand Canyon. But this relatively small amount must serve the needs of more than 30 per cent of the Mountain States' residents—plus several million Southern Californians.

The Colorado drains some 240,000 square miles of country in seven states—a country of endless enchantments. Some of the river is two miles above sea level, some of it a mile down at the bottom of Grand Canyon. The biggest tributary (by volume), Green River, starts in the Bridger Wilderness Area below Gannett Peak, Wyoming's highest, in the Wind River Range. The second-biggest tributary, the almost unknown San Juan River, splashes down from Wolf Creek Pass in southern Colorado. Other rivers in the Colorado system in order of size are the Gunnison; the sparkling Roaring Fork; the Yampa; the Dolores, which the Spanish explorer Father Escalante named; and the Animas, flashing down its canyon from Silverton, Colorado, to join the San Juan in New Mexico.

Everything about the Colorado is mixed up and debatable, as can be seen from a discussion of just what *is* the Colorado. The river, as it was once defined, had two major divisions: the Upper Colorado and the Lower Colorado. The dividing point between these two sections was a place in Utah where the Colorado is joined by the Green River. Major Powell and others put the Colorado's total length at 1,700 miles. But that mileage was measured from the Colorado's mouth in the Gulf of California to the source of the Green River, which is by itself 730 miles long. Green River is 300 miles longer than the part of the river above the junction with Green River. The Upper and Lower Colorado together travel a total distance of only 1,440 miles. Well, if Green River was so much longer than the Upper Colorado, why wasn't the Green called the Colorado? It wasn't big enough, some said. Green River carries 4.6 million acre-feet of water annually. The Upper Colorado carries 6.3 million acre-feet as estimated in Canyonlands National Park, Utah, near the Green-Colorado junction.

But the matter is much more complicated than that. Before 1921 the term "Colorado River," a name bestowed by the Spaniards, referred only to the 1,000 miles below the mouth of the Green. The section above the mouth was called Grand River by Coloradans, who applied the "Grand" part in the 1880s to the new Grand River towns of Grand Valley and Grand Junction. Meanwhile, Utah citizens kept demanding that the longer Green River be recognized as the main stream by having its name changed to Colorado River as well. Coloradans wanted none of that. It had always irked them that a Colorado River existed that was not in Colorado. And they realized the value to them if the Colorado River officially began deep inside Colorado and carried the state's name, signifying to the other Mountain States—and to California—that the whole of it was not merely the Colorado River but *Colorado's* river. In 1921, while the Utah legislature was not in session, the Colorado legislature changed the name of Grand River to Colorado River, declaring that the Grand carried more water

than the Green and therefore was the main stream, even if the Green was 300 miles longer. Congress confirmed the change.

The official Colorado begins as cheerful rivulets 10,000 feet up in the lovely Never Summer Mountains northwest of Denver. The source area is called "Little Yellowstone" because of the presence of yellow outcrops of rock amid the stands of aspen and spruce. The rivulets are only a few miles from the Milner Pass summer picnic tables on Trail Ridge Road, which crosses Rocky Mountain National Park above the timber line, but they are not visible from that vantage point. Specimen Mountain blocks the rivulets from the view of picnickers in the pass munching their fried chicken and tossing snowballs at each other.

The Colorado increases in size in the fragrant hay meadows of Middle Park when Blue River ripples down from Hoosier Pass and the Breckenridge skiing area to join it at the ranch center of Kremmling. Then it hurries through the nut-brown canyons and striated cliffs of western Colorado, and near Moab, Utah, it enters the red-rock chaos of Canyonlands National Park and begins its awesome trip through 600 miles of gorges to Lake Mead and Hoover Dam. As it flows through Utah the river changes character. The attractive blue mountain stream becomes a dull yellow glint at the bottom of canyons—an aloof comment on the inconceivable age of the universe and the inconsequence of man. The sheer canyon walls are pages of a book telling the history of the planet, the warpings and breakings of the earth's crust, the comings and goings of seas, the slow evolution of life.

Major Powell's party boated through the shoals and rapids between these walls in 1869 after surviving the lesser but still relatively deep gorges of Green River—Flaming Gorge, Lodore, Whirlpool, Desolation and others. Wisely, most of the settlers of Utah and northern Arizona stopped far short of these formidable passages of the Green and the Colorado, and commerce and emigrants detoured around them to the north and south. To this day, the area is largely uninhabited, although its beauty is striking. The first of the spectacular gorges begins at Moab, Utah, running 70 miles through Canyonlands National Park as far as the mouth of Green River. The rapids of Cataract Canyon rush on for 40 miles, followed by 180 miles of Lake Powell, the major's memorial, which floods Glen Canyon behind Glen Canyon Dam at Page, Arizona.

From just below Page, Marble Canyon extends approximately 60 miles south before widening and deepening into the immensity of Grand Canyon

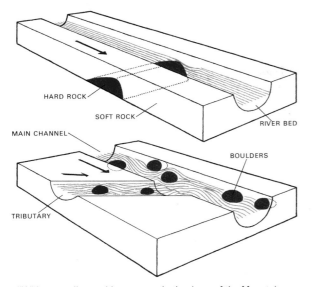

"Whitewater," or rapids, common in the rivers of the Mountain States, is caused by irregularities in the river's bed. In a bed made up of hard and soft rock layers *(top diagram)* the softer rock erodes faster, leaving the hard rock and creating a washboardlike surface that causes turbulence. Boulders, broken off the surrounding canyons or carried to the river by its tributaries *(lower diagram),* also cause rapids. Whenever fast-moving water encounters these obstructions on the uneven bed, it foams, creating "whitewater."

near the northern edge of Grand Canyon National Park. Grand Canyon has quite a variety of declared lengths. Some say it is 217 miles long. Others throw in Marble Canyon's 60 miles for a total length of 277 miles. One hundred and four miles of Grand Canyon lie in Grand Canyon National Park. Forty miles more are in Grand Canyon National Monument, which adjoins the park on the west. But the canyon is alleged by some to end 75 miles farther downstream at Grand Wash Cliffs in the Lake Mead Recreation Area. The spectacle of the Colorado River ends there too, as far as canyon histrionics are concerned. Below Lake Mead and Hoover Dam the river undergoes another radical transformation, becoming a broad, shallow desert stream carrying what remains of its 15 million acre-feet toward the Gulf of California.

To sum up, it is these six drainage basins—the Continental Divide's eastern-slope systems of the Missouri, Arkansas and Rio Grande and the divide's western-slope systems of the Columbia, Colorado and Great Basin—that gather the water annually available to the people of the Mountain States. The controlled use of this water by humans dates back to the practices of the ancient Indians of the Southwest. Some of the Indians raised corn in their almost rainless desert by building irrigation ditches along the Salt River. The ditches lay around present-day Phoenix, Arizona, frequently in the same places where ditches today carry water to the citrus groves, swimming pools, air conditioners and golf courses of the Salt River Valley. To the east, along the Rio Grande below Taos in New Mexico, Spanish colonists after 1600 also made attempts at irrigation, as the Pueblo Indians had been doing for centuries.

Early American explorers, soldiers and traders tried unsuccessfully to make navigable waterways out of the shallow Arkansas, the two Plattes, the Big Horn, the Snake and the Yellowstone, assuming that these streams had full year-round flows like Eastern rivers. But Brigham Young and his Mormons, after beginning their pioneer Utah settlement in 1847, rapidly learned that they could not count on the kind of rainfall that filled Eastern rivers and watered Eastern crops. Soon after arriving at Great Salt Lake, they began tapping City Creek to water their fields. Over the ensuing years they created an irrigation system that enabled them to survive and prosper in their arid promised land. The Colorado gold rush of 1859 inspired irrigation systems in the Arkansas River's drainage area and on the South Platte around Denver. Eleven years later a group of settlers led by Nathan Meeker founded Greeley, Colorado, on Cache la Poudre River 50 miles north of Denver. Meeker's men studied the Mormon ditches and went to work on an irrigation system of their own.

The builders of the early ditches realized that the legal rights to the use of water in the West, where streams often ran very low—and even dried up—had to be different from water rights in the East, where stream beds generally had plenty of water in them. Back East, a man got the use of stream water by buying land on either bank of the stream. A reasonable amount of the water flowing past his property was his to take out and use, and nobody could deprive him of that use. This practice created few problems; since there was ample water available, there was plenty left over for downstream holders. This kind of water right, derived from old English law, was called a riparian right, "riparian" meaning "of a bank of a river."

In place of this Eastern riparian right, Western irrigators followed mining practices for a new kind of "first come, first served" water right. From the time of the California Gold Rush, Western miners had been staking placer claims along the banks of creeks where gold was caught in loose sand. They diverted the water from the stream to their sluice boxes, or to dry gulches of gold-bearing sand in the vicinity, and used it to wash away the sand from the heavier gold. By common consent, the first miner to stake such a claim on a creek acquired also the first, the *prior*, right to appropriate—to use for his work—a fixed amount of the creek's water. When the creek ran low, only enough water might be available to meet the rights of this first miner and a few other early birds. That was fair and square —"first come, first served."

The irrigators of the 1860s adopted this "water right by prior appropriation" doctrine, and it became the legal basis of runoff distribution arrangements in most of the Mountain West. In addition, it was generally accepted that a man's water right was real property separate from his land. If he sold the land, he could retain the water right and apply it "to beneficial use" somewhere else in the same watershed. Or he could sell the water right with its priority intact. By 1900 many thousands of rights involving every river and creek in Colorado, for example, had been recorded in huge red leather books kept at the office of the State Engineer, who had charge of Colorado's water. The rights by then were being issued not just to farmers but to everybody who had a definite use for water—to cities and railroads, to factories and hotels, to real-estate promoters, and to companies building ditches and selling water from them. As the Colorado Constitution puts it: "The right to divert the unappropriated waters of any natural stream to beneficial use shall never be denied."

Virtually every recorded right, by this time, had been "adjudicated" by a Colorado district court as to the date of the owner's priority and the amount of water he needed to divert from his particular stream for his beneficial use. When the water in a given Colorado watershed became scarce, the State Engineer determined how far it would go among its appropriators and set a cutoff date—1880, for example, meaning that owners of water rights dated later than 1880 had to shut the head gates of the ditches through which they drew water from the river until more of it was available. The State Engineer had a water commissioner in each watershed district to enforce his cutoff orders, at gun point if necessary.

No institution in the West was more American, more democratic, fair and youthfully optimistic than this doctrine of "water right by prior appropriation." It was an invitation to every mountaineer to get his share of the land's most precious resource by finding some good way to use it. The doctrine was an invitation also to Congress, which passed the Reclamation Act in 1902, authorizing the Department of the Interior to set up large-scale irrigation projects. One of the first of these was the Salt River Project in Arizona, which began delivering its first irrigation water from behind Roosevelt Dam in 1907. Still a grand old pile, the dam was designed to store 1,382,000 acre-feet from Salt River, a branch of the Colorado via Gila River, and regulate its flow to the fields of carrots, cotton, oranges and corn around Phoenix. Though built by the federal Bureau of Reclamation, the dam actually got there as a result of grassroots action. The farmers of the Salt River Valley had formed an association, obtained money for a plan and won Congressional approval for the dam by pledging their lands to repay the federal government eventually for the cost of construction. To supply power for construction, a small, 900-kilowatt hydroelectric plant was added to the plan. The power plant was to have important consequences.

From the start the demand in Salt River Valley for Roosevelt Dam electric power was so great that the plant was enlarged to a capacity of 4,500 kilowatts within five years after its opening. And so at Salt River the Mountain West pragmatically hit on still other beneficial uses for its 130 million acre-feet of runoff. Each river canyon had potential dam sites. Gravity would force water at the penstocks of the dams to turn turbines to generate power. Sale of the power would help pay for the dams and their beneficial uses—irrigation, flood control, domestic water supply and recreation.

The success of Roosevelt Dam led to its epic descendant, Hoover Dam, which was completed by the Bureau of Reclamation in 1936. Hoover, 726 feet high, backs up the Colorado River for 115 miles to form Lake Mead along the Nevada-Arizona border below Grand Canyon. Lake Mead can store more than 28 million acre-feet of water—nearly twice the annual flow of the Colorado. The lake and the dam are part of a $245 million project that irrigates more than a million acres in California, Arizona and Nevada and produces 1.3 million kilowatts of power. By regulating the flow of the Colorado, Hoover Dam in addition made possible the construction of Parker Dam on the Arizona-California border and the construction of the Colorado River Aqueduct from Parker, which supplies water to 10 million people in Los Angeles and 118 other California cities.

Hoover Dam rose out of the same beneficial-use doctrine of prior appropriation and the same grassroots action that had produced Roosevelt Dam. But there was a difference. The grassroots promoters of Hoover Dam were primarily Southern

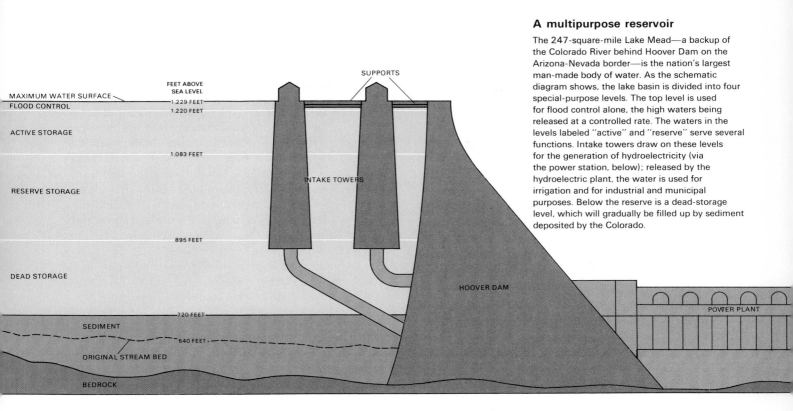

A multipurpose reservoir

The 247-square-mile Lake Mead—a backup of the Colorado River behind Hoover Dam on the Arizona-Nevada border—is the nation's largest man-made body of water. As the schematic diagram shows, the lake basin is divided into four special-purpose levels. The top level is used for flood control alone, the high waters being released at a controlled rate. The waters in the levels labeled "active" and "reserve" serve several functions. Intake towers draw on these levels for the generation of hydroelectricity (via the power station, below); released by the hydroelectric plant, the water is used for irrigation and for industrial and municipal purposes. Below the reserve is a dead-storage level, which will gradually be filled up by sediment deposited by the Colorado.

Diagram labels:
MAXIMUM WATER SURFACE
FLOOD CONTROL
ACTIVE STORAGE
RESERVE STORAGE
DEAD STORAGE
SEDIMENT
ORIGINAL STREAM BED
BEDROCK
FEET ABOVE SEA LEVEL
1,229 FEET
1,220 FEET
1,083 FEET
895 FEET
720 FEET
640 FEET
SUPPORTS
INTAKE TOWERS
HOOVER DAM
POWER PLANT

Californians. Some of the beneficial uses that they put before Congress were seacoast uses far from the watershed of the Colorado River—242 pipeline miles, to be exact. The basic question was: Whose river was it, anyhow? And there were a couple of other important questions: Would the state of Colorado have to start curtailing the use of the water in its own river so that Los Angeles could get bigger and richer? Was Arizona's growth to be blighted simply because it could not conjure up for Congress an immediate beneficial use?

For years the debate raged throughout the Colorado River Basin states—state versus state, states versus Congress, and everybody versus the U.S. Supreme Court. Consistently, the Court held that Congress was the final authority over the use of interstate waters under the commerce, property and general-welfare clauses of the Constitution. And, as a property owner, the federal government had priority over all other holders of water rights. Hoover Dam, for instance, was federal property committed to supply power. If Lake Mead's storage level fell below 14.5 million acre-feet, both the power production and water-supply commitments of Hoover Dam would be threatened. State officials upstream from the dam would be obligated to take steps to raise the lake's storage level by shutting

down head gates or releasing water from their own storage reservoirs no matter what water rights their constituents otherwise held.

Naturally, the states using the Colorado did not want to be asking Congress or the Supreme Court to settle their water disputes all the time. To avoid this, they established the Colorado River Compact among themselves in 1922, and Congress approved it in 1929. It worked well enough to inspire a great many more compacts among the Mountain West states to apportion the water they share.

The Colorado River Compact assigned 7.5 million acre-feet of the Colorado's annual flow to be used above Lee Ferry in the four Upper Basin states—Wyoming, Colorado, Utah and New Mexico. Another 7.5 million acre-feet was assigned to the three Lower Basin states—Arizona, Nevada and California. By a later compact (1948), the four Upper Basin states agreed on the amount of water each of them could use from their 7.5 million acre-feet. This compact helped the four to agree in 1956 on the complex Colorado River Storage Project of multipurpose dams, which include Glen Canyon on the Colorado and Flaming Gorge on Green River in Utah, the three-dam Curecanti Unit on the Gunnison in Colorado and Navajo Dam on the San Juan in New Mexico. A proposed seventh dam,

The two graphs at right show how the flow of the Colorado River, a major source of water for the Mountain States, is now apportioned, and how it is expected to be used in 1975. Under the terms of the Colorado River Compact *(top graph)*, which took effect in 1929, the states of the Upper Basin—Colorado, New Mexico, Utah and Wyoming—and the Lower Basin—California, Arizona and Nevada—were each allotted 7.5 million acre-feet of the Colorado's water annually. Since 1944 Mexico also has been allotted 1.5 million acre-feet, bringing the total to 16.5 million. Experience has shown, however, that the Colorado can supply only 15 million acre-feet a year, and the Lower Basin and Mexico have used water not required by the less needy Upper Basin. A new, more realistic division of the Colorado's water *(bottom graph)* has been projected for 1975 by the U.S. Bureau of Reclamation.

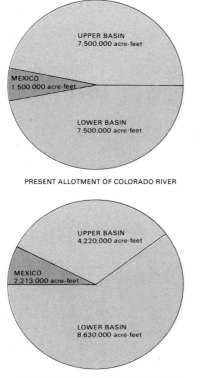

PRESENT ALLOTMENT OF COLORADO RIVER

UPPER BASIN
7,500,000 acre-feet

MEXICO
1,500,000 acre-feet

LOWER BASIN
7,500,000 acre-feet

UPPER BASIN
4,220,000 acre-feet

MEXICO
2,213,000 acre-feet

LOWER BASIN
8,630,000 acre-feet

PROJECTED USE OF THE COLORADO IN 1975

to be situated at Echo Park on Green River in Dinosaur National Monument, was dropped from the project because of a national uprising of conservationists against it.

Meanwhile, Arizona, California and Nevada could not agree on a division of the Lower Basin's annual 7.5 million acre-feet. And so in 1963 a Supreme Court decision had the effect of dividing the water for them, giving 4.4 million acre-feet to California, 2.8 million to Arizona and the small remainder to Nevada. By this time the building of Hoover-style multipurpose dams had become a favorite Western outdoor sport. Everywhere grassroots groups—"water conservancy districts"—were cooking them up by the hundreds and thereby appropriating great quantities of the Mountain States' annual 130 million acre-feet. Among the larger projects of the conservancy districts were the Fort Peck Dam on the upper Missouri, Hungry Horse on the Flathead, Boysen on the Wind, Yellowtail on the Big Horn, Palisades on the Snake, Pathfinder and Glendo on the North Platte, John Martin on the Arkansas and Elephant Butte on the Rio Grande. Some of these monsters were built primarily for irrigation by the Bureau of Reclamation, as required by the Reclamation Act. Some were built by the Army Corps of Engineers, whose dams

must relate to flood control and navigation. Some were put up by investor-owned utilities, such as the Idaho Power Company, the builder of Brownlee, Oxbow and Hells Canyon power dams on the Snake River.

As a climax to this frenzy of dam construction, the seven Colorado River Compact states, egged on by the Bureau of Reclamation and the Secretary of the Interior, petitioned Congress in the mid-1960s to approve what they called the Colorado River Basin Project, which would have been one of the costliest water schemes in U.S. history. They asked the federal government to spend $1.8 billion on a whole new series of dams that promised some benefit to residents of Los Angeles, California; Las Vegas, Nevada; Albuquerque, New Mexico; Salt Lake City, Utah; and practically everybody else in or adjoining the 240,000 square miles of the Colorado's watershed. However, a top-heavy 75 per cent of the total amount—$1.25 billion—was to be spent to bring relief to residents of central Arizona, who were facing serious water problems because of the postwar growth of Phoenix and Tucson. This Central Arizona Project part of the new plan involved pumping 1.2 million acre-feet of Colorado River water up to central Arizona through 400 miles of aqueducts costing $500 million. The pipes, canals and pumping stations were to be paid for by the sale of power from two more dams on the Colorado —in Grand Canyon and in Marble Canyon. These two dams alone would together have cost $750 million. Like the rest of the Colorado River Basin Project, they were expected to pay for themselves eventually, and to return the cost of their construction to the federal government, but they would have flooded 140 miles of Grand Canyon and Marble Canyon. The flooding would have eliminated living space for bighorn sheep and other canyon wildlife, destroyed unusual deep-canyon flora and removed rare geological formations from view.

The same conservationists who in the 1950s had blocked the proposed dam at Echo Park in Dinosaur National Monument protested even more loudly against building dams in either Grand Canyon or Marble Canyon. Congress heeded the protest and shelved the bill, and the Department of the Interior withdrew its support of the two dams. Not all the Congressmen based their nays on objections to flooding parts of a unique and beloved geological phenomenon, at the edge of a national park. Uppermost in several Congressional minds was the knowledge that the Colorado River has over the years been producing an average of only 15 million acre-feet of runoff. It had been doing far better than

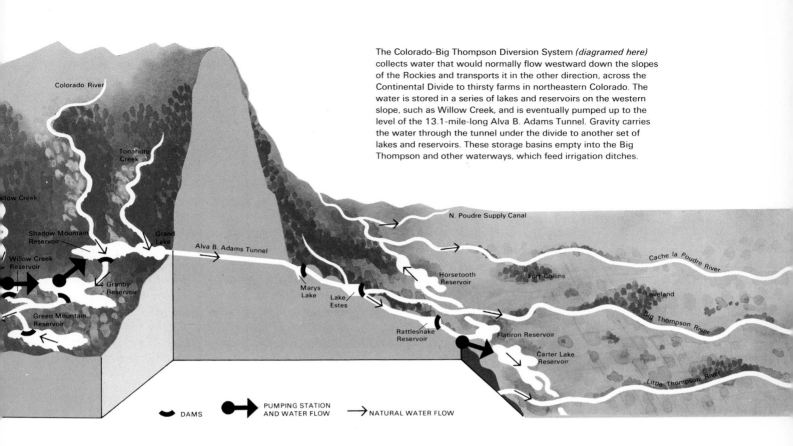

The Colorado-Big Thompson Diversion System *(diagramed here)* collects water that would normally flow westward down the slopes of the Rockies and transports it in the other direction, across the Continental Divide to thirsty farms in northeastern Colorado. The water is stored in a series of lakes and reservoirs on the western slope, such as Willow Creek, and is eventually pumped up to the level of the 13.1-mile-long Alva B. Adams Tunnel. Gravity carries the water through the tunnel under the divide to another set of lakes and reservoirs. These storage basins empty into the Big Thompson and other waterways, which feed irrigation ditches.

that in the years before 1922, when the Colorado River Compact was drawn, and the Congressmen knew that the compact, based on that greater average flow, allocates 15 million acre-feet among the seven compact states, that another 1.5 million acre-feet of runoff has been promised to Mexico by treaty, and that still another 1.5 million acre-feet is estimated to evaporate annually from Lake Mead, Lake Powell, Lake Mojave and Lake Havasu. In short, the Colorado is a bankrupt river. It owes at least three million more acre-feet of water annually than it takes in. So some of the Congressmen wondered if it were wise to spend $1.8 billion of federal funds to improve the distribution of water that was in fact nonexistent.

Not only does the Colorado owe more water than it takes in, but this intake is increasingly affected by a practice called transmountain diversion. It involves in this particular case the use of ditches and water tunnels to divert water from the drainage area of the Colorado on the western slope of the Continental Divide to drainage areas on the eastern slope. The process can be visualized as a sort of tug of war over the water between western-slope users and eastern-slope users. Near the Colorado's lower western reaches are Los Angeles and Phoenix and Tucson, all burgeoning incredibly and

needing more and more water. Near the river's source to the northeast, just over the Continental Divide, is metropolitan Denver, population one million, and also very thirsty. South of Denver is Colorado Springs, fond of lawns, pools and golf courses, and then there is Pueblo, with a water-consuming steel mill. The Colorado Springs and Pueblo metropolitan areas together have 325,000 residents, and a great many more coming. For water to supply their needs, however, these cities are on the wrong side of the Continental Divide. When it rains and snows along the divide above the eastern-slope cities, two thirds of the moisture falls on the western slope. That is why the South Platte and Arkansas Rivers on the eastern slope have such minuscule flows—less than two million acre-feet a year between them. And that is why eastern-slope cities and farmers in Colorado have been diverting water from the western slope over or under the Continental Divide by ditches and tunnels for almost a century.

Transmountain diversion has increased enormously since 1953, when only 133,770 acre-feet of water, mostly from the Colorado River, was taken from one watershed to another. Today federal and municipal engineers are moving the water through the ruggedest of mountains and transporting it hundreds of miles in eastern-slope creek and river channels with the delight of children playing in a sandbox. (They cannot just steal the water; they have to compensate users on the western slope—usually by building storage dams on the western slope that catch and hold the Colorado's excess runoff for release when the river gets low.) During the 1950s the $160 million Colorado-Big Thompson fantasia of reservoirs, dams, electric power plants and canals was completed. It can deliver 310,000 acre-feet of Colorado River water annually to the sugar-beet fields of Weld and Larimer Counties by way of a 13-mile tunnel under Rocky Mountain National Park. Denver's $200 million water system was augmented in 1964 when facilities were opened that enabled the city to draw an annual 150,000 acre-feet through the divide from Blue River in a 23.3-mile tunnel.

In 1954 a similar diversion system helped neighboring Colorado Springs win the nation's prize military plum, the new Air Force Academy. To ensure the academy of an adequate water supply, the city guaranteed to transport Blue River water through the divide at Hoosier Pass and on east to Pikes Peak. Later Colorado Springs and the Denver suburb of Aurora began bringing 74,000 acre-feet annually to their filter plants from Homestake Creek, a Sawatch Range stream more than 140 miles away. Some years hence still another 70,000 acre-feet will be drawn from the lovely Fryingpan River, which runs down to the Roaring Fork below Aspen to join the Colorado. The Fryingpan supply will go through the divide in a 5.3-mile tunnel to the headwaters of the Upper Arkansas and on down that blue, bubbling stream to Pueblo and other Arkansas Valley towns and to the valley's melon growers. This $180 million Fryingpan-Arkansas Project will produce electricity too.

So the drain increases year by year on the overworked Colorado, and on the other overworked rivers in the southern part of the Mountain West —the Rio Grande, Arkansas and South Platte. Residents on these streams are finding all their "great values [measured] in acre-feet," just as Major Powell predicted, and they have good reason to worry. And yet some hydrologists are not hysterically concerned. They point out that, despite constant exhortations from water officials and the press, it seems to have occurred to few Westerners to stop wasting their water—not even to central Arizonians whose vital underground supply, 60 per cent of their total, has sunk from an average depth of 70 feet in 1940 to 200 feet, and is sinking 10 feet more each year.

These experts sometimes say that Bureau of Reclamation men exaggerate water crises and power needs because they have whirled turbines so long that they cannot stop and give somebody else a crack at making electricity—nuclear people or coal-steam people, for example. Prudent irrigation practices alone, the hydrologists insist, would stave off disaster through the rest of the 20th Century. In addition, billions of gallons could be reused if Western cities took the trouble to treat sewage properly. In the meantime, cheap ways to desalinate sea water seem certain to be developed, and these could solve Los Angeles' problem and that of Salt Lake City, where residents may find themselves able to drink Great Salt Lake with pleasure. And rain makers may learn at last how to induce clouds to sprinkle their water evenly over the land instead of just along the Continental Divide.

Some Westerners expect improvements in water distribution to come out of the Water Resources Planning Act of 1965, which authorized the creation of federal-state commissions to develop "the Nation's water and related land resources through sound, comprehensive and coordinated planning." The hope is that the federal-state commissions will be able to persuade groups of states to consider the development and use of entire river basins, much as the Colorado has been developed, rather than to continue dealing with river development on a state-by-state basis. Westerners are also looking with interest at the Western States Water Council, a group formed in 1965 by the governors of 11 Western states. It is possible that the Western States Water Council will consider a further step toward equitable apportionment—the transfer of some of the Snake's 40 million acre-feet and the Missouri's 20 million acre-feet to supplement the overdrawn 20 million acre-feet of the southern rivers.

If such transfers should not suffice, the arid states of the West could turn to the hydrologist's dream of dreams, the North American Water and Power Alliance (NAWAPA) conceived by the California engineer Ralph M. Parsons. NAWAPA is designed to bring millions of acre-feet of water annually as much as 2,500 miles from Alaska and western Canada to the United States and to Mexico through a supercolossal network of tunnels and canals. It would cost $100 billion, produce a 500-mile-long reservoir in British Columbia 16 times the size of Lake Mead, and build power dams by the dozen, including one in Alaska 1,700 feet high.

Even in Major Powell's Mountain West, where bigness is commonplace, those oceans of acre-feet from the far north would make quite a splash.

The capricious Colorado

The changeable 1,400-mile-long Colorado River is one of the most fascinating waterways on earth. It starts as a mountain rill, 10,000 feet high among the peaks of northern Colorado; it ends as a mere trickle of moisture in the salt flats of northern Mexico. Between its sylvan beginning and its soggy end, it—and its hundreds of branches—flows placidly between mile-high bluffs, churns over evil rapids, and fills numberless mountain-ringed lakes to entice sportsmen and nature lovers alike.

No less than the esthetic appeal of the river is its practical value. The Colorado is one of the most exploited and regulated of the world's rivers, its waters collected and parceled out by scores of dams to fill the need of much of the Southwest—and Southern California—for irrigation, drinking water and hydroelectric power.

This mountain rivulet, high in the Never Summer range on the western edge of northern Colorado's Rocky Mountain National Park, forms the headwaters of the Colorado River. Such small streams serve as channels—"draws" in the West—for melting snow.

A slow but powerful carver of canyons

Over millions of years of inexorable flow to the sea, the Colorado River has carved gorge after gorge into the high plateaus of the West. Flowing through Utah, it scours deep passageways through the Canyonlands area *(below)*. But its most impressive gorge by far is the more than 200-mile-long Grand Canyon *(right)*, whose towering rock walls soar an average of one mile above the river bed. To protect this precious asset from man's abuse and save it for man's enjoyment, the federal government has established two preserves that cover a 1,362-square-mile area and encompass most of the canyon and the rugged cliffs and templelike formations on its rims.

A sinuous "meander" of the Colorado River twists through a gorge in Utah, upriver from the Grand Canyon. Such deeply cut channels were formed when the river eroded through soft material and then was trapped between the hard sides of the rock-ribbed canyon.

Majestic, nearly vertical bluffs of the Grand Canyon dwarf two riverboats *(center of the channel)* as they float down the Colorado near the canyon's mid-point. In this area the walls rise to a height of 5,000 feet, of which only 1,500 feet are visible here.

High adventure
along the mighty river

In 1869 explorer John Wesley Powell guided his small boat through the perilous rapids of the Grand Canyon. For almost a hundred years few were brave enough to emulate this feat. But recently professional guides have greatly reduced the dangers of the wet, bucking trip, and running the rapids has become a popular sport among visitors, thousands taking the thrilling ride each summer. Equally attractive are the quieter pleasures to be found along the Colorado, where caverns stretching deep into canyon walls invite exploration and quiet tributary creeks wait to be fished. Though the Colorado and its tributaries have been intensively exploited by man, those areas that have not been disturbed remain among the loveliest in nature's domain.

Huge, rugged rubber pontoons, of the sort used by the U.S. Army
for pontoon bridges, plunge a group of adventurous tourists through
churning rapids on the section of the Colorado ominously known as
the "widow maker." The trips take from one to two weeks, the
boats being pulled ashore at night so that the passengers can camp.

Riverboat passengers *(next page)* disembark at Redwall Cavern in
the Marble Gorge section of the Colorado. Though many caves pock
the walls of the river's gorges, this is one of the few at water level.
Its deep, cool interior offers relief from the 100° summer heat.

Rising over the Gunnison River, a tributary of the Colorado, the Morrow Point Dam nears completion. Like many dams in the Colorado River system, it has several functions, including water storage, irrigation, flood control and the generation of electric power.

The brilliant green of an alfalfa field in southern Arizona, watered by a slowly rotating overhead pipe, sharply contrasts with the lifeless and parched desert land surrounding it. Only with constant irrigation can this arid region be made habitable for man.

Bringing the desert to life

The waters of the Colorado River are literally vital to man in the dry segments of the Mountain States. These waters are the lifeblood of this area; its bed, the beds of its tributaries, and its countless irrigation canals and aqueducts are the veins and arteries that carry the vital liquid to farm and city; its dams, power and pumping stations are the pulse beats that drive the waters into useful channels. So arid is much of the area through which the Colorado flows that just allocation of its waters remains a source of lively controversy throughout the West and Mexico. Few rivers have been so tampered with by man (*map, following pages*), whose works along the Colorado all testify to this determination to utilize every drop of water that the river provides.

A river system in harness

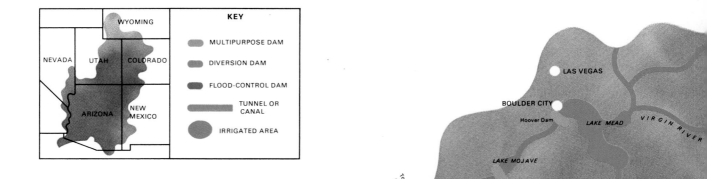

KEY

- MULTIPURPOSE DAM
- DIVERSION DAM
- FLOOD-CONTROL DAM
- TUNNEL OR CANAL
- IRRIGATED AREA

WYOMING

NEVADA · UTAH · COLORADO

ARIZONA · NEW MEXICO

LAS VEGAS

BOULDER CITY

Hoover Dam · LAKE MEAD · VIRGIN RIVER

LAKE MOJAVE

Davis Dam

LAKE HAVASU

COLORADO RIVER

To Southern California

To Coachella Valley

To Imperial Valley

Headgate Rock Dam

Palo Verde Dam

Senator Wash Dam

Parker Dam

COLORADO RIVER INDIAN PROJECT

RIVER

Imperial Dam

Laguna Dam

Alamo Dam

COLORADO

YUMA

YUMA PROJECT

GILA PROJECT

GILA RIVER

PRESCOTT

FLAGSTAFF

Painted Rock Dam

PHOENIX

Horseshoe Dam

Granite Reef Dam

SALT RIVER PROJECT

Theodore Roosevelt Dam

LITTLE COLORADO RIVER

Ashurst-Hayden Dam

Coolidge Dam

SALT

RIVER

TUCSON

GILA

RIVER

The map at right, tipped on its side to spread most of the Colorado River Basin over these two pages, locates many of the major projects—either completed or under construction—that divert and conserve the water of the Colorado system as it flows through six Mountain States *(inset map, above)* and into California and Mexico. The key structures along the Colorado and its tributaries are the dams, of which there are literally hundreds. They range in size from tiny, temporary "beaver" dams built by Indians from mud and brush to the 726-foot-high steel-and-concrete Hoover Dam, and only 86 of the more important ones are marked on the map. More than half of these installations are multipurpose structures *(orange ovals)* used for flood control, irrigation, the generation of hydroelectric power and the storage of water reserves. Others are employed solely for flood control *(purple ovals)*, and some function only as "diversion" dams *(pink ovals)* that channel water into irrigation canals for farmland *(green areas)*. Many of the reservoirs created by multipurpose dams feed water into canals, pipelines and tunnels *(pink bars)* that supply farms, towns and industries far beyond the borders of the Colorado Basin. One such aqueduct carries water to Southern California *(upper left)*, and delivers one billion gallons of water a day to the nearly 10 million residents of 119 cities. All of the dams pinpointed here, with the exception of Horseshoe Dam *(left center)* are installations in which federal agencies have been involved. To avoid confusion, the many dams built and operated by state and private authorities —as well as about 20 small federal dams—are not shown.

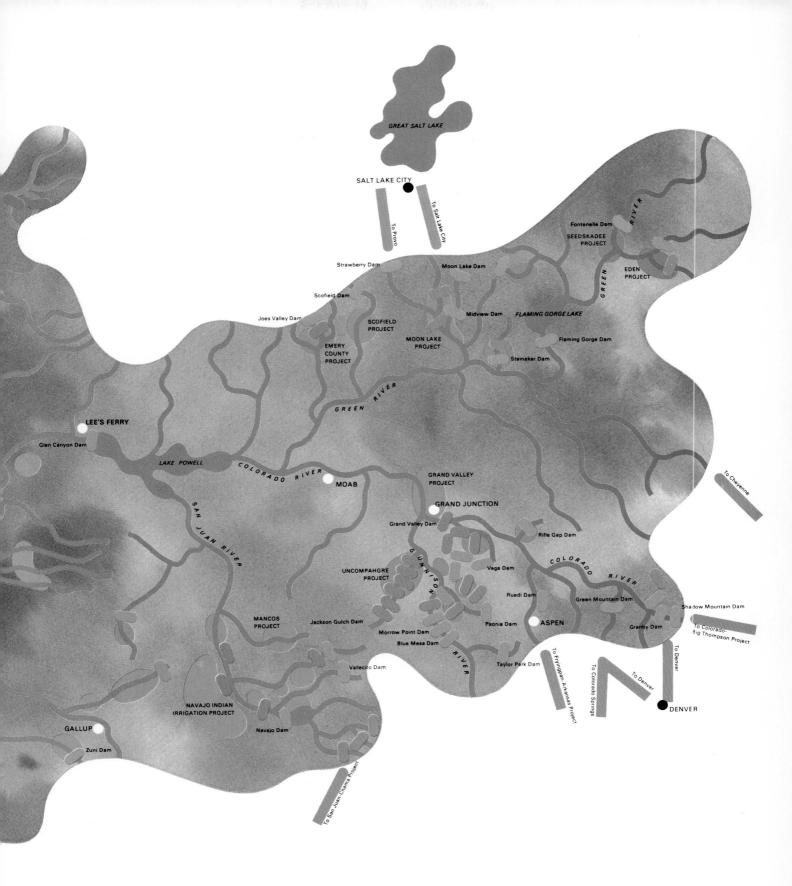

GREAT SALT LAKE

SALT LAKE CITY

To Salt Lake City

To Provo

Fontenelle Dam

SEEDSKADEE PROJECT

GREEN RIVER

Strawberry Dam

Moon Lake Dam

EDEN PROJECT

Scofield Dam

Midview Dam

FLAMING GORGE LAKE

Joes Valley Dam

SCOFIELD PROJECT

MOON LAKE PROJECT

Flaming Gorge Dam

EMERY COUNTY PROJECT

Steinaker Dam

GREEN RIVER

LEE'S FERRY

Glen Canyon Dam

GRAND VALLEY PROJECT

To Cheyenne

LAKE POWELL

COLORADO RIVER

MOAB

GRAND JUNCTION

Grand Valley Dam

SAN JUAN RIVER

Rifle Gap Dam

Vega Dam

COLORADO RIVER

UNCOMPAHGRE PROJECT

GUNNISON

Ruedi Dam

Green Mountain Dam

Shadow Mountain Dam

MANCOS PROJECT

Jackson Gulch Dam

Paonia Dam

ASPEN

Granby Dam

To Colorado-Big Thompson Project

Morrow Point Dam

RIVER

To Denver

Blue Mesa Dam

Taylor Park Dam

To Fryingpan-Arkansas Project

To Colorado Springs

To Denver

Vallecito Dam

DENVER

NAVAJO INDIAN IRRIGATION PROJECT

GALLUP

Navajo Dam

Zuni Dam

To San Juan-Chama Project

71

A lake for sailing
and an exhausted river's end

The great dams that supply water and power may seem unrelated to recreation, but the artificial lakes behind them, often of surpassing beauty, have now become busy centers for tourists. To Lake Mead National Recreation Area alone come four million people a year to swim, fish and sail in its three reservoirs or gaze at the mountains and their reflections in the clear waters. Yet such projects exact a price from the river. Far to the south in Mexico, where once the Colorado flowed majestically into the Gulf of California, the river now lies exhausted, its waters used up, its bed but a salty mud flat.

Framed by the Black Mountains, the waters of Lake Mead are a perfect setting for an afternoon under sail. The lake backs up 115 miles from Hoover Dam, the highest concrete dam in this hemisphere and the key to an irrigation system for Southern California.

In a tepid end to an epic journey, the last remnants of the Colorado's water trickle toward the sea. The Colorado is so thoroughly utilized by man that at the Gulf of California *(top of picture, below)* nothing is left but brackish wastes ejected from irrigation systems.

4

New Horizons
for the Navajo

The venerable Bureau of Indian Affairs, a division of the Department of the Interior, has estimated that there are something more than half a million Indians in the United States. Almost 200,000 of them live in the Mountain States. They make up 30-odd tribes and occupy some 38 million acres of reservations and Indian lands, mostly in areas that they roamed centuries ago—Blackfeet and Crow on the high plains of Montana; Nez Percés in the Clearwater Mountains of northern Idaho; Shoshone in Wyoming's Wind River Valley; Utes in southern Colorado and northeastern Utah; Paiutes around Pyramid Lake in Nevada; Hopi on their Arizona mesas. There are Pueblo Indians in New Mexico and Arizona villages—communities that were in existence long before the coming of the white man. Apache are to be found in New Mexico and Arizona, and there are also smaller tribes like the Havasupai, who dwell at the bottom of remote Havasu Canyon in Arizona and get their groceries delivered by helicopter.

All the tribes are a fascinating lot, and they are

as different from one another as are the nationalities of Europe. The quiet, gentle, medium-sized Nez Percés are a fish-eating river people who raise Appaloosa horses and love them above all things. The tall, handsome, cattle-raising Crow hunt deer and elk in the foothills of eastern Montana and use their hides in their crafts. The short, corn-growing Hopi are among the original settlers of the Indian West and still perform their ancient Snake Dance to supplicate the rain gods.

Some white Americans have made cults of Indian study. They see in all these tribes a sense of elemental values, a coming to grips with environment that the whites miss in their own culture with its technological zeal for blunting the pain and toil and feel of life. In Arizona and New Mexico, particularly, cultists go at copying everything the Indians of that area do, hoping their virtues will rub off. The whites eat the Indians' foods, wear their clothes, sing their songs, dance their dances, and think mystic thoughts about sun, rain and animals. There are academic students of Indians too. "In the Southwest," one of them has said, "the Indian family consists of momma, papa, three children and an anthropologist."

The Navajo are the largest tribe in the region—and, in fact, in the country. They already number

At a meeting of the Navajo chapter of Tohatchi, New Mexico, officers *(on dais)* and members listen as a woman argues for a change in zoning laws. In the Navajo's system of government, the elected chapter officers act as advisers to the tribal lawmakers.

more than 100,000 and are multiplying rapidly. One out of every five Indians in the United States is a Navajo, and the tribe is producing babies at a rate twice that of the United States as a whole. The Navajo own far more real estate than any other tribe. Their vast, irregularly shaped reservation—painted deserts, deep, grassy canyons, forested mountains, and surrealist sandstone gardens spotted with piñon and juniper—occupies most of the northeastern corner of Arizona and northwestern New Mexico and a bit of southern Utah. All together it covers 15 million acres, almost 24,000 square miles. That makes it a little bigger than Massachusetts, Connecticut and New Hampshire put together. In addition, members of the tribe own or lease an estimated 3.5 million acres of nonreservation lands in the area.

The Navajo are generally sturdy, stubborn, temperamental, artistic, humorous, patient, conservative and uncomplaining. They call themselves the *Diné*, the People. While the People are not exactly representative of all of the Mountain West tribes, they face problems that are common to most of their fellow Indians. A close look at modern Navajo life provides a revealing glimpse of the position of these original Americans in the middle of the 20th Century.

The Navajo are remarkable these days because of the daring things they are up to. After a century of hard times they are beginning to move away from their old problems—chronic unemployment, poor health, political impotence, confusion about their status in courts of law and a general refusal to adjust to a world they never made. They are finding ways at last to live fruitful lives in non-Indian America.

The ancestors of the Navajo seem to have lived in northwestern Canada before filtering down into the Southwest. It is believed that they were not a highly organized tribal group at first, but a simple collection of hunting clans. They became a more settled people as they adopted the farming practices of the sophisticated Hopi and other Pueblo Indians, who had arrived in the Southwest much earlier. They got more ideas after the Spanish colonists reached the Rio Grande at the close of the 16th Century.

The colonists brought with them their marvelous horses, as well as sheep and goats. The Navajo Indians took to these European novelties and added stock raising and the weaving of sheep wool to their farming culture. They fell deeply in love with their sheep, goats and horses and arranged their lives to suit the needs of these wonderful new creatures. Navajo life came to center around the isolated family hogan, or house—a snug, thick-walled dwelling made of earth and logs, with a smoke hole in the center and an entrance facing due east to catch the first light of dawn. Since it took as many as 65 acres of their high, arid land to support a single sheep, each Navajo family lived far from the next family so that everybody's sheep would have plenty to eat.

The wide spaces, the climate, and the reliable supply of good meat from their sheep and goats apparently agreed with the Navajo. By the time of the Civil War the handful of clans had become an estimated 12,000 people scattered over the same general area that they are scattered over now—from near Farmington, New Mexico, 200 miles west to the Colorado River; from Rainbow Bridge, Utah, 150 miles south to the Petrified Forest National Park in Arizona.

The Navajo began thinking of themselves as a tribe during the winter of 1863-1864 when U.S. troops trapped several hundred Navajo families near their sublime Canyon de Chelly, in northeastern Arizona, and starved them into surrender by killing their sheep, burning their corn and cutting down their peach trees. The Navajo's offense was that they had been raiding widely and stealing livestock from white settlers. The soldiers herded them and most of the rest of the Navajo on a heart-rending "Long Walk" of some 300 miles to a sort of concentration camp 40 miles square at Bosque Redondo, in eastern New Mexico. The brown eyes of the Navajo go hard today when one of them mentions the Long Walk.

The officials of the Bureau of Indian Affairs thought that the move to Bosque Redondo was wise and benevolent. The People would become righteous and rich by learning English and irrigation methods as well as how to raise vegetables on small plots the way white farmers raised them. It did not work. The Navajo could not raise crops in the poor soil, few of them learned English, and even fewer could grasp white ideas of property, profit and progress. Some of these concepts ran counter to their own ideas. Besides, they were desperately homesick for their space and sheep and goats and horses. Many died of disease at Bosque Redondo. The rest sat around despairingly, dreaming of springtime in the Chinle Valley below the Black Mesa with the lambs and children frolicking about the dirt floor of the hogan and the loom squeaking cheerfully. After four frustrating years the Bureau of Indian Affairs gave up its concentration camp and sent what was left of the People back to their

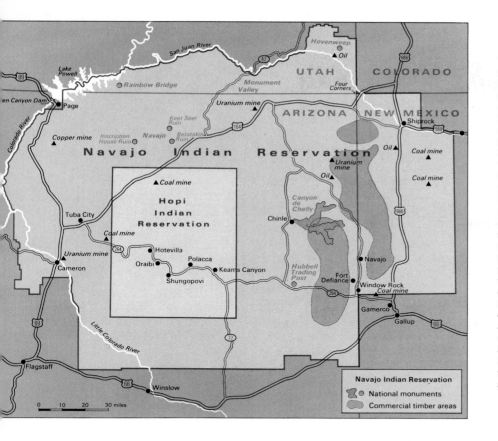

The Navajo Indian Reservation *(left)*, covering parts of Utah, Arizona and New Mexico, is about the size of the state of West Virginia. The rugged, arid countryside cannot support a healthy agricultural economy, and for many years the reservation could offer little but abject poverty to the Indians who lived there. Then about 1950 the Navajo, using federal funds, began long-range road-building programs that are still uncompleted. Partly because of new and improved roads, tourism and, most important of all, industry have grown. Companies such as Fairchild Semiconductor, manufacturers of transistors, built plants on the reservation and provided jobs for the Indians. The tribe even formed a company of its own, the Navajo Forest Products Industries, and built a multimillion-dollar sawmill. When uranium, coal and oil were found on the reservation, mining and oil companies moved in, and they, too, needed Indian workers. Many Navajo still live off the land, but the days of total dependence on agriculture seem to have passed.

land and their lonely hogans to resume sheep raising.

In 1887 Congress decided to try a different policy for all Indian tribes by passing the Dawes Severalty Act, which permitted the breaking up of tribal land into plots to be allotted to individual Indians. It seemed reasonable to assume that when an Indian held a plot he would give up the tribal ties that the white man felt were impeding his progress toward modern living. Tens of thousands did take plots. But the Indians were often cheated out of them by white speculators and settlers; many an Indian turned over valuable property for a bottle of cheap whiskey or a gun. By 1934 the country rang with clamor about disinherited Indians and demoralized tribes. The total size of Indian reservations had dwindled in half a century from 132 million acres to 49 million.

The allotment policy was ended in 1934 by President Franklin Roosevelt's Indian Reorganization Act. This complete about-face shifted emphasis from the individual back to the tribe and attempted to make at least partial restitution by giving back to the tribes some of the land that had slipped away through the allotment system. The new act had beneficial effects, but by 1950 the Navajo, fertile as ever, faced new crises of unemployment and overpopulation on the reservation. To meet these

and similar problems plaguing the neighboring Hopi tribe, Congress that year passed the Navajo-Hopi Long Range Rehabilitation Act. It included an authorization of $88.57 million to be spend over a 10-year period for schools, hospitals, roads and irrigation facilities. In 1958 an additional $20 million was authorized to improve the all-weather roads that transverse the Navajo Reservation. Many of these roads are completed and Window Rock, the capital of what the vacation brochures call "Navajo-land," invites tourists from several directions. One of the most interesting jumping-off places for a visit is Gallup, New Mexico, a high, untidy desert city of 17,000 people, mostly of Spanish, Mexican and Indian descent. Gallup is the main urban center off the reservation, the place to which the People go to trade and to find entertainment. The town's handsomest building is the Indian hospital, which the U.S. Public Health Service built in 1960. Less inspiring is the dingy row of bars and pawnshops fronting on the highway. Many of the customers going in and out of these places are likely to be disheveled, middle-aged Navajo men more or less in their cups, behaving just like any sad drunks in any dingy part of Philadelphia, St. Louis or Butte, Montana. On the main street of the town can be seen Navajo women, in to shop in their voluminous

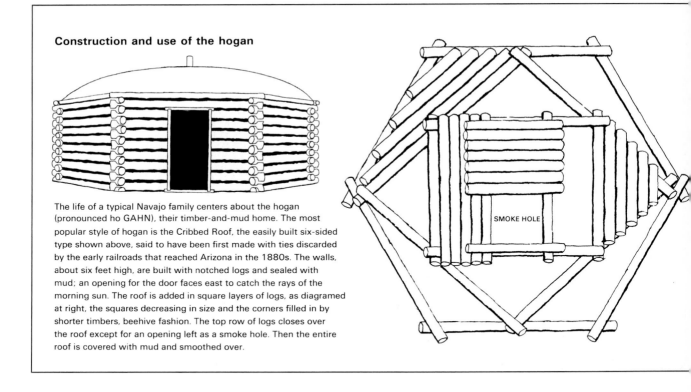

Construction and use of the hogan

The life of a typical Navajo family centers about the hogan (pronounced ho GAHN), their timber-and-mud home. The most popular style of hogan is the Cribbed Roof, the easily built six-sided type shown above, said to have been first made with ties discarded by the early railroads that reached Arizona in the 1880s. The walls, about six feet high, are built with notched logs and sealed with mud; an opening for the door faces east to catch the rays of the morning sun. The roof is added in square layers of logs, as diagramed at right, the squares decreasing in size and the corners filled in by shorter timbers, beehive fashion. The top row of logs closes over the roof except for an opening left as a smoke hole. Then the entire roof is covered with mud and smoothed over.

SMOKE HOLE

skirts and velveteen blouses. The picturesque skirts are supposed to date back to Bosque Redondo and the 1860s. The story is that Army wives gave the Navajo women their old hoop skirts. The Navajo women discarded the hoops, but they permanently adopted the full skirts.

North of Gallup the road winds through what seems to be the biggest agglomeration of junk yards and secondhand stores on earth. They may offend the sensibilities of tourists, but they serve an essential purpose. The average rural Navajo has only a tiny cash income. He buys used washing machines and stoves and farm equipment as he advances toward the Machine Age. (His pickup truck, however, is likely to be a late-model Ford or Chevrolet or GMC.) Leading past the junk yards, the road toward the reservation continues to the Navajo Shopping Center at Gamerco and to the Yah-Te-Hay Supermarket, whose wares show how simple life still is in the isolated hogans. The goods include harnesses, bridles, halters, axle grease and whiffletrees and all the other horse-and-wagon things out of an age long gone. There are wooden barrels for hauling water in dry parts of Navajoland where a family may be miles from a spring. There are sacks of flour for making bread, and bolts of colored cloth for the voluminous skirts and blouses. Heavy, tan

work shoes, blue jeans, scarves, headbands, sashes and black sombreros are on sale for the men, and blue, black and white sneakers are available for the women.

It is 20 miles from Yah-Te-Hay to the Navajo capital of Window Rock. The quiet land, tipped with rimrock at the horizon, rolls away in sage and grass. Dirt roads wind off and out of sight to hogans somewhere in the distance, leaving the highway at points marked by little log shelters where Indian children wait for school buses to pick them up. Navajo pedestrians are numerous on the road. If they speak English, they may ask a non-Indian motorist for a lift. If not, they seem to be embarrassed by the language problem and usually thumb rides only from other Indians. The hitchhikers are no particular highway hazard, but the sheep and horses are. And so are Indians who have stopped their pickups by the road to chat with friends. An approaching pickup is a warming sight. Usually the cab holds at least five people. The open rear seems to be for grandmothers, small children, dogs and goats.

On the reservation, Window Rock Boulevard winds a mile or so to the capital itself past the new blue-and-cream tribal police building. Window Rock is more a scattering of ideas than a town—

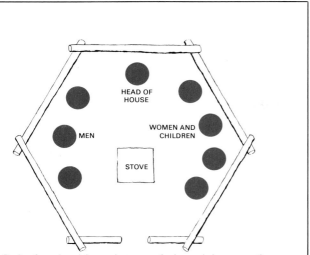

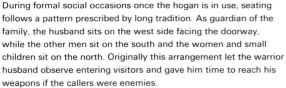

During formal social occasions once the hogan is in use, seating follows a pattern prescribed by long tradition. As guardian of the family, the husband sits on the west side facing the doorway, while the other men sit on the south and the women and small children sit on the north. Originally this arrangement let the warrior husband observe entering visitors and gave him time to reach his weapons if the callers were enemies.

some ideas fulfilled and others awaiting development. The rural background of the People makes them a bit timid in their urban planning, and no settlement on the reservation can be called a town in the modern sense of having posted city limits, a main street, and well-defined residential and business sections.

The capital lies in a beautiful grove of trees cradled in a number of striking sandstone formations. One bright red upthrust has a great hole in it revealing the bluest of skies in back. This is the stunning rock window that gives the place its name —*Tsehanhodzani* in Navajo, which means "perforated rock." The town proper seems to begin with the tribe's small motel and cafeteria and the offices of the tribe's weekly newspaper, *The Navajo Times.* Just beyond is what nucleus the town possesses—a group of federal and tribal buildings and circles of homes for Indian and white employees on the bluffs above.

A great many trees shade the lawns and the sidewalks that wind around the red stone official buildings—a rambling L-shaped one that contains the offices of the Bureau of Indian Affairs and the Navajo Tribal Council, and the extraordinary Tribal Council Chambers. This big stone structure is shaped like a hogan. The interior, spotless and

gleaming, has a high ceiling of peeled logs radiating from the center. A full circle of wall murals depicts the Long Walk and other scenes taken from Navajo history. Arrayed before the murals are 74 handsome desks, each with a name plate on it and a big chair for each one of the 74 Tribal Council delegates.

The Navajo Tribal Council was organized in its present form in 1938 by the Bureau of Indian Affairs as the governing body of the tribe. Its importance has grown enormously since the mid-1950s, when large corporations began discovering quantities of oil and gas on tribal land that they had leased through the council. Uranium is now being found, too, and helium and coal. Royalties from these properties support the tribal fund, which at times reaches more than $70 million. The Tribal Council is responsible for the disposition of this fund and of income from tribal investments. The tribe receives additional income from a long-term lease it has granted to a group of public-utility companies that operate a new steam power plant located on the reservation southwest of Farmington, New Mexico. This huge plant uses coal that is mined on the reservation. When all its units are operating, the plant will generate at least two million kilowatts for six major suppliers of electricity from Texas to California.

The Tribal Council is a democratically elected body. The chairman and vice chairman run for office every four years and are salaried officials; the chairman receives $18,000 a year, the vice chairman $16,000. Each of the 74 council delegates also holds office for four years and is elected by the voters of his own community, which is like a congressional district. Tribal voting is by secret ballot, and since many of the People are illiterate, the ballots carry photos of the candidates next to the voting squares.

The tribe has the rudiments of a two-party system, with a New Guard faction opposing an Old Guard group. Things grow red-hot with excitement all over Navajoland during election campaigns. In 1966, for example, the incumbent tribal chairman, Raymond Nakai (New Guard), was energetically opposed by Samuel Billison (Old Guard). The two men attended a series of political meetings around the vast spaces of the reservation and heard themselves called thieves and imbeciles in the heat of the campaign. There were incidents— at least one fist fight broke out, and a reporter for *The Navajo Times* was ejected from a New Guard meeting. The voters accepted the outcome peacefully enough, however; the New Guard's Raymond

Indian tribal government

Ever since the first incursions of the Spanish in the 16th Century, the Indians have been forced by their conquerors to form governments that could be dealt with by the white men. The structures of the Pueblo Indians and Navajo tribe are shown below. Both governments are democratic, but their forms differ. Although the Indians were granted U.S. citizenship in 1929, the federal government retains veto power over Indian legislation.

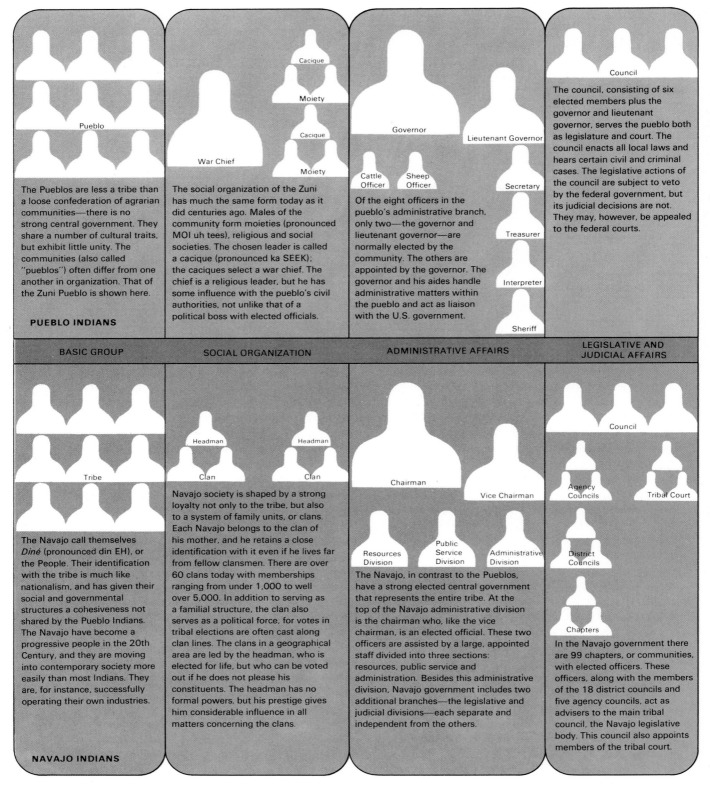

PUEBLO INDIANS

BASIC GROUP

Pueblo

The Pueblos are less a tribe than a loose confederation of agrarian communities—there is no strong central government. They share a number of cultural traits, but exhibit little unity. The communities (also called "pueblos") often differ from one another in organization. That of the Zuni Pueblo is shown here.

SOCIAL ORGANIZATION

Cacique · **Moiety** · **Cacique** · **Moiety** · **War Chief**

The social organization of the Zuni has much the same form today as it did centuries ago. Males of the community form moieties (pronounced MOI uh tees), religious and social societies. The chosen leader is called a cacique (pronounced ka SEEK); the caciques select a war chief. The chief is a religious leader, but he has some influence with the pueblo's civil authorities, not unlike that of a political boss with elected officials.

ADMINISTRATIVE AFFAIRS

Governor · **Lieutenant Governor** · **Cattle Officer** · **Sheep Officer** · **Secretary** · **Treasurer** · **Interpreter** · **Sheriff**

Of the eight officers in the pueblo's administrative branch, only two—the governor and lieutenant governor—are normally elected by the community. The others are appointed by the governor. The governor and his aides handle administrative matters within the pueblo and act as liaison with the U.S. government.

LEGISLATIVE AND JUDICIAL AFFAIRS

Council

The council, consisting of six elected members plus the governor and lieutenant governor, serves the pueblo both as legislature and court. The council enacts all local laws and hears certain civil and criminal cases. The legislative actions of the council are subject to veto by the federal government, but its judicial decisions are not. They may, however, be appealed to the federal courts.

NAVAJO INDIANS

Tribe

The Navajo call themselves *Diné* (pronounced din EH), or the People. Their identification with the tribe is much like nationalism, and has given their social and governmental structures a cohesiveness not shared by the Pueblo Indians. The Navajo have become a progressive people in the 20th Century, and they are moving into contemporary society more easily than most Indians. They are, for instance, successfully operating their own industries.

Headman · **Clan** · **Headman** · **Clan**

Navajo society is shaped by a strong loyalty not only to the tribe, but also to a system of family units, or clans. Each Navajo belongs to the clan of his mother, and he retains a close identification with it even if he lives far from fellow clansmen. There are over 60 clans today with memberships ranging from under 1,000 to well over 5,000. In addition to serving as a familial structure, the clan also serves as a political force, for votes in tribal elections are often cast along clan lines. The clans in a geographical area are led by the headman, who is elected for life, but who can be voted out if he does not please his constituents. The headman has no formal powers, but his prestige gives him considerable influence in all matters concerning the clans.

Chairman · **Vice Chairman** · **Resources Division** · **Public Service Division** · **Administrative Division**

The Navajo, in contrast to the Pueblos, have a strong elected central government that represents the entire tribe. At the top of the Navajo administrative division is the chairman who, like the vice chairman, is an elected official. These two officers are assisted by a large, appointed staff divided into three sections: resources, public service and administration. Besides this administrative division, Navajo government includes two additional branches—the legislative and judicial divisions—each separate and independent from the others.

Council · **Agency Councils** · **Tribal Court** · **District Councils** · **Chapters**

In the Navajo government there are 99 chapters, or communities, with elected officers. These officers, along with the members of the 18 district councils and five agency councils, act as advisers to the main tribal council, the Navajo legislative body. This council also appoints members of the tribal court.

Nakai won the election and settled into office without trouble.

The Tribal Council is the creature of the Bureau of Indian Affairs, but it does not like to remember that. Many of its actions reflect the burning desire of most of the People to get out from under federal paternalism into full management of the tribe's affairs. The Navajo are American citizens with all the constitutional rights that everybody else has, including the right to vote in national and state elections, to draw Social Security, to come and go as they wish, to get drunk or stay sober. But at the same time they are in a sense wards of the federal government, which holds their reservation in trust for them in what the government deems to be the best interests of the tribe. Final authority over the spending of tribal funds and over practically everything else that happens on the reservation is vested not in the Navajo Tribal Council but in the Secretary of the Interior, acting through the Window Rock area director of the Bureau of Indian Affairs.

By endorsing or not endorsing projects of the Tribal Council, the Secretary of the Interior in effect controls the amount of power that the council wields. This situation has existed since Bosque Redondo days, but it is not supposed to last forever. The presumption is that the trusteeship will be terminated when the People are ready, by reason of their educational and economic progress, to take complete charge of themselves and their property. Since World War II the council has been given more and more responsibility, but during the mid-1960s there appeared to be little expectation that the trusteeship could be terminated in the immediate future.

The members of the Tribal Council are understandably anxious to enlarge their authority even further. At one hearing in the tribal chambers, the Finance Committee blasted both the Secretary of the Interior, Stewart L. Udall, and the Indian Bureau area director, Graham Holmes, who was present, for investing tribal funds in certain Arizona banks without consulting the council. The committee's angry views went out over the loudspeaker first in Navajo and then in English. The committee's final statement was addressed directly to Holmes. As translated, it went: "Next time, you and Secretary Udall had better huddle with us before you run with the ball."

One grows fond of Window Rock after a few days' stay there. The little capital in its sandstone garden has a beguiling simplicity about it, a neatness and freshness and an air of confidence and good cheer. It is pleasant to chat at the Indian Bureau refreshment stand with the pretty Navajo stenographers who chatter away in a mixture of English and their own expressive language. Their dresses and hairdos are like those of any other modish American girls of today. The nearby cafeteria is a place of contrasts during the lunch hour—impassive, sombrero-wearing sheepherders just in from their hogans to see the sights, and suave Navajo men who work for the Indian Bureau and dress like conservative Phoenix businessmen.

The brisk confidence of many younger Navajo men traces back, one hears, to World War II, when 375 of them served in the U.S. Marines as radio and field telephone operators in the Pacific theater. Sending voice messages to each other, they used a "code"—their native language—that Japanese eavesdroppers could not break. The Navajo Marines found themselves admired and accepted as equals by non-Indians. In addition their Marine Corps paychecks—and those earned by their brothers who served in other branches of the armed forces or worked in wartime factories—taught them that the white man's money could buy many comforts, and that an educated Navajo need not be condemned to a life of penury. Many of these men were therefore most receptive to the educational goals of the 1950 Rehabilitation Act.

Since the passage of that act, programs in Navajoland have expanded rapidly. In 1950 a little more than nine million dollars was authorized to be spent on Navajo and Hopi problems. During 1965 alone, the bureau spent $71 million on the Navajo Reservation, including $33 million for new schools and almost $28 million for teachers' salaries and welfare programs. The office of Navajo Economic Opportunity had a 1965 budget of $1,738,736 for assorted "community action" programs—preschool training, youth recreation, job placement and aid to small business.

Graham Holmes, the man in charge of these expenditures, is a soft-spoken, reflective lawyer from Oklahoma, who has worked with Indians most of his life. "Our aim," he says, "is simple—my aim, the Secretary of the Interior's aim, the aim of the Commissioner of Indian Affairs, Robert Bennett, who is part Oneida Indian, by the way. We want the Navajo—and all the other Indians out West for that matter—to free themselves of the need to be dependent on anybody. We want them to have the option to do what they please—to stay on the reservation or to leave it and make careers elsewhere."

Holmes believes that good education is the key to

solving the Indians' problems. He feels that nothing sets up a Navajo child quite so much as finding that he can learn to speak English, that requisite tool in the white man's world. He stresses that practically every Navajo child is getting to school these days, whereas only one child in 10 attended school a decade ago. In the new scheme of things, Navajo youngsters want careers that demand more of their minds than sitting out in a field tending sheep, even if the reservation would support enough sheep for them to watch, which it won't. As Holmes puts it: "They want real opportunity so that they can afford to own a pickup truck and a modern home. Yet the youngsters hate to leave this spacious land. I don't blame them. So it is a matter of timing. The Indian Bureau and the Tribal Council have to make jobs for them just as fast as they come out of school." Nearly 2,000 Navajo boys and girls are graduated from high school each year. A number of these graduates go to college on scholarships paid for by income from the Tribal Council's $10 million scholarship fund. The scholarships have not produced many Navajo doctors or lawyers yet, but Holmes is sure that the number is bound to increase in the years ahead.

One of the best authorities on programs directed by the Navajo Tribal Council is Howard Gorman, a perennial council member and one of the most distinguished of modern Navajo. Gorman is a gentle, chunky, bespectacled, graying man who wears a big turquoise ring and the clothes of the well-to-do rancher that he is—whipcord breeches, plaid shirt, string tie, tan sombrero. He lives west of Window Rock in a comfortable bungalow that he built with his own hands. The walls of his parlor are adorned with arrowheads, a bow and arrow, and several landscapes that he himself painted. Like most of the People, Gorman much prefers the outdoors to the indoors and enjoys taking visitors out into his back yard to have a quiet talk and to show them his horse, his ewe and his dog. "You can see I'm a Navajo," he tells them.

Navajo in the ancient tradition he may be, but Gorman is a strong supporter of Tribal Council programs designed to bring a measure of stability and prosperity to the People. During the mid-1960s he headed the committee in charge of the 204-man Navajo police force, a well-trained body of men who patrol the reservation in radio-equipped cars. He is pleased with the fact that the council has spent large sums to build civic centers in Window Rock, Chinle and Tuba City, in which concerts are given and tribal dances and basketball games are presented. More money was also spent to build dozens of chapter houses—small community centers—that have gone up lately at a cost of about $65,000 each. The chapter houses, Gorman explains, are expected to break down the isolation of the hogan dwellers who live in places far from paved roads, like Navajo Mountain in Utah and Kaibitoh in the Arizona desert west of the ruins at Betatakin and Keet Seel. The council has also used tribal funds for warehouses at Window Rock, Shiprock and Tuba City. The warehouses are stocked with lumber and supplies used to build or repair hogans or other structures for indigent Navajos.

Gorman's eyes gleam when he rattles off tribal plans—cheap electricity from the big Four Corners plant to serve every Navajo dwelling, a visitors' center at Four Corners, tourist facilities on the shores of Lake Powell, and more tribal parks like that breathtaking study in stillness, Monument Valley. He likes to talk of the factory that the Fairchild Semiconductor company has installed in a building the council built in Shiprock. Fairchild has been employing hundreds of Navajo girls to assemble transistors. But the Tribal Council's proudest achievement, Gorman feels, is an enterprise called Navajo Forest Products Industries, which the tribe owns and operates in the ponderosa hills north of Window Rock. In 1958 the council appropriated $7.5 million to build its great sawmill, one of the most modern in existence, in a brand-new town, Navajo. Practically everything in the town is Navajo, starting with Navajo pines cut by Navajo lumberjacks and hauled to the mill by Navajo drivers operating big blue Navajo-owned trucks. At the mill, Navajo workers turn out 48 million board feet of lumber annually. Navajo salesmen market this lumber throughout the country.

Howard Gorman is a persuasive and eloquent man. After hearing him in his back yard, with his ewe and horse and dog seeming to be listening to the conversation too, visitors are apt to find themselves convinced that the Navajo are making a massive assault on old problems. But Gorman wonders how long it will take, this long walk to salvation for the People, and for all the Indians of the Mountain States. "We have to do it all ourselves, the way we built the lumber mill," he says, "or it's no good. Your way is one way—material wealth and success, progress. The old way is the Navajo way, the way we love—the way of the sheep, the hogan, our land and sky and all our little rituals to keep well, to keep happy, to keep evil away. We can't go your way too fast, and we can't go *all* the way your way. Only far enough to stand tall, as we say. How much longer? Who knows?"

A woman of the Santo Domingo Pueblo in New Mexico displays Indian craftwork that includes an Apache papoose basket and pottery from the Santa Ana Pueblo. The wares of many tribes are sold by the Santo Domingans, who serve as the middlemen.

A revival of Indian crafts

The crafts of the Mountain States Indians are generally thought of as ancient, handed down from the times before Columbus' discovery of the New World. Some of them are very old. Women of the Papago tribe, for example, fashion strikingly patterned baskets of the same desert grasses used by their forebears 2,000 years ago. But the fine silver for which the Navajo, Zuni and Hopi are known was not made until 100 years ago, and the Navajo did not begin to weave their colorful rugs until the end of the 19th Century.

Nearly all of these skills almost died out at the beginning of this century as factory-produced goods supplanted handmade wares in everyday use. But traders, anticipating tourists' demand, encouraged a revival of native arts, and today the best work blends a new artistic vigor with ancient traditions of craftsmanship.

Photographs by Richard Noble

COCHITI FIGURINES

Unique local forms and decorative styles identify pottery, most of which is made in the villages, or pueblos, of the Pueblo Indians of New Mexico and Arizona. The vessels below are shown in Acoma Pueblo; the figurines at left were made in Cochiti. The sources of the pots and bowls at left below are listed beneath the pictures.

SAN JUAN

SAN ILDEFONSO

ZUNI

ZIA

HOPI

PAPAGO

A flourishing prehistoric art

Even pottery making, among the oldest of Indian arts, has changed with the times. The methods of potting are the same as they were more than 1,500 years ago—rolled strips of clay are coiled layer upon layer, smoothed, decorated and then baked in a cow- or sheep-dung fire. But the vivid designs that make the finished vessels prized by collectors continue to evolve, and some wholly new forms are now made. Along with traditionally decorated vessels, such as the delicately wrought ware made by the craftswomen of the Acoma Pueblo (below), are many that are new. The Cochiti figurines shown at the top of the opposite page, for example, were first made in the 1870s, when they were a commercial failure; they only became popular about 1950.

Silversmithing, a new Indian craft

It was only in the mid-19th Century that Indians learned silversmithing, yet since then the Navajo, the Zuni and the Hopi have developed the art to a high degree. The Navajo were taught by itinerant Mexican smiths in the 1850s; a scant 20 years later the Navajo were the teachers, this time of the Zuni, and in 1898 the Zuni skills were passed on to the Hopi. The three peoples have developed their own techniques and designs: the Navajo have retained their preference for heavy and simple work; the Zuni produce lighter pieces that are usually inlaid with turquoise *(below);* and the Hopi pattern their designs after those found on ancient Indian pottery.

Robert Lee Toshewana of the Zuni Pueblo *(below),* an apprentice silversmith, displays work done in his village, some of it, such as the necklaces, characteristic of Zuni design. The pictures at right show the difference between the jewelry of the Navajo and the Hopi.

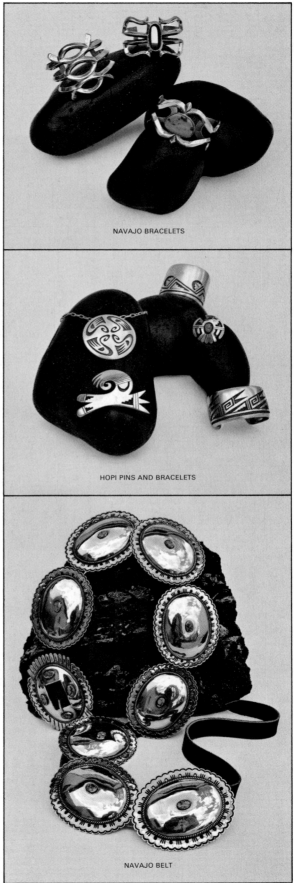

NAVAJO BRACELETS

HOPI PINS AND BRACELETS

NAVAJO BELT

CHINLE

GANADO

Geometric designs from Navajo weavers

Although the Navajo have been weavers of rugs for little more than half a century, their work is renowned throughout the world, both for its beauty and strength and for the imaginative use of color and line. Every Navajo rug is unique—each weaver develops her design and chooses her colors as she works at her loom. The pattern generally indicates the place in which it was woven: the balanced geometric groupings of black, tan and white in the Two Gray Hills rug *(below, right)* are recurring themes in rugs of that part of Arizona. There are exceptions to this rule, however. The Storm Pattern *(below)* and Raised Outline *(bottom, far right)* are not known by their place of origin but by their design.

WESTERN RESERVATION

STORM PATTERN

GALLUP

KLAGETOH

TWO GRAY HILLS

RAISED OUTLINE

Working at her homemade loom, Mary Holiday, a Navajo woman, weaves a rug outside her home in Monument Valley, Arizona, while a neighbor looks on. Like all Navajo weavers, she works without a pattern, developing the design and choosing the colors as she goes along. Mrs. Holiday is not a professional weaver, but a housewife with children and the family flock of sheep to attend. Making rugs, however, is her avocation —as it is for most Navajo women —and she performs all of the tasks involved herself, shearing the wool, carding and dyeing it before starting to weave. A small finished rug may take her as many as 350 hours, nine normal work weeks, and may bring about $50.

Beauty from woven twigs and grasses

The art of basketry is the oldest known surviving craft of the Indians of Arizona and New Mexico. Artifacts 11,000 years old have been found in some areas. The Papago are the chief bearers of this tradition, producing most of the contemporary Indian baskets. But the craft has suffered so much recently from the competition of commercially made products that many experts feel it will not survive. Fewer of the beautiful Papago baskets, of bear grass, split willow, yucca and a pod called devil's-claw, are woven each year; it is estimated that by the end of the 20th Century, no Indian basket weavers will remain, and the art will be lost forever.

Lucy Pablo, who lives on the Papago Reservation in southern Arizona, weaves baskets of traditional designs. Although the Papago produce the bulk of Indian basketwork, other Indian groups produce excellent work, as shown by the highly varied examples at right.

PIMA BOWL

NAVAJO PLAQUE

HOPI PLAQUE

JEMEZ TRAY

APACHE BOWL

HOPI PLAQUE

SANTO DOMINGO BOWL

HOPI TRAY

The kachinas—Hopi rain spirits

Against a cloudy southwest sky, Hopi dolls loom menacingly. But they are not meant to frighten. The dolls represent some of the 250-odd kachinas, or spirits, that the Hopi believe control the rainfall in their arid land. During seven months of the year, January through July, Hopi men don kachina costumes and masks and perform ritual dances to assure essential rain for their own and other Hopi villages in northern Arizona. The dolls representing the kachinas are carved in painstaking detail for Hopi children, who use them to learn the names and appearances of the spirits. In the past the dolls found their way to the shelves of trading posts only when the young ones were through learning—and playing—but today Hopi men also carve the kachina figures specifically for the tourist trade.

Montana cattlemen move a herd of breeding stock to a nearby water hole during the five-day, 60-mile drive from the open grazing land near Ennis to the sheltered, winter range at Dillon. In the spring they will make this rugged trip back to the Ennis area.

5

Pleasures and Pains of Ranching

A beef cattle ranch is a summing up of most of the rural pleasures and pains that make the Mountain States what they are. Some of the pleasures derive from the titillating climate, so divinely good—most of the time. Some derive from the beauty of the setting and the grandeur of space, the generous space of the ranch within the larger majesty of Western space. There is the pleasure of hunting and fishing out the back door, though ranchers claim that they don't have much time to play. Even ranch smells are fine, for the spirit—wet hay and sage, piñon smoke, cows breathing out wild onion, food stewing in molasses, and always manure, glad promise of fertility.

Against the pleasures are plenty of pains. Ranchers have no control over the prices they receive for their cattle. The prices are set by processes inconceivably abstruse. The amount is what everybody except the rancher thinks the price should be—it is set by operators of feedlots, who purchase cattle from the rancher to fatten them for market, by packing houses, chain stores, housewives, plain gamblers and a hundred parasites in between. If a rancher holds cattle on his land for a better price, they soon eat him out of house and home. When prices are satisfactory, all kinds of disasters may foul up his plans. His cows may refuse to mate or his bulls become impotent. Disease may flare in the herd and put him in difficulties for years. The whimsies of rain and snow are a constant harassment. Because of these vagaries, a man can only hope for the best while expecting the worst, and the worst is more likely to happen. If by some miracle everything goes just right, a ranch will turn a modest profit. More often, it is a treadmill of striving to break even, a job never done.

There are around 12 million cattle on the ranches and public lands of the Mountain States. They forage everywhere except high above the timber line, the steep grades and thin air of which seem to offend their conservative natures. It is an eerie feeling to Jeep deep into some national forest—up Medano Creek above Great Sand Dunes National Monument in the Sangre de Cristos, for example, or in the Shoshone River country of Wyoming's Absaroka Range—and be startled by a movement in the willows. One expects a mountain lion, or at least a bear, but it turns out to be a cow placidly chewing her cud with a calf at her side bumping away at her udder. Occasionally a hunter will shoot at such a movement in the brush, and down comes the poor cow—the "slow elk" of hunting talk.

Of the eight states, Montana and Colorado have the greatest number of cattle, nearly three million each, followed by Wyoming, New Mexico and Arizona, each with more than a million. Idaho also raises about a million head, although it could support much larger herds—the Snake River Plain has enough water for many more ranches. But that great irrigated area is the richest of croplands and the vegetable money-makers crowd out the beef cattle there. Utah has around 750,000 cattle; Nevada 560,000. One reason that these two states do not raise as many cattle as their neighbors is their extreme aridity. On the big desert ranches of Utah and Nevada it can be a very long way between clumps of grass and water holes. From the Reno-bound highway west of Delta, Utah, a motorist may see a cow, its ribs showing, and drive miles before seeing another. A square mile of such wasteland will keep scarcely two cows alive—in sharp contrast to the 25 head per square mile that a ranch with good grass supports.

The cattle industry of the Mountain States, like that of the West as a whole, owes its origin to the Spaniards. Domesticated cattle did not exist in the New World until the conquistadors first brought Moorish varieties across the Atlantic from Spain in the 1520s. Through the centuries some of the Spanish imports evolved in the mountain valleys of northern Mexico and in Texas into the lean, wild beef breed that Texas Americans came to call Longhorns, a reasonable name for animals with horns curving out from their heads for several feet.

The Longhorns were not raised systematically. They just raised themselves, as deer and elk do, and roamed at will on both sides of the Rio Grande. A remarkable technique for herding them on horseback was invented and perfected by Spanish and Mexican vaqueros. Later it was adopted by pioneer Texas cowboys of the 1830s and used by them before the Civil War to drive Longhorns to markets in New Orleans, in St. Louis and in Chicago. The Texans took over the Mexican roundup system, the highly trained Mexican cutting horse to cut troublesome animals out of the herd, and the Mexican saddle of embossed leather with a high pommel and an upward-projecting cantle to support the rider's back. The Texans retained Spanish words when they adopted the lasso (from lazo, meaning "slipknot"), the lariat (from la reata, meaning "tie rope"), the corral ("pen"), the remuda of spare horses, the bronco (meaning "rough" or "crusty" and applied to Mexican cow ponies), and the sombrero (from sombra, meaning "shade").

The graceless beasts these Texans corralled were, as the late J. Frank Dobie described them in his classic book, The Longhorns, "the bedrock on which the history of the cow country of America is founded." The breed turned up in the Rockies after the Colorado gold rush of 1859, when Texas cowboys drove some Longhorns north from Texas and New Mexico for the purpose of supplying beef to miners around Denver and South Park. The Civil War put a temporary stop to the Longhorn drives, but they resumed with a rush at the war's end, and, all of a sudden, before anybody realized what was happening, the Longhorn was creating an industry and making enormous contributions to the growth of the Mountain West. The gold rushes of the late 1850s had begun that growth, but the numbers of people they brought to the vast public domain that then constituted the Mountain States were relatively small. Only a few more settlers were attracted by the Homestead Act of 1862, which offered a ridiculously inadequate spot of free land for arid Western conditions—a man could scarcely raise enough food to feed a family on the 160 acres that the act allotted him. Who wanted land nobody knew what to do with?

And then the Longhorns were rediscovered. They were still lean, intractable and inefficient in making meat out of grass, but during the Civil War they had been multiplying like rabbits down in the Texas bush; the grassy wastes below the Brazos River were drowning in them. Moreover, there was suddenly a rich market hungry for their beef. The population of the Eastern Seaboard was growing and expanding, in the postwar boom people had money to spend for meat, and the extension of the

The flavor of the Old West is portrayed in realistic detail in these works by the frontier's best-known artists, Frederic Remington and Charles Russell. Remington, whose *Stampeded by Lightning* at left captures the frenzy of a runaway herd, quit Yale to see at firsthand the Western life that would be the subject of most of his paintings, drawings and sculpture. Russell started as a rancher, but after some years his growing activity as an artist commanded enough commissions to keep him busy full time. His sketch above of the oldtimer he called *Cyuse Bill* was probably done in a Montana saloon.

railroads provided an efficient way to get it to them.

By 1867 the rails had reached as far west as Abilene, Kansas, and the Chisholm Trail began to bring in Longhorns, tens of thousands of the critters pouring along like floodwaters after a cloudburst, a million and a half all told in about four years. From Abilene and succeeding railhead cow towns they were shipped to Eastern markets, producing revenue for the railroads as they pushed on to Denver and Cheyenne and Salt Lake City, to Billings and Great Falls, Montana.

At the same time, the Texas cowboys drove more millions of Longhorns along the trail blazed by the pioneer cattleman, Charles Goodnight, through New Mexico into Colorado and Wyoming and on to Montana. These cattle began to be used almost at once to stock Mountain West preserves as big as a New England state. These vast areas were fiercely guarded territories, private in the sense that each was grazing grounds for herds owned by one man —a brand-new kind of tycoon, the cattle king— men like John W. Iliff of Colorado, Moreton Frewen and Alexander Swan of Wyoming, Pierre Wibaux and Granville Stuart of Montana, and John S. Chisum of New Mexico. Yet the land the cattle king used was not his property; it was part of the federally owned public domain. The open-range

kingdoms did not last long. In the early 1870s Congress passed an act designed to increase the size of free homesteads; steel plows appeared, as well as barbed wire and cheap windmills. These developments together made Mountain States farming more practical and encouraged more farmers to follow the gold seekers and cattlemen to the Rockies and to fence off their crop-growing homesteads along the best streams of the public land.

The fencing of the range changed not only cattle ranches but the cattle themselves. As good, free land and the indispensable running water became scarce, the cattle kings had to fence land of their own to stay in business and go through the shattering experience of paying for the property. That meant a shift from open range to ranch operation and to an increase in raising and feeding costs. To meet these increased costs, cattlemen needed an animal that could transform grass into beef more efficiently while making tastier and higher-priced meat at the same time. The skinny Longhorns had to be improved by crossing them with better stock, mainly Hereford, Angus and Shorthorns imported from the British Isles. The effect was to breed the Longhorns out of existence. Unpoetic justice! For 20 years after 1867, they were the heroes of a Western epic that thrills us still whenever we look at the paintings of cattle drives by Charles Russell or Frederic Remington, or read Owen Wister and Zane Grey, or watch television cowboys riding hell-bent for leather through the gunsmoke of Dodge City. But the Longhorn disappeared in the process of showing the Mountain West how to succeed.

Its demise coincided with the awful drought and blizzard years of 1886 and 1887, when countless cattle froze or starved to death and ranchers went broke on spreads from southern Colorado to the Canadian border. But this apparent disaster turned out to be a blessing in the long run. It encouraged cattlemen to establish wise practices to preserve cattle, like the stock-piling of hay as winter feed. It made necessary a halt to the overgrazing that had been so excessive in some regions as to ruin the grass for a generation. As ranching recovered in the 1890s, it gradually lost much of its blood-and-thunder romance and became a respectable business. This transformation was hastened, after the turn of the century, by conservation laws that restricted grazing on publicly owned lands.

A lot of the free public domain in the Rockies was still left for the ranchers to use after the blankety-blank homesteaders had fenced off the choicest parts. There were some growls from the ranchers when President Theodore Roosevelt reduced the free-use area by setting up national forests and installing a fee system for grazing a regulated number of cattle on them. Much later, in 1934, the Taylor Grazing Act imposed a similar fee system for much of the rest of the public domain that lies outside the national forest areas. But the establishment of the national forest and Taylor grazing areas ultimately proved valuable to the ranchers for it has helped make certain that economical forage will always be available.

The national forest grazing area of the Mountain States now totals 71,200 acres. The lucky cattlemen who hold forest permits pay modest fees of around 55 cents per month per animal to graze in the forests. The Taylor Act grazing districts in the eight states total an additional 141,242,000 acres. Forage is scant in these semidesert grazing districts, which are much drier and several thousand feet lower than the high country of the national forests. Taylor grazing fees are consequently lower —by about 20 cents—than those charged by the government for forest grazing.

The differences in climate, which so sharply influence grazing fees on the public lands, set the pattern of ranching throughout the Mountain States. The exigencies of water divide the cattle range into two parts—where it snows in winter and where it does not snow. The snow line runs irregularly west to east through southern Nevada, southern Utah and southern Colorado and makes northern ranching quite different from southern ranching. Each region has its advantages and disadvantages. North of the snow line, in Colorado, Wyoming, Montana and Idaho, cattle graze all year round because there is some rain in summer and snow in winter to supply to stock ponds and to keep the ground moist.

However, ranchers in these relatively wet areas must be prepared to carry their stock through periods, usually brief, of deep snow and blizzards; they have to keep at least a ton of hay per cow on hand in sheltered feeding areas. On the lower desert ranches of Arizona and New Mexico, there is no need to put up hay or to spend money for shelters because of the mild climate. But desert ranches on the average have to be much larger than mountain ranches to support the same number of animals. There is much less forage and very little moisture on the surface. Since a cow will not graze far from water, ranchers in the deserts have to dig wells—sometimes very deep wells—at intervals of two or three miles and pump water up into surface tanks. In this way the cow is persuaded to clean up all the forage between tanks.

If these few details of ranch operations suggest that cattle raising is today a complex business—as much technology and economics as old-fashioned farming—that is true. Somebody once defined a Mountain States ranch as a farm with 10 times more grazing land than cropland. It ought not to be much smaller than a couple of square miles— 1,000 acres perhaps—to be productive. Ranches of 20,000 acres are a handy size. Some in the Elko region of Nevada are as much as 100 square miles —64,000 acres. The price of a ranch bears no relation to what it is earning, or not earning. Since World War II, land prices have gone sky-high as the population and wealth of the nation have increased. All sorts of city people—doctors, especially, and oilmen and lawyers—are putting their surplus money into ranches, perhaps responding to childhood dreams of riding fence, breaking broncs and shooting it out with rustlers. Giant corporations buy ranches too, attracted in a measure by low real-estate taxes and by income-tax deductions that can develop from depreciation on animals and machinery. With so many buyers and so few sellers, a mountain ranch worth barely $25 an acre in terms of its beef production may bring $100 an acre as an investment these days.

This costly real estate is all cow pasture, but not all in the same way. Something like 80 per cent of the cattle ranches in the Mountain States are called "breeding" or "cow-and-calf" operations. These usually have winter feeding areas in the low, protected valleys and summer feeding areas high in the hills. The cows are bred in June or July to drop their calves the following spring. The calves and their mothers are then driven into the hills and stay there until October, when the calves, by then weighing around 400 pounds, are weaned. They may be sold then, or, depending on grass and market conditions, sold later as yearling steers and heifers at weights up to 700 pounds. The buyer may be one of the big feedlot operators who will gorge them for six months to fatten them up to 1,100 pounds or so before selling them to packers in Denver or Omaha or Chicago. The whole cycle, from a calf's birth to its appearance as a steak in the supermarket, takes about 18 months.

Occasionally a cow-and-calf man will sell his weaned calves to another type of rancher known as a "grower," who has grass going to waste and wants to turn it into meat by feeding it to the young stock. The growers—who account for about 15 per cent of the ranchers—are reckless types who like to gamble that the price of cattle per hundredweight will be as high or higher when they sell their animals to the feedlots as when they bought them. If the price should drop, the growers will have nothing to show for their grass and their labor.

The elite among Mountain States ranchers are the remaining 5 per cent—those who raise purebred animals or scientifically crossed strains that they sell to the commercial breeders—the plain cow-and-calf men—to improve the quality of the calves. To start a purebred business, a rancher ought to have at least one million dollars at his disposal. Some purebred spreads are show places, with painted fences, artificial lakes full of ducks, and vast barns with push-button feed mixers, calving stalls equipped like hospital operating rooms, and hot and cold showers to clean up the bulls for exhibition. The most famous of the purebred operations is the 60,000-acre Wyoming Hereford Ranch near Cheyenne, which dates back to the 1870s. The ranch spends $50,000 a year on feed alone and has a crew employed to do nothing but chaperon prize-winning bulls and heifers on the national stock-show circuit.

The dark-red, white-faced Hereford that is the Wyoming Ranch's specialty has been the most popular beef breed in the mountains since the 1880s. It was developed in England as an ox to haul plows and was first brought over to the United States in 1817 by the Kentucky statesman Henry Clay. The coal-black Aberdeen Angus, a native of the Scottish Highlands, is also popular. Since the 1950s, the Charolais, a whitish animal of French origin, has made headway both on its own and as a cross with the flop-eared, humpbacked Brahman (an import from India) to produce cream-colored cattle called Charbray. Other modern mixes include the Santa Gertrudis, a Shorthorn-Brahman cross created at the King Ranch in Texas, and the Beefmaster, a Hereford-Shorthorn-Brahman cross bred by Tom Lasater on his 25,000-acre Lasater Ranch at Matheson, Colorado.

Of whatever breed, cattle are not exactly lovable animals. They are not at all bright. They cannot be housebroken or taught to shake hands like a dog. Nevertheless, every cattle ranch is exclusively dedicated to their comfort. The average rancher is a marvelous host, but if word comes to him that a calf is being born wrong end first, he drops his guest in the middle of a sentence, dons his galoshes, and heads for the corral on the run.

The "average rancher" is, of course, a statistical myth. Like the cattle they raise, Mountain States ranchers are of every kind and condition. Tom Lasater and his wife, Mary, were born to the business, both being members of distinguished old Texas ranch families. They began moving their cattle north from Texas in 1949 to get away from rising land prices. Still another rancher of distinguished lineage is Andrew Marshall Jr., a Bostonian and Harvard graduate who came to northern New Mexico in 1950 to run the 96,000-acre Fort Union Ranch, which used to be the site of a big Army base set up to control the Indians after the Mexican War. The adobe remains of the Army base form today's Fort Union National Monument. The ranch was acquired in the 1880s by Marshall's great-grandfather, the lawyer-soldier-politician, General Benjamin "Beast" Butler, and it is now owned by Marshall and 200-odd relatives of his, descendants of the general. All the children of these 200 owners are entitled to spend their summers working at Fort Union Ranch if they wish to, and many of them do wish to. In consequence, Marshall and his wife, Peggy, spend more time in summer riding herd on these eager young New England cowhands than they do managing the cattle.

There is no lovelier spread in all the Rockies than the Wallop Hereford Ranch, which lies along Little Goose Creek and rises up into the canyons of the Big Horn Mountains near Big Horn, Wyoming. The ranch belongs to Wyoming-born Oliver Malcolm Wallop, who has maintained it with the trimness and dignity of an English estate. Wallop's father came to the U.S. from North Devonshire in 1883 and later joined with Malcolm and William Moncreiffe of Scotland to make Little Goose Creek Valley a polo and hunting paradise for sportsmen. The elder Wallop returned to England in 1925 to become the eighth Earl of Portsmouth.

Quite a different tradition, pioneer American this time, is upheld by Louis Gold. A well-to-do Colorado rancher, he lives serenely in a one-room homestead shack on his Tarryall River spread below Bison Peak exactly as he lived half a century ago, ready with his six-shooter to discourage any caller trying to sell him plumbing or electric lights. Another native, Channing Sweet, a Princeton track star in the 1920s and son of a governor of Colorado, won a Chicago debutante for a wife partly because she yearned for the romantic life of a rancher on Sweet's cow-and-sheep spread southwest of Denver. But it took time for her to adjust to the sight of her Princeton hero milking a balky Hereford cow or to the sound of coyotes yipping at one another outside the ranch house in the early evening.

Perhaps the most beloved and colorful of Mountain States ranchers is the famed octogenarian of Hayden, Colorado, Farrington R. Carpenter, whom President Franklin Roosevelt appointed in 1934 as his first Director of Grazing under the Taylor Act. He is known universally as "Ferry," and his yellow ties, red galluses, loud cowboy shirts and whipcord britches, his stories of pioneer life, and his scathing contempt for the ranching status quo are known from Texas far north into Canada. "I'm against standing still," Ferry likes to say. "Let's move somewhere, even if it's in the wrong direction."

He lives on the banks of the beautiful Yampa River in a huge ranch house consisting of several antique log cabins hooked together and disguised with white clapboard. The rooms are filled with books, cowhide rugs, paintings of Carpenter bulls, photos of Carpenter children and grandchildren, and awards of every kind. Ferry filed in 1907 on a Yampa Valley homestead while still a Princeton undergraduate, added to it during his years at Harvard Law School, and settled down at Hayden as a lawyer and Hereford breeder. He recalls that the valley at the time was full of lonely bachelor cowboys "and only one lady, Mrs. Murphy, who was happily married to Mr. Murphy." To solve the bachelor problem, Ferry began luring girls from back East to teach in a school that he organized for the express purpose of making pretty girl teachers necessary. The luring chore went on and on because the teachers married the bachelor cowboys rapidly and had to be replaced by more teachers. Ferry

married one of them himself, Eunice Pleasant. Two years after Eunice died in 1954, Ferry married still another of his early teachers, Rosamond Perry, who had been a widow for some years.

Ranch life in the Mountain States today is purest luxury compared to what Carpenter found it to be in 1907. All sorts of machinery helps the rancher to improve his property with stock ponds, erosion-control terraces, new fence, trails for access to pastures and so on. He and his cowboys use Jeeps instead of horses to get around the place, though they may saddle up the horses as of old when it comes to some chores, such as driving cattle into the hills for summer grazing. Rural electricity, up-to-date home water and sewage systems, deep wells, submersible pumps, refrigeration and the rest have made living in the most howling of desert and mountain wildernesses at least as comfortable as city living, and often more so. Because of good roads, fast cars, even airplanes, ranch families move around socially as much as urban families. Ranchers and their wives are better educated on the whole than their parents were and they have wide intellectual interests. Their children attend fine consolidated schools whose teachers are able to train them to meet college entrance requirements anywhere.

For all the modern conveniences, however, ranching remains, as it always has, a pain in the neck. Cattle get sick and die, drought ruins pasture, beef prices fall while ranching costs rise. Still, the average cattleman in the Mountain States would not trade places with anybody in the whole wide world. To him, his home on the range is everything the sentimental old song says it is. The rancher and his wife and children stay out where the deer and the antelope play because they can stand it. They can depend on their own resources to stand 50-below cold if they live in Montana, soaring heat in Arizona, floods and dust in Colorado, drought everywhere. They can stand gales, leaking ditches, the contretemps that go with windmills, dawn-to-midnight toil, coyotes stealing the chickens, pack rats stealing the silverware, beavers stealing the creek. They can fix anything—cars, radios, plugged toilets. They can doctor themselves and their animals. They can spot overgrazed land at a glance and can look at a steer's outside and know what he has inside where the steaks are.

Sometimes they get fed up and move to town, but soon they are sick of being fenced in and hurry back to the pain in the neck. For their ranch brings them a delicious taste of freedom, the joy of being able to tell the world to go to hell if they feel like it. And that makes it worth all the trouble.

Formed 70 million years ago, cloud-shrouded Pikes Peak rises in central Colorado. By geological standards the peak is not an old formation, but its core is rock that was part of a mountain range that rose, only to be gradually worn down, 230 million years ago.

Origins of a rugged landscape

The 863,887 square miles of the Mountain States comprise a huge geological museum —a majestic display of terrain in which can be traced the changes that have made this region one of the most dramatically beautiful in the world. Here are remnants of the predecessors of the Rocky Mountains, themselves more than 70 million years old. Here, too, are ancient sea beds, whose multihued layers of sediment were laid down inch by inch over the ages, compressed to rock hardness, then raised thousands of feet above the level of the waters that created them. Still visible are hard, upthrusting formations created by volcanoes. On the following pages this history is retraced—in maps that show the region as it probably appeared at significant geological moments and in photographs of contemporary landscapes that reflect past epochs.

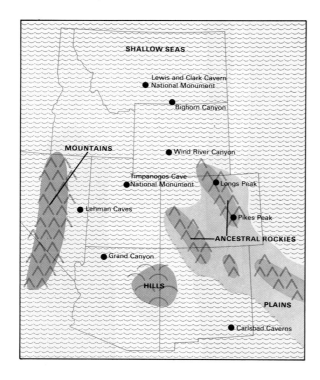

This map, like those on the following pages, locates the most important geological features *(marked in capital letters)* of an ancient period in relation to landmarks of the present day. In the very remote past, between 310 and 230 million years ago, the Mountain States were largely covered by shallow seas interrupted by a few mountains, hills and low-lying plains. The hills and the range to the west have been eroded away, but the materials that once made up the Ancestral Rockies to the east are still to be found in such contemporary features as caves and canyons and far below the surface of mountains like Pikes Peak *(page 103)*.

A labyrinth of limestone from an ancient sea bed, Lehman Caves lie within Wheeler Peak, Nevada. The porous rock of which they are made was formed of limy mud and the shells of tiny invertebrate organisms that eons ago fell to the bottom of the inland sea.

The jagged, spectacularly colored cliffs of the Kaibab Plateau *(background)*, out of which the Colorado River has cut the mile-deep gorge of Grand Canyon, tower 7,000 to 10,000 feet above sea level. But more than 300 million years ago this high plateau was the bottom of the sea that covered much of North America.

Mountainous islands
from a huge sea

For millions of years most of what is now the Western United States lay beneath a vast sea. Then, about 310 million years ago, heat and pressure within the earth created a dramatic change: mountains that geologists call the Ancestral Rockies rose to dominate the waters. These peaks eventually formed a chain that ran from Wyoming to Texas. When they rose, they carried upward with them the rock of the sea bed—soft sandstone, limestone and similar material that in some places has since been hollowed into caves (*bottom, left*). The mountain building lasted about 80 million years, but even as the Ancestral Rockies were rising, wind and water were wearing away at the peaks, carrying gravel, sand and silt back into the surrounding sea.

Low hills and swamps where dinosaurs roamed

By 230 million years ago, the geologic forces that had raised the Ancestral Rockies had ceased, these primeval mountains had been completely worn away, and the inland waters were again unbroken by land. Then the eastern floor of the sea tilted up, exposing hills and pushing the waters westward. Rain created streams that carried sand and silt away from the uplifted hills to build deserts *(far right)* and swampy lowlands that came to cover most of the Mountain States. The climate became tropical and dinosaurs roamed the swamps. As time passed, great amounts of rock debris were carried into the swamps from low hills that bordered the region and were in their turn solidified into sedimentary rock. By 160 million years ago the hills, like the Ancestral Rockies, had been worn almost entirely into the sea. But always, in the innards of the earth, heat and pressure were seeking an outlet, preparing once more to create new land from the ocean bottom.

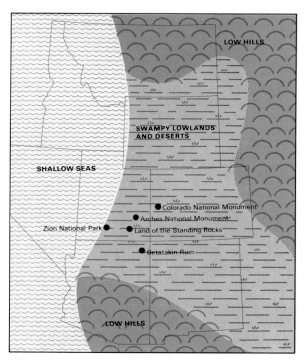

After the disappearance of the Ancestral Rockies and other formations during the 70-million-year period that began 230 million years ago, the Mountain States looked much as they do on the map above. Low hills, on the north, east and south, were separated by swampy lowlands and deserts in which erosion had formed sand dunes still seen in modified form in such places as Zion National Park and the Colorado National Monument.

A towering cliff that overshadows the Betatakin Ruin *(left)*, a Pueblo Indian village abandoned in the 14th Century, was originally sand dunes formed when part of the region consisted of swamp and desert. The sand was made into rock when water bearing solidifying minerals seeped through it. The rock was later carved and scoured by winds.

Vestigial remains of the great desert sand dunes, an eroded formation in the Land of the Standing Rocks *(right)* rises a few miles south of Moab, Utah. The stratified sedimentary rock of which it is composed once covered thousands of square miles of the surrounding area, but millennia of erosion have destroyed all but a few such structures.

An abrupt reversal
of land and sea

For 100 million years, during a period that began 160 million years ago, the Mountain States were subjected to a violent upheaval that geologists call the Laramide Revolution. The crust of the earth, weakened and strained by the weight of water and silt, gave way to pressures generated internally. The surface buckled and folded, and great mountain ranges again rose from the sea, this time in the west. Ranges like the Wasatch *(top, right)* replaced the western sea, while to the east the remaining low hills were submerged, and great swampy areas were created between mountains and sea. When the Laramide Revolution ended, a large part of the U.S. was still under water. But this new sea was shallower and less extensive than its predecessors. The level of the entire land area had been raised significantly, presaging the sea's eventual disappearance.

Mounds of Mancos Shale, named for nearby Mancos, Colorado, rise treeless from the plain. This oil-bearing shale consists of petroleumlike organic matter—the residue of microorganisms that once inhabited the swamplands—intermixed with silt and clay washed down from the western mountains 100 million years ago.

The most dramatic accomplishment of the Laramide Revolution (160 to 60 million years ago) was the transposition of land and sea; the landscape shown at the right was almost the opposite of its predecessor *(page 106)*. Mountains that, somewhat altered by time, form such existing ranges as the Sawtooth and Wasatch were thrust up by processes called folding and faulting *(pages 112-113)*. At the same time, the deposits that now make up the petroleum-rich Mancos Shale *(red dots)* were accumulating in the shallow seas.

The rugged peaks of the Wasatch Range thrust up in an ambling line in northern Utah. The range consists of a block of stratified rock that folded over as a result of subterranean pressures during the Laramide Revolution and was subsequently weathered to its present form.

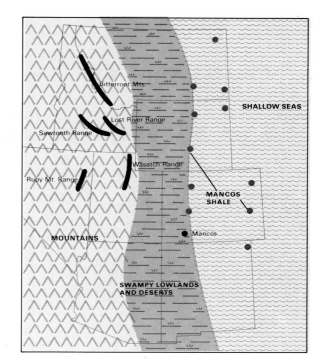

Terrain raised and shaped in volcanic fire

The Laramide Revolution (*pages 108-109*) prepared the base of the Mountain States; the period just following built upon that base. From 60 million years ago almost to the present, the land rose in a progression of steps that ended a mere two million years ago, the beginning of the ice age. By then this entire part of the continent had been raised above sea level and the waters had drained from the land. A major force in this reshaping was vulcanism, or volcanic activity, which created mountains and plateaus. The period was one of awesome fireworks, of lava forcing its way upward and spouting forth from volcanoes. Today such activity, although no longer of an explosive nature, continues in some parts of the region and is visible in the form of hot springs and geysers in Yellowstone National Park.

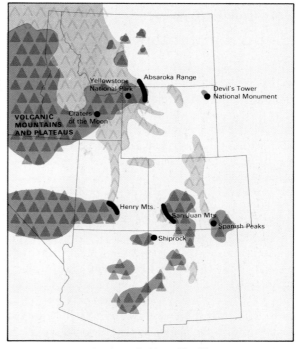

Devil's Tower, a reminder of past volcanic activity, rises in solitary splendor in Wyoming's Black Hills. It was formed when molten lava pushed its way up through an opening in the earth's crust, then cooled and hardened. Rain and wind have since worn down the soft sedimentary rock that once surrounded this hard material, leaving the tower—an example of what geologists call a volcanic plug.

Mist rises above Yellowstone National Park, Wyoming, a plateau formed of once-molten lava and still seething with subterranean volcanic activity. Its hot springs and geysers are a result of rain water seeping underground and passing over superheated rocks.

Volcanic activity during the period from 60 million years ago to two million years ago created many of the great peaks of the Rocky Mountains—and some of today's most notable landmarks, such as the Craters of the Moon, Shiprock and the San Juan Mountains. Centers of volcanic activity are shown on the map above by dark-shaded triangles. Mountains formed by other geologic processes —explained on following pages—are indicated by the inverted V's.

The evolution of modern mountains

Vulcanism was not the only force at work during the 60 million years following the Laramide Revolution; the Mountain States were again subjected to two other mighty geologic processes: folding and faulting. Folding results when movements of rock deep within the earth push and pull on the surface, wrinkling it, the wrinkles becoming great folds of mountains. Faulting develops along lines of weakness, or faults, in the crust. Triggered both by folding and by subterranean pressures, the earth's crust slips along the fault line, and the crust on one side rises above the crust on the other side or falls below it. Great masses of the earth moving in this way form what are called fault-block mountains. Usually the break is a clean one, and fault-block mountains like the Tetons *(right)* present sheer cliffs rather than the more sloping sides seen on folded mountains. In the Mountain States both types are found side by side with mountains of volcanic origin.

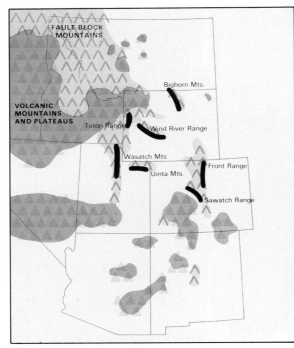

In the map above, similar to the one on the preceding page, fault-block mountains—formed by the processes of folding and faulting—are shown by inverted V's alongside their neighboring volcanic mountains *(shaded triangles)*. A few of the present-day ranges that were thrown up by folding and faulting are shown on the map, including the Tetons, the Wasatch and Uinta Mountains, the Front, Wind River and Sawatch Ranges, and the Bighorn Mountains.

Rising with dramatic suddenness behind the crystal-clear water of Jenny Lake, the steep-sided peaks of the Tetons of western Wyoming soar to more than 13,000 feet. A fault-block range, these mountains came into existence approximately 10 million years ago.

The great sculpting
of the ice age

During the present geologic era, which began two million years ago, the temperature of the earth has gone up and down several times, abruptly changing the climate of the entire planet. In periods of low temperature, enormous quantities of the earth's water became locked in great glaciers that extended as far south as New Mexico. Forming first in high-altitude areas of heavy snowfall, the sheets of ice grew and slipped slowly down the mountainsides. Their movement was almost imperceptible—a few feet a year at the fastest—but the glaciers acted like giant bulldozers, carving the rock, smoothing jagged crags, rounding V-shaped valleys, and leaving their trash piles of rock and earth, called moraines, where melting finally stopped their progress. The glaciers were the geologic artisans, smoothing the rough features of earlier eras. When they retreated for the last time, only 12,000 to 15,000 years ago, they left the terrain almost exactly as it appears today.

Cottonwood Pass, high in the Colorado Rockies, is snow-covered the year round. At the very top, the snow compacts from its own weight, forming rivers of ice that inch downhill as glaciers, honing the peaks to jagged sharpness, like small echoes of the ice age.

Grinnell Glacier, one of 60 in Glacier National Park, Montana, makes its tireless way down the valley floor that it has been shaping and smoothing for millions of years. Each year the moving ice river deposits hundreds of tons of rock and earth at the mountain's base.

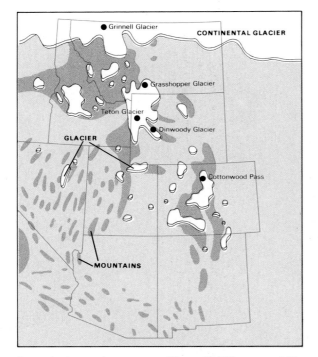

Successive ice ages between two million to 18,000 years ago laid glaciers in nearly every part of the region. As this map indicates, the heaviest concentration of ice *(white areas)* was in the north, where one huge continental glacier left no land uncovered. Smaller ice masses capped mountain peaks even in relatively warm New Mexico. The glaciers advanced and retreated four times during the period, and today only a few small ones *(black dots)*—Grinnell, Teton, Dinwoody, Grasshopper—remain. Scientists do not know whether the last retreat was final. Some believe that the glaciers may return to resume their work of sculpting and planing.

Poisoned by the hot-spring water that surges around them, lifeless trees stand in Mammoth Hot Springs in Yellowstone National Park. This area was once rich in evergreens; the underground volcanic activity that heats the springs is slowly altering the landscape.

Portents of change in today's landscape

The story of the repeated building up and destruction that has created the Mountain States terrain through past millennia has not ended. The process of geologic change goes on, and in this region it is frequently more visible than it is elsewhere. Glaciers persist and grind their way down the slopes of the high mountains; volcanic activity that brought towering peaks into existence still transforms the earth in areas like Yellowstone National Park *(above);* streams falling from mountain heights continuously carry sediment to lowland valleys, where winds heap it into giant dunes *(right),* piling up layers that may someday lie again beneath some future sea.

A lone clump of grass manages somehow to survive in the desert
dunes of White Sands National Park in New Mexico. The dunes are a
result of the continuing process of erosion, wind and water at work
constantly wearing down mountains and moving them to lowlands.

6

Elusive Treasures Underground

In the largest man-made excavation in the world, Utah's Bingham Canyon open-pit copper mine, a three-story-high electric shovel drops its 20-ton load of ore into a rail car. The mine has produced more copper—nearly eight million tons—than any other in history.

Precious and useful metals have been the will-o'-the-wisp of the Mountain West since the rushes of 1859, when gold in quantity began to be found in Colorado and Nevada and, three years later, in Montana. The lure is as irresistible now as it was then—the dream of unimaginable affluence and power, the sort of rapturous *could be-could be* that one feels in Harold's Club in Reno, yanking the slot-machine handle and waiting for the torrent of jack-pot quarters.

It is by no means a petty bewitchment. Every sort of Western mining man from unschooled prospector to highly trained geophysicist is caught in the same web of universal forces that have caused more than $34 billion worth of metals to be dug out of the region in the past 100 years. Of the eight Mountain States, Arizona has been by far the biggest producer in that period; its mines have yielded about $11 billion worth of metal, more than 80 per cent of it copper. Its great copper mines include the venerable Morenci near Clifton, the San Manuel northeast of Tucson, the Copper Queen-Lavender Pit at Bisbee, the New Cornelia at Ajo and the Ray open pit east of Phoenix.

Utah ranks after Arizona in metal production with $6.5 billion worth. Most of that has come from Kennecott Copper Corporation's Bingham Canyon open pit, one of the richest mines of any kind on earth and an astonishing example of man's ability to dig: it measures two miles across and one-half mile down. This great gash has given up so much gold as a by-product of its copper that it stands (after South Dakota's Homestake) as the nation's second-largest gold mine. Montana's total metal

production since 1862, some five billion dollars' worth, has come mainly from a legendary pile called Butte Hill, the so-called "richest hill on earth," just off the Continental Divide. Though Montana is nicknamed the Treasure State, implying state-wide metal wealth, nearly all the treasure lies in the few thousand acres of Butte Hill, which includes the city of Butte. The mines of the hill are owned by the Anaconda Company and they produce virtually all of the state's copper, 90 per cent of its silver, 80 per cent of its gold, 75 per cent of its zinc and 65 per cent of its lead.

Idaho is the state of all states for silver and is also a storehouse of lead. The narrow Coeur d'Alene District, in the beautiful rain-forest area of northern Idaho, is only 10 miles wide and 30 miles long, but it produces practically all the valuable ores. Some two billion dollars' worth of metal has come from there, including more than one billion dollars in lead and $650 million in silver. Among the Coeur d'Alene mines is the old Bunker Hill and Sullivan, from which more than 110 million ounces of silver and nearly 2.5 million tons of lead have been taken over the years, and the nation's three top producers of silver—the Sunshine, Galena and Lucky Friday mines, in that order. Colorado and Nevada have some live mining camps these days but the two states are known more for the past glories of their mining towns—Nevada's Virginia City, Tonopah and Goldfield; Colorado's Leadville, Cripple Creek, Georgetown, Silverton and Creede. Currently, a touch of the old Nevada excitement has been inspired by the Carlin Gold Mine that began operating in 1965 near Elko. Colorado's metal production consists chiefly of the $70 million worth of molybdenum taken annually from the Climax Mine north of Leadville. New Mexico and Wyoming have trailed the others in output, but they too are becoming important producers now as they discover new sources of uranium.

All this Western mining activity has ebbed and flowed rather like the tides—but unpredictably. A certain metal is needed desperately by a lot of people all of a sudden, and there you are. A new rush to the Rockies starts overnight, a rush to the canyonlands of Utah, perhaps, or the alkali deserts of Wyoming, or the highlands of the Southwest, or up the steep, aspen-dotted gulches of the Continental Divide to grassy moraines and tarns at 12,000 feet above sea level, and on over the passes to possible bonanzas on the far side. Perhaps the sudden new need is for lead, as occurred long ago when Americans fell in love with indoor plumbing. Governments may get to devaluating their currencies,

which causes the hoarding of gold and silver coins and attendant shortages. The demand may be medical (cobalt can be made radioactive for cancer therapy). More zinc may be needed for the batteries of electric automobiles. A cry may go up for large quantities of titanium, a light, heat-resistant metal of many uses in the aerospace industry.

Gold, of course, is one of the most remarkable of metals, so beautiful, so eternally valuable, so emotional in its appeal—something everybody has yearned to have and to hold since the days of Adam and Eve. Silver is nice, too. During the last 40 years of the 19th Century, the search for gold and silver preoccupied everybody in the Mountain West. These two metals, the standards for international exchange, were needed in ever-increasing amounts to keep pace with the vast expansion of world trade.

But the demand for other metals—the ones that now make up most of the Mountain States' mineral wealth—was practically nonexistent until long after the gold and silver rushes had begun. Before telephones and electric lights were invented in the late 1870s, copper ore was considered to be a relatively worthless rock that had to be hauled out of gold and silver mines and disposed of. But copper was an excellent conductor of the impulses that transmitted speech and made Thomas A. Edison's incandescent lamps light up. By the early 1900s power and telephone lines made of copper were creeping around the earth. So copper was *it*, the new darling of the Rockies mining community.

The element molybdenum was identified in 1782. However, nobody had found a use for it as late as 1879 when Sergeant Charles J. Senter, recently retired from the Indian wars, staked what he hoped would prove to be gold claims at 12,000 feet above sea level on Bartlett Mountain in Colorado. The claims changed hands several times and eventually became the Climax Molybdenum Mine. The mine's gray metal began coming into modest demand before World War I as an alloy—in light-bulb filaments, for instance—but it was not until the 1920s that a young chemical engineer for the Climax Company, Brainerd F. Phillipson, induced Eastern steel manufacturers to use molybdenum in considerable quantities to produce harder steel alloys. Climax sold the then-amazing total of 718,000 pounds of molybdenum from Bartlett Mountain in 1925; by 1965 sixty million pounds of it were being used each year, most of it in steel production.

And so the ebb and flow continued—silver and gold, copper and lead, zinc and molybdenum. Then came the frenzy over uranium. The demand for this last metal was minute before World War II, and only small amounts of it were coming out of the Mountain States. Its uses were gentle, such as giving a soft glow of color to glass—yellow, green or red. In 1945 the first atomic bombs containing uranium 235 ungently tore up the New Mexican desert and two Japanese cities. More nuclear bombs capable of blowing up the world were made as fast as more uranium could be obtained. Suddenly a once-ignored mineral became the key to the future of the world, and the United States grew aware that the country might need vast quantities of the ore from reliable sources, secure within its own borders.

To encourage prospecting, the Atomic Energy Commission, which directs nuclear affairs, in 1948 opened offices in Grand Junction, Colorado, near a source of supply: flat beds of uranium ore known to lie in the broken, arid wilderness on both sides of the Colorado-Utah line. Some of the beds were in a type of rock stratum known as the Morrison formation; some in the older, deeper Shinarump conglomerate. Both strata could be found exposed in the walls of canyons if a man knew where and how to look for them.

Shortly after the Grand Junction offices opened, the uranium country began filling with the same kind of excited, determined fortune hunters who had roamed the West in the boom days of gold and silver. By 1952 thousands of house trailers and tents were scattered about the sage desert of the vast Colorado Plateau, and thousands of people were wandering through the canyons looking for Morrison and Shinarump strata and staking claims on any rock that made a Geiger counter click as it responded to the gamma rays given off by radioactive uranium. Though the metal they sought and the methods of finding it differed from the metals and methods of the 1860s, the modern prospectors followed the same old will-o'-the-wisp. They wanted to escape the bondage of ordinary mortals by getting filthy rich in a hurry. Their failures were the same as those of the pick-and-burro men, too. Most of them had nothing to show for their toil and expense by 1958, when the Atomic Energy Commission announced a cutback in purchases.

There were exceptions to finding nothing, however, and there are two prospectors in particular whose stories make bright, adventurous pages in the history of mining. Their high courage and persistence and incredible energy symbolize the mining spirit as it has been through the years, as it is now and will be for a long time to come. One of these two modern prospectors, Charles Augustus Steen, was born in the hamlet of Caddo, Texas, worked his way through high school and in 1943

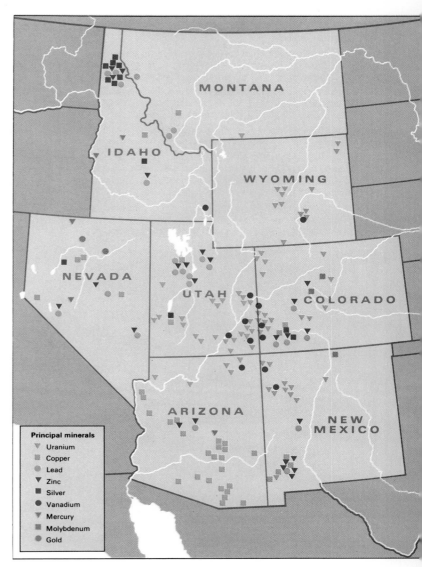

The Mountain States region is one of the world's richest mining centers, yielding more than a billion dollars' worth of essential ores each year. Arizona alone is the source of more than half of the copper dug in the U.S., about a tenth of the total world output. Yet Utah has the nation's largest copper mine, the Bingham Mine of the Kennecott Copper Corporation. Nearly half of the country's silver comes from Idaho, most of it from the cluster of mines in the state's northern tip, while much molybdenum, a metal used to make high-strength steel alloys, is mined in Colorado. The Climax Mine in central Colorado by itself yields more than half of the molybdenum produced in the U.S. Valuable by-products are also obtained from the operating mines shown above. The Mineral Park Mine in Kingman, Arizona, for example, is primarily a copper mine, but yields large quantities of molybdenum, gold and zinc as well.

The miner's life

1. Pack horses trudge toward isolated mines in the mountains near Telluride, Colorado, carrying barrels of fresh water, the miners' only supply. Delivered at the mines, the water cost five cents a bucket.

2. Square-set timbers, fitted together to form hollow cubes, support the Independence Mine in Cripple Creek, Colorado. In large chambers, waste rock was packed into some of the cubes for more strength.

3. Miners from the hills near Georgetown, Colorado, pose stiffly for a photographer. Although their pay was high for the period—about three dollars a day—living costs and gambling losses left little surplus.

4. A quiet street in Upper Creede, Colorado, basks in the mountain sunlight. But Creede itself saw around-the-clock gaiety, prompting one visiting journalist to write, "There is no night in Creede."

5. Like a scene from a Western movie, a saloon in Tombstone, Arizona, swings with activity as "upstairs girls" draw customers to the gambling tables and a barroom piano player looks on in the background.

was graduated from the Texas College of Mines with a degree in geology. He was a slight, impulsive, forthright youngster who hated knuckling under to any boss. He hoped to escape bosses forever by finding a gold mine worth a million dollars. But grubstakes were hard to come by and he had to earn a living in the meantime, particularly after marrying a Texas girl named Minnie Lee Holland, who produced a child every year or so. Steen held various geology jobs for oil companies until he was black-listed in the late 1940s for talking back to one boss too many.

The next few years for the Steens and their four small sons were filled with the distress of poverty and the happiness and zest of having a go at a dream together. Minnie Lee was as determined as was her husband to find that million-dollar, boss-escaping mine (it became a uranium mine instead of a gold mine after the AEC's announcement). Starting in 1950, they rambled over the desert in a secondhand Jeep and a house trailer, looking for uranium from Dove Creek in southwestern Colorado past Utah's Big Indian District and on as far north as Cisco, Utah. They could not make ends meet on the small grubstakes supplied by relatives and friends. Once, when even the beans and oatmeal ran out, Steen shot a deer out of season for food. During part of a winter, they heated their board shack in Cisco with coal picked up along the Denver and Rio Grande railroad tracks. There were delays while Steen was away trying to borrow money to pay doctor bills and to fix his dilapidated drill rig.

People said that he was bound to fail because he did not look for uranium where the AEC said it ought to be. Actually, he was a shrewd and imaginative geologist who knew what he was about. He studied Shinarump strata and at last staked 12 claims 52 miles south of Moab, Utah, in the Big Indian District, an area described in AEC reports as "barren of possibilities." He had reached the bottom financially, having sold the house trailer for cash to keep going.

On July 3, 1952, he placed his drill rig over a spot where he hoped to find uranium-bearing ore at a depth of 150 feet. The diamond drill broke off at 75 feet. Steen hurried to nearby Cisco in his Jeep to find a tool to fish out the drill, as an afterthought taking along a bit of core rock from the drill hole. In Cisco, Steen put a friend's Geiger counter over the piece of core rock as a matter of routine. The needle hit the top of the scale. Steen recalled later, "I dashed out the door and ran a block to our shack, jerked open the door and yelled

to Minnie Lee, 'We've hit it, we've hit it! It's a million-dollar lick!' Minnie Lee replied, 'Boy, you've been out in the sun too long.'"

Minnie Lee was not the only skeptic, and Steen had a great deal of trouble persuading people of the value of his claim. But eventually his core hole became Mi Vida (My Life) Mine, one of the richest in history, with reserves estimated to be worth $100 million. Within a year of the discovery a million dollars' worth of uranium ore had been taken out of Mi Vida. Minnie Lee and the four boys were off the beans and oatmeal. Charles Augustus Steen had a fiery red Lincoln and a private airplane for openers, and plans for a mansion on a bluff above Moab. Later, he sold his uranium properties for many millions and moved to Reno, Nevada, to live the life of a mining tycoon.

While Steen was struggling out in the desert to make his wild dream come true, a totally different sort of prospector was also following the will-o'-the-wisp. His name was Vernon Pick, and he was a big, ruggedly handsome, largely self-taught man approaching 50. During the 1940s, Pick had laid plans to spend the rest of his days quietly and comfortably in Two Rivers, Minnesota, where he owned a profitable, diversified business that, among other things, had a substantial mail-order trade in rewound electric motors. On May 9, 1951, the former flour mill that housed the business went up in smoke. Pick had loved the business and the old mill. He could not bring himself to try to rebuild. He and his wife, Ruth, bought a house trailer with $6,000 of their insurance money and headed for California to look for work in the aircraft industry. In Colorado Springs they heard about the uranium rush, caught the mining bug and landed in Grand Junction, where Ruth set up housekeeping in the trailer. An Atomic Energy Commission expert suggested to Pick that the Shinarump conglomerate around Hanksville, Utah, might be the place to look for his fortune. Pick's notion of a fortune was more modest than Steen's million dollars. Pick decided he would settle for $50,000.

While Steen was probing the area south of Moab, Pick drove a panel truck across the Colorado and the Green Rivers to Hanksville, a green dot west of Moab in an immensity of huge red buttes and pebbly washes. The Dirty Devil River comes down there past Hanksville from a seldom-visited area called the San Rafael Swell and flows southeast to the Colorado. Hanksville residents saw that Pick was the rawest of amateur prospectors—so raw that they suspected him of being some sort of mining spy. But he proceeded to prove that he could prospect tirelessly, going out alone for two weeks at a stretch in the desert canyons running toward the San Rafael Swell. He would drive the panel truck up a wash as far as the sand would allow and continue on foot with his scintillometer, a more sensitive (and expensive) detector of gamma rays than a Geiger counter.

As the winter months of 1951-1952 passed, Pick came to look like an oldtime desert rat, his face deeply tanned, his big felt hat soaked with sweat, his heavy shoes battered and his pants caked with grime. He enjoyed the beauty of the desert and learned about thirst and the fear of getting lost. He caught glimpses of mountain lions and once he came upon the remains of a dinosaur. For a long time he was full of confidence, even in the spring of 1952, when noonday temperatures began rising as high as 120 degrees. But when June came, he had only $300 left of his insurance money. He faced up to the plain fact that he had failed to discover his $50,000 mine. He would do well to get Ruth to California and close out his Utah dream in some dull factory job.

But one last try. From his road-end camp Pick could see in the north one canyon that he had not explored. It was the canyon of the Muddy River, a silt-laden branch of the Dirty Devil, flowing down from the San Rafael Swell. Early on a June day he walked away from the panel truck, carrying his pack and canteens and scintillometer—65 pounds in all. He reached the canyon mouth that evening. He spent two days more fighting his way up the hot gorge of the Muddy. He crossed the river 27 times and collapsed at the end of the fourth day's grind with stomach cramps, a pulse rate of 130 beats a minute and an idea that he might be dying from drinking poisoned river water. Next morning he decided to move camp into the shade of some nearby trees to rest. While carrying gear to the site, he noticed that his scintillometer needle was jiggling back and forth as he passed rocks that had fallen from an outcrop high up on the face of the canyon. Suddenly he forgot all about his cramps and weariness. He scrambled 400 feet up the steep slope to the outcrop and chipped off a piece. It was yellow —the color of carnotite, a major uranium ore frequently found in Shinarump strata. The scintillometer needle hit the top of the scale.

In a day or two he made it back to his truck and on to Hanksville to tell his friends about his mine. And that is why Mr. and Mrs. Vernon Pick eventually did get to California after all. Instead of arriving penniless, they were richer by the more than nine million dollars (six million dollars after taxes) that Pick received for his mine from the Atlas Corporation. The Picks settled down to live happily ever after on a large tract of land in the Santa Cruz Mountains south of San Francisco. Here some of the Pick millions have gone into a full-scale research-and-development laboratory devoted to electronics and electromechanics. For Pick, it was in effect back to Two Rivers, Minnesota, and the dear old mill.

During the mid-1950s, overproduction from bonanzas like Steen's and Pick's brought on a uranium glut and a period of gloomy predictions that there would never be another U-boom. The gloom lasted until 1966 when the Atomic Energy Commission disclosed that American utility companies had placed orders for the building of 21 new steam-generating plants to be powered by nuclear energy. The first really big nuclear power plant had been ordered only three years before by the Jersey Central Power and Light Company, and this phenomenal increase caused a huge revision upward of uranium needs.

The result was a second uranium boom, especially in New Mexico, where more than 30 uranium mines were developed in the mid-1960s in the Haystack Butte-Ambrosia Lake country some 15 miles northwest of the town of Grants. One of the mines in this area, the Anaconda Company's Jackpile, contains some of the largest known uranium deposits in the world. The AEC thinks that the New Mexico uranium-ore reserves consist of some 30 million tons, or nearly half the estimated U.S. reserves of 61 million tons. In 1964 New Mexico produced about $38 million worth of uranium ore. Utah's output was valued at $26.3 million, mostly from Steen's Big Indian-Lisbon Valley area. Wyoming, never much of a metal state in the past, produced uranium ore worth $23 million in 1964, chiefly from the sandy rimrock of the Gas Hills, just west of the Rattlesnake Range, and from Shirley Basin northeast of Rawlins.

In the Mountain States today, prospecting for uranium or anything else tends to be more and more the province of specialists exploring for large mining companies. Rich strikes are not likely to be found sitting out in plain view any more. Every likely outcrop has been examined and assayed over and over. Most of the good ores that remain are hidden far beneath the surface and can be detected only by very costly processes. In 1961, for example, when the Newmont Mining Corporation acted on a U.S. Geological Survey report that gold probably existed north of Carlin, Nevada, its well-equipped exploration crews spent months mapping and staking claims in the area. Eventually they picked a two-square-mile tract and in 1962 began sinking exploratory drill holes. Two were worthless. But samples from the third, when analyzed by Carlin geologists, brought evidence that gold indeed lay far below the surface in an area that oldtime prospectors had sniffed over a hundred times in a hundred years.

During 1964, heavy earth-moving machines shoveled off more than two million tons of dirt lying over the ore to create an open-pit operation. An automated cyanide mill to refine the gold was built and the first bars of gold were poured in April 1965. The ore had turned out to have good commercial value—$11.50 worth of gold per ton. Drilling had indicated that the tract contained at least 11 million tons of ore. Newmont officials said that their investment of $10 million would be returned to the company within five years. Ten million dollars! Time was when, with luck, another kind of gold seeker in Nevada could make as rich a strike on a grubstake of a burro, a pack and a bottle of whiskey.

The big companies dominate exploration, but there are still modern prospectors like Steen and Pick roaming around on their own in their long-billed caps looking for that fortune. Many today are, however, better financed, grubstaked by the federal government under the Office of Minerals Exploration (OME) program of the U.S. Geological Survey. The OME advances a qualified miner 75 per cent of his costs if he is in search of silver and 50 per cent if he is looking for other minerals, and he reimburses the government on a royalty basis if he finds anything. The miner may be well heeled enough to prospect in a helicopter towing a long, orange tube containing a device that detects underground silver deposits. Or he may ride the wilds in an air-conditioned, Cadillac-powered camper equipped with electric blankets and a refrigerator full of beer, and with a Jeep hooked on behind. The Jeep can ascend any sandy wash and climb a cliff if necessary, hauling itself up with a winch installed behind the front bumper. The camper may hold a library of maps and mining reports, a mobile laboratory for geochemical and spectrographic analysis, and sometimes even delicate navigation instruments to tell the prospector where he is in relation to dots on the maps indicating places recommended for exploration.

Though prospecting methods have changed, federal mining laws have not—and that fact both confers benefits upon the Mountain West and creates certain problems for the region. In the days of the California forty-niners, the miners made local laws to suit themselves. The intent of the local laws was to help miners in every possible way and was reflected later in the Federal Mining Act of 1872. The act still governs the staking of mining claims and not only makes the extraction of valuable minerals legally possible but enables modern prospectors to feel as sure as the California pioneers that they are kings of the West. As we have noted, virtually the entire Mountain States region began as U.S. public domain and much of it still is. Today anybody has a right to stake a mining claim on most of this public land—national forests and grazing districts, for example—although certain areas, such as national parks and monuments, dam sites and Indian reservations, have been declared off limits to prospectors' claims.

Even some kinds of private Western land are open to the prospector. He can stake a claim on somebody's ranch without asking the owner's permission if the government reserved the mineral rights on that particular ranch when it was conveyed by patent to the original homesteader. The government did reserve such mineral rights in many Mountain States homesteads in the early 1900s, notably on the enlarged stock-raising parcels granted to individuals by the Homestead Act of 1916. When some of these 640-acre homesteads of 1916 became an expensive subdivision not so long ago in Tucson, a clever group staked out mining claims in people's back yards, apparently in the hope that the homeowners would feel compelled to buy out the claims. The U.S. Bureau of Land Management declared the claims invalid, but the problem could crop up again elsewhere in the region.

Mining claims under the federal law are of two kinds—lode claims and placer claims. Say a man finds an outcropping of rock with veins of something valuable within it or, by drilling, discovers a valuable underground vein. That is the basis of a lode claim. He can reserve it for himself by staking around it a parcel of land 1,500 feet long and 600 feet wide—about 20 acres. Then he posts his name on the claim with the discovery date, goes to the courthouse of the county in which the claim lies and pays the county recorder a small fee for each page that the description of the claim takes up in the recorder's claim book. So he has his lode claim. He can hold it and take for himself every bit of ore that it contains without any further legal action. He can hold it without mining it extensively just as long as he does at least $100 worth of work on it each year. If he wants to own the land contained within the boundaries of the claim, he must do a total of $500 worth of work on it, have it surveyed, apply for a patent at the nearest office of the Bureau of Land Management and pay a small fee.

Perhaps the prospector finds metal lying around loose on the ground or scattered in underground beds. Such ground is called a placer, and the prospector can claim 20 acres of it by marking its boundaries with posts. After that, he goes to his county courthouse and records his placer pretty much as in the case of a lode claim. In theory, there is nothing to prevent a prospector from staking out all of the vast, unclaimed area of the public domain, but as a practical matter claims are confined to land worth working.

Inevitably more such land will be found, perhaps in areas that no one today suspects of bearing anything worth claiming—for there are no satisfactory answers to the whys of metal distribution throughout the world. Why is there so little tin and nickel in the United States? Why is Arizona so overloaded with copper, providing more than half of the U.S. supply and 10 per cent of the world's? Seventy-five per cent of the molybdenum concentrates produced in the Free World come from that one Bartlett Mountain at the top of Fremont Pass in Colorado. The mineral gilsonite, used in the manufacture of such varied product as inks, varnishes, fuel and roofing materials, is mined exclusively in the vicinity of Vernal, Utah. Recently much has been made of the fact that the world's largest deposit of oil shale lies in an ancient lake bed in northwest Colorado near other deposits in northeastern Utah and southwestern Wyoming.

The belief is that as many as two trillion barrels of oil, at least three times the world's known reserves of petroleum, are locked up in the sedimentary rock of this lake bed awaiting the perfection of practical processes of extraction. The oil shale lies in layers from 300 to 2,500 feet thick that are laced with a substance known as kerogen. Under heat and pressure, kerogen releases a vapor that can be condensed into crude oil. All together, the formation is said to contain enough oil to supply the U.S. for several centuries at the present rate of consumption of some three billion barrels a year.

Eighty per cent of these oil-shale lands belong to the federal government and are controlled by the Department of the Interior, for in 1930 they were withdrawn from mineral entry—that is, from the claims of prospectors—to be held as a reserve against national emergencies. Since before World War II both the U.S. government and groups of oil companies have operated pilot plants to find ways of getting oil from the rock at a cost competitive with oil taken from wells. When such processes are perfected, and mining begins in the area on a large scale, the Mountain West will be presented with a huge bonanza. At the same time it will face enormous problems—such as where to put the thousands of oil-shale workers in the narrow Colorado River Valley, where to get the necessary extra water and where to dump the de-oiled shale. These problems will have to be solved in the decades ahead, as will those of working this inconceivably vast new oil source into the existing worldwide frame of the petroleum industry.

The Mountain West, then, is a great storehouse of things people find themselves needing at one time or another. In wartime some of these things—such as copper, molybdenum, uranium, lead and zinc—are important to national security. In peacetime their availability stimulates science and invention everywhere in the U.S. Their presence, in addition, is another reason why the Mountain States form a region-at-large, so to speak, in which all Americans share an interest.

Western mining is a continuing story. The early explorers, the Indian fighters, the buffalo hunters, the trail-driving cowboys came and went, but the miner in one guise or another will roam the wilderness as long as we can foresee. Back in the late 1850s, men from Georgia, like William Green Russell and John Gregory, found pay dirt near Denver and started the great rush to the Rockies. Soon after, John W. MacKay and others began piling up silver wealth from Nevada's Comstock Lode. Pat Casey, an illiterate Irish immigrant, made a fortune from his mine at Central City, Colorado, in the late 1860s. The grocer Horace Tabor became the world's reigning silver king at Leadville in the 1880s. Marcus Daly and William A. Clark built their Montana copper empires during the 1890s. The carpenter Winfield Scott Stratton received $11 million dollars for his Cripple Creek, Colorado, gold mine at the turn of the century. In the 1950s, when such bonanza days were said to be dead and gone, along came Steen and Pick to strike it at least as rich as any prospector of the past.

The fact is that the hidden treasures of the Mountain West will long be there, waiting for somebody to find them and start a new rush into the wilds. The lure of the will-o'-the-wisp, man's gambling spirit, his burning desire to get very rich in a hurry, is inexhaustible. He knows that the odds against him are enormous, but he will not be deterred from trying. The important thing is the quest.

Long boarded shut, stores along Main Street in Silver City, Idaho, once served a population of 4,000. During the town's life span, nearby mines produced $28 million worth of silver. The last resident, "Two-Gun" Willie Hawes, left Silver City in the 1960s.

Nostalgic ghosts of a roaring era

In the era of the 19th Century mining booms the names of such towns as Silver City, Rhyolite, Elkhorn and a hundred others rang like gold and silver bells across the nation. Today they are ghost towns, their names all but forgotten. A few were born in the 1850s, given life by forty-niners who left California to prospect in the Mountain States. Then gold was discovered in quantity in the Rockies, and wagons streamed into the mountains from both east and west. If the mines were rich enough, the tent slums that sprang up nearby were soon supplanted by wooden houses, brick banks and opera houses. But even the best surface finds petered out. From miles away would come news of richer lodes, and thriving towns were abandoned almost overnight to the sagebrush and lizards they had replaced.

Photographs by Evelyn Hofer

Its garish red-and-green exterior has turned a weathered gray, but fancy lettering still identifies the Cosmopolitan, a once-elegant music hall in Belmont, Nevada. In the 1870s, 10,000 people lived in silver-rich Belmont, and they packed the hall to see such plays as *Maid with the Milking Pail* and *Uncle Tom's Cabin*.

The balcony of Fraternity Hall, a club that once echoed to the merrymaking of those who struck it rich, looms over the main street of deserted Elkhorn, Montana. During the last decades of the 19th Century, Elkhorn mined $14 million worth of silver, and the balcony was a favorite vantage point when gun-toting gentlemen on the street below ironed out their claims to mines—or ladies.

Among the usual paraphernalia of a hotel office, a photograph of Louis Dupuy, founder of the Hotel de Paris in Georgetown, Colorado, still stands on the long-departed owner's desk. The French cuisine of the hotel's dining room rivaled any in the country, and guests were at pains to enjoy it: Dupuy had no qualms about asking patrons to leave if they failed to enjoy a soufflé or a fine imported wine.

Tattered posters cling to the walls of Piper's Opera House in Virginia City, Nevada. Perched almost on top of one of the richest deposits of minerals in the West, the Comstock Lode, Virginia City could afford the best; Piper's was as sumptuous a hall as could be found, and its stage was graced by nationally known performers, including the Barrymores, Lillian Russell and Enrico Caruso.

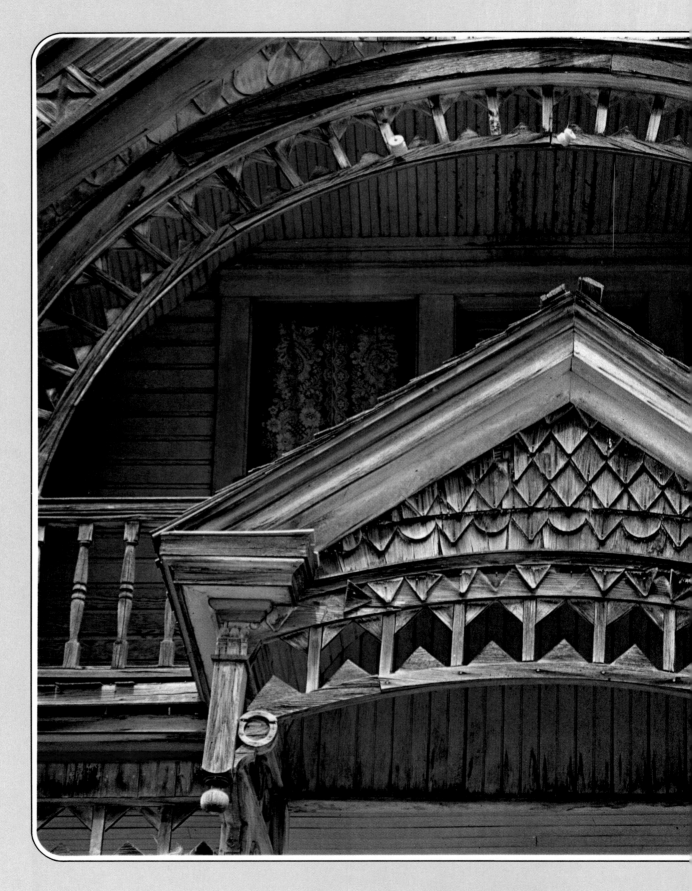

Among the most imposing houses in the once-booming mining town of Silver City, Idaho, was the mansion built by one of the city's wealthiest men, J. W. Stoddard, who owned a thriving cattle ranch, held large interests in mines and operated a Silver City sawmill. As this detail showing its second-floor balcony indicates, the house was edged with the intricate fretwork called gingerbread that was popular during the 19th Century. But if Silver City favored such styles in its architecture, its atmosphere was somewhat other than Victorian, as the town newspaper, the *Owyhee Avalanche*, noted in 1865: "The saloons and Justice's office at Silver City have been doing a rushing business during the present week. . . . He who gluttonously patronizes the bar is liable to account to the bench." On another day the newspaper had sadder news: "Mr. Cox, recently of Silver City, was killed by Indians Wed. morning. Himself and family were moving in a wagon to Boise. . . . His wife drove on rapidly and escaped. . . ." The fortunes of the city rose and fell with the activity in the silver mines; output dropped in the 1870s, then picked up again in the following two decades. More than 4,000 people lived there in the late 1860s. Today, the silver mines played out, Silver City is only a stopping place for tourists.

When a mining town struck it rich, the new prosperity was immediately proclaimed in grandiose, lavishly furnished public buildings, hotels and restaurants. Some examples of this ostentation are shown in these photographs. The top left picture shows a crystal-and-silver salt-and-pepper service in the Hotel de Paris in Georgetown, Colorado. The fringed lamp stands on the judge's bench in the old Esmeralda County Courthouse in Goldfield, Nevada. To its right is a marble lavatory, installed in the expensive Hotel de Paris, and at far right is one of the hotel's iron stoves. The dresser and matching mirror frame of black walnut in the bottom left photograph stand in Teller House, a hotel in Central City, Colorado, and the brick-sided cooking range was imported by the hotel from Europe. At far right, in another room in Teller House, is the furniture of socially ambitious Baby Doe Tabor, wife of a fabulously successful operator who got his start by selling a share in a Leadville, Colorado, mine for one million dollars. Her picture stands on the table at the rear.

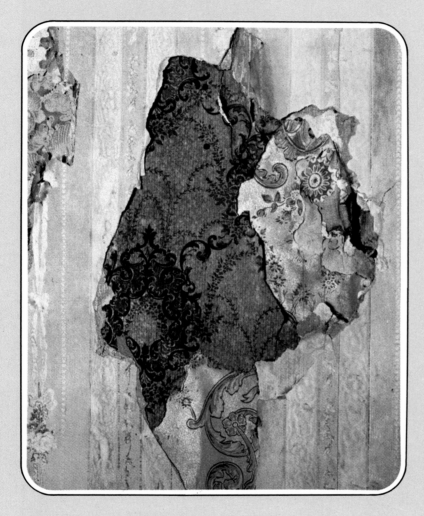

Bits of fancy wallpaper cling tenaciously to the plaster of an Elkhorn, Montana, residence. In the boom days, the Elkhorn mines produced several thousand dollars' worth of gold and silver every day, and the town's residences reflected that fact: wallpaper imported from France, furniture crafted by the best cabinetmakers of Europe, Oriental rugs and incredibly ornate Tiffany lamps.

A wooden grave marker, its inscription erased by time, is one of the few remains of Rhyolite, Nevada, long emptied of both gold and people. The mine was found in 1904 by a star-crossed prospector, "Shorty" Harris. Elated by his first chance at big money, Harris celebrated—and gambled away his claim for $800; eight years later three million dollars had been taken from "Shorty" Harris' claim.

7

The Children of Joseph Smith

Nothing out there in the mountains and deserts of the wondrous West is more wondrous than that phenomenon of tradition, industry, faith and discipline, the Church of Jesus Christ of Latter-day Saints. These Mormons, as they are usually called, or Saints, as they like to call themselves, are not only to be found in the Western United States. Two and a half million of them fructify the whole earth in their own intensely energetic way—not only in the U.S. but in Finland and Brazil, in South Africa and England, in Japan and Rarotonga among other places. Salt Lake City is the Mormon mecca, however. In the surrounding 400,000-square-mile area of the Mountain West that Brigham Young called "Deseret," and which covers Nevada, most of Arizona and parts of Idaho, Wyoming, Colorado, New Mexico, California and Oregon in addition to Utah, live a million of them. Here, from 1847 on, the first Mormon settlers tackled the problems of Western life, solved the bulk of them and passed the solutions along to the "Gentile" (that is, non-Mormon) hordes that followed after them. The

A gilded statue of Moroni, the angel who appeared in the visions of Joseph Smith, founder of the Mormon faith, caps a spire on Salt Lake City's Mormon Temple. The four-million-dollar structure, completed in 1893, is the center of the Mormon world.

Mormons were the pioneers who taught the pioneers.

Most of the Deseret Saints live in Utah—700,000 of them, in a recent estimate, or 70 per cent of the state's population. Idaho has 178,000 Mormons, Arizona 83,000, Nevada 40,000, Wyoming and Colorado about 27,000 each, Montana and New Mexico 18,000 each. Mormon "hatcheries," a nickname for the elaborate Mormon missions, student seminaries and institutes, are producing thousands of converts each year. The missionaries—12,000 of them in all—feel that it is just a question of time before the rest of the eight million residents of the Mountain States will become Saints and begin what the Mormons consider to be the only spiritually and materially satisfying way to live on this earth and in the exclusively Mormon hereafter.

Despite its international membership, the Mormon Church is a purely American creation, a do-it-yourself institution without precedent in history. Almost every male Saint is some kind of Church official with specific responsibilities. Almost every male is a priest also—from age 12 to 19 he holds some degree in what is called the Aaronic priesthood; from 19 on he holds a degree in the Melchizedek priesthood. Huge Mormon Temples are built, Church lands farmed, Church businesses manned, Church services held, missions operated and guided tours conducted by these amateur priests, most of whom give their labor without compensation. There is no professional Mormon clergy.

The Church follows the Scripture of the Bible much as other Christian sects do. But it has, in extraordinary addition, a scripture of its own, the previously mentioned Book of Mormon, and a prophet of its own, Joseph Smith Jr. The Book of Mormon tells, in the literary style of the Bible, how a man close to God, Lehi, sailed with some other Israelites from Palestine across the Atlantic to America about 600 B.C. Lehi's party developed into two American nations, the Lamanites and the Nephites. Some centuries later, Jesus Christ, after His Resurrection, visited these New World Israelites briefly, teaching the Gospel, ordaining disciples and making a second center in America for His Christian church.

The Book of Mormon goes on to explain that around 400 A.D. the Lamanites and Nephites had a falling out and fought a battle in Cumorah, "a land of many waters, rivers and fountains," which appears to have been the Finger Lakes country of upstate New York. In this Cumorah battle (or shortly thereafter) the Lamanites, whom the Saints believe to be ancestors of the American Indians, killed all the Nephites except a young man named Moroni—the "i" pronounced "eye" and the accent placed on the second syllable.

Moroni was the son of Mormon, the last Nephite prophet, who had previously written a history of the Nephites in characters that the Saints call "reformed Egyptian." The characters were scratched by the Prophet Mormon on golden plates—thin gold sheets eight inches square held together with three rings in loose-leaf-notebook style. Moroni buried this golden-plate history on a hill called Cumorah—a minor prominence located four miles south of present-day Palmyra, New York, which is 15 miles south of Lake Ontario and 20 miles east of Rochester. Then Moroni died and went to heaven. By 1820 A.D., when Palmyra had become a boomtown on the proposed route of the Erie Canal, Moroni had become an angel whom the Lord employed to send messages to His prophets on earth.

In that same year, Joseph Smith Jr. was a blond-haired, blue-eyed boy of 14 living on a farm near Hill Cumorah, where Moroni had buried Mormon's golden plates 14 centuries before. He was the sort of boy Mark Twain would have admired—merry, zestful, loving, mischievous, curious, precocious, gregarious, imaginative and quite irresistible, to men and women alike. He was unschooled but far from illiterate, being a student of the Bible and of Indian lore. Religion interested him, but he had no use for the Christian sects around Palmyra. He felt that they wasted so much time quarreling over Church forms that they neglected Christ's teaching.

According to Mormon belief, the Lord shared Joseph's low opinion of the established Churches and chose Joseph to restore Christ's original Church in full detail—the Twelve Apostles, the First Council of the Seventy (seven men who preside over the missionary work done by groups called Seventies), and other bodies. Its name would be the Church of Jesus Christ of Latter-day Saints and Joseph would be its Prophet and First President. During the boy's 10-year period of contemplation—in Palmyra and later in Harmony, Pennsylvania—the Lord and his Son, Jesus Christ, John the Baptist, and the Apostles Peter, Paul and John all appeared to him. He entered the Aaronic and Melchizedek priesthoods and acquired the authority of a prophet to utter the divine will and announce future events.

The angel Moroni returned to earth several times to help Joseph find Mormon's golden plates on Hill Cumorah and to explain their significance. Joseph was a handsome, muscular six-footer of 21 when he finally dug up the plates from Hill Cumorah and took them to a house in Harmony to translate the reformed Egyptian characters into English. He was able to do this by looking at the characters through two magic transparent stones that Moroni had buried with the plates. He dictated his 350,000-word translation of the plates to a friend and got to the end of the Prophet Mormon's history in less than three months.

Our concern here is the Mormons of Deseret, but an understanding of Joseph Smith is the main step to understanding his two and a half million spiritual children in the eight Mountain States and elsewhere. Every Saint has something of Joseph's loving spirit in him, something of his sublime confidence and his faith in his restored Church of Jesus Christ. The Saints do not simply accept Mormon doctrine. They *believe* the Book of Mormon. They believe that Joseph's Church came from revelations that the Lord put in Joseph's mind, and it seems likely that Joseph believed it too.

In the spring of 1830 Joseph published his translation of the plates as the Book of Mormon and formally organized the Mormon Church with himself as Prophet and First President. Shortly thereafter, he reported that Moroni had taken the plates back. During the next 14 years, Joseph developed the policies that have made the Church today such a fast-growing, aggressive and colorful theocracy, and these policies reflect his own pragmatic personality. Joseph put all his vitality, his exuberant joy of living, into Mormon doctrine. Puritan ideas of hell-fire and predestined damnation because of original sin were not for his Saints. Joseph believed that a man suffered the torments of hell only because of his own foolishness.

The authority of the President of the Church of Jesus Christ of Latter-day Saints, Joseph said, was fundamental. Whatever the President wanted done had to be done by whomever the President called upon. The member might have to leave for England the next day to seek converts or he might be called to ride horseback to Missouri to plan a new Mormon town. The Church was not merely a helpful item in each Mormon's life, along with his wife and children and career. The Church was his whole life. His family and career were threads in the fabric of the churchly whole.

To the gay, supercharged Joseph, a strong and growing Church was a happy, industrious Church. A man should go to church as much for the dancing and singing and sports and theater work as for religious inspiration. These social activities under the Lord's approving eye were great fun, brought the membership close together, taught them the blessings of cooperation and kept them out of mischief. Joseph also insisted that in addition to studying Church history and working and playing hard, his people should have as many children as possible. Procreation increased the membership. For a Mormon, making money was fun and holy too. A Mormon did not need to be ashamed of being acquisitive, of grabbing his share of material things. His prosperity was the Church's prosperity because he tithed—a tenth of his earnings went into the Church treasury. And if Mormons made money out of one another that was good, too. It tended to keep control of Mormon enterprises within the Church.

All these churchly goings on, of course, took physical strength. A devout Mormon must do nothing to weaken his body, which housed an eternal spirit. That is why Joseph issued his "Word of Wisdom" in 1833, which counseled Saints not to drink tea or coffee or alcoholic beverages or to use tobacco.

From the start, Gentiles opposed Joseph's upstart Church and harried its members from New York State westward in a rising crescendo of violence. This persecution, the worst in the nation's religious history, included murders, rapes and beatings, the burning and looting of Mormon homes and barns, and the theft of Mormon livestock. It culminated in Carthage, Illinois, on June 27, 1844, when a Gentile mob went after the Prophet and his brother in a jail where they were being held on treason charges and murdered them both. Joseph's

martyrdom at 38 was an eerie echo of the martyrdom of Christ, also in his thirties.

Gentiles of the period resented the Mormons for many reasons—for their confounded confidence that theirs was the only true Church, for having their own defense army, a formidable body known as the Nauvoo Legion (named for the Illinois town that was their headquarters at the time), and for their organized industry, which dominated the economy of any community in which they settled. Early in 1844 the Gentiles had fumed when Joseph decided to run for President of the United States on a "Theodemocracy" ticket. When Joseph was reported to have received the Lord's sanction for plural marriage because the Old Testament was supposed to have sanctioned it, the Gentiles protested bitterly. Mormons still are at odds as to whether Joseph was a polygamist. A small schismatic group, the Reorganized Church of Jesus Christ of Latter Day Saints, says that he was not. Those who say that he was give him anywhere from 27 to 50 wives.

The Saints argue among themselves about why Joseph may have wanted his Mormon men to have all the wives they could handle. Some declare that he felt that polygamy reduced promiscuity and made it easy for widows to get husbands. Some say there were not enough men to go around. Polygamy made good Mormon mothers of women who would otherwise have been spinsters. A few speak of the Prophet's good looks, great vitality and gentle ways, roll their eyes and murmur, "Maybe Joseph just liked women."

Joseph himself said little about the wives he did, or did not, have, or about other interesting aspects of his strange, short, heroic, frantically busy life. Fawn McKay Brodie, who wrote an excellent but frank biography of Smith in 1945, quoted him as saying to an audience just before his murder: "You don't know me; you never knew my heart. No man knows my history, I cannot tell it; I shall never undertake it. I don't blame anyone for not believing my history. If I had not experienced what I have, I could not have believed it myself."

It has been noted that the Church, which approved plural marriages openly in 1852, ceased to sanction them in 1890. But it is said that there are Saints in Deseret today who refuse to repudiate any of Joseph's sanctions and have extra wives even though the practice is against the law of the Church and of the land. In 1966 these fundamentalists were publicly supported in the medical journal *Geriatrics* by Dr. Victor Kassel, a Gentile Salt Lake City physician, who found that the group living guaranteed by polygamy protected the health of elderly persons. "Studies have demonstrated," Dr. Kassel wrote, "that married couples subsist on a more adequate diet than do widows and widowers. The lonely women, who were once excellent cooks, have no one for whom to prepare a complete meal. There is no incentive to cook. . . . On the other hand, where there is a group of people living together as a family, eating in the company of one another, the story is different. Mealtime regains its social atmosphere; appetites return."

After Joseph Smith's death the Mormons fled from their persecutors in Illinois to sanctuary in Utah. Under President Brigham Young's leadership from 1844 to 1877, they laid the groundwork for today's blooming Deseret by courage, will power and incredible industry. The setting of Salt Lake City and its environs, between the slaty-blue Wasatch Mountains and Great Salt Lake, has striking similarities to the section of Palestine where Christ lived. Both areas are tablelands with scant rainfall and with cool oases of trees and flowers produced by irrigation. The low mountains around Jerusalem are cut by many canyons, as is the higher Wasatch Range. Palestine's Dead Sea is just as salty as the larger Great Salt Lake. The fresh-water Sea of Galilee is about the same shape as fresh-water Utah Lake, though not as large. The River Jordan, which flows some 65 miles from the Sea of Galilee to empty into the Dead Sea, is about the same length as Utah's Jordan River, which flows from Utah Lake to empty into Great Salt Lake. When Mormon artists want to show how ancient Israelites in the Holy Land looked before they sailed to America, they just go out somewhere in the red rocks of Utah and paint away.

Whether this Biblical setting is approached from Manassa, Colorado, or from Rexburg, Idaho, or from the White Mountains of Arizona, or from Wyoming's Star Valley, the highway is sprinkled with hints of the splendors to come. The traveler may happen on one of the six Mormon Temples in Deseret where marriages are celebrated and ceremonials held. Gentiles are not allowed inside these Temples and the design of the buildings makes it difficult to peek in. Especially impressive from the outside is the oldest of them all, the dazzling white Temple in St. George in southern Utah, which was completed in 1877. You may visit the grounds of the somewhat Egyptian Temple in Mesa, Arizona, set in a lush park of date palms and cypress trees, and with "No smoking please" signs spiked around the weedless lawn. Nothing serious will happen to you if you smoke on the grounds, but you have a feeling that if you do, your distinguished Mormon guide will bow politely and depart, leaving you and the rest of the tourists stranded. Nobody smokes.

New Mormon chapels, often in the shape of crosses, appear regularly along the road to Salt Lake City, most of them built of tawny brick with slender black or white steeples, shingled roofs and high, arched, mullioned windows. They are always the handsomest buildings in their towns. Mormon men and women bustle about their chapels tenderly, mowing the greenest of lawns or getting ready for a dance or a funeral or a basketball game or Sunday services or a barbecue out back. Chattering Mormon children fly on their bicycles over the new chapel sidewalks. The nearer Salt Lake City is approached, the more numerous the tawny brick buildings become; many of them actually are Mormon homes constructed in the same general style as the chapels, and having the same kind of weedless lawns and new sidewalks and chattering children and aura of loving care. Even the mammoth assembly of tawny bricks that is Brigham Young University at Provo exudes this air of saintly pride and joy.

Driving down out of the Wasatch Mountains en route to Salt Lake City, the visitor encounters the This Is the Place Monument, starring President Young, at the foot of Emigration Canyon. The stone monument is peopled with pioneers in statues and bas-reliefs—one of the proudest presentations of a heritage in the nation. From the monument it is not far into Salt Lake City. On the north side of the city rises the domed Utah State Capitol, with its terraced gardens, Mormon Battalion Monument —commemorating a Mormon fighting unit in the Mexican War—and a delightful non sequitur, a huge statue of Massasoit, a 17th Century Indian chief from Massachusetts, whose Utah-born sculptor presented it to the state. After seeing the capitol, a visitor may move on to Welfare Square, which contains an enormous supermarketlike dispensary from which Mormon-made food and clothing are distributed to needy Saints. Next, one may stop at Brigham Young's home, the Beehive House, or at his burial plot—a bit disappointing because only three of his 27 wives are buried with him, perhaps as a result of a disagreement among his 56 children. A visitor may dine in luxury on the top floor on the Church-owned Hotel Utah, bringing his own bottle and ordering setups since liquor by the drink is banned in Utah. Other customs may bemuse the tourist. Most coffee-scorning Mormons turn their coffee cups upside down when they sit down in a Utah restaurant, and some turn the cup handles to point north or south as a sign to the waitress that they would prefer tomato juice or orange juice.

Temple Square occupies 10 acres in the heart of the city, and is the heart of the Mormon world. It is one of the world's great tourist attractions; more than a million people flock to see it each year. The many-spired Temple was begun in 1853 and was finished in 1893. Its lines suggest the silvery contours of the Wasatch Range above it, but it has a quaint grace and beauty of its own. Its highest spire is surmounted by a 12-foot-high gold representation of the angel Moroni, blowing hard on a three-foot trumpet. Near the Temple is the great whale-shaped 1876 Tabernacle, used for large meetings and for the Sunday morning concerts of the 375-voice Mormon Tabernacle Choir, which has broadcast coast-to-coast since 1929. Elsewhere are a statue of Joseph Smith, a statue of the Mormon pioneers pushing their handcarts across the plains, a new visitors' center, the small but architecturally unusual Gothic Assembly Hall, and the Sea Gull Monument, honoring the birds that answered the prayers of the pioneers in 1848 by devouring a horde of grain-consuming crickets.

Temple Square is always teeming with visitors. But they stay away from the Temple itself, which has no public entrances and looks as though nobody had been inside in years. That is an illusion. At certain hours, especially before sunrise, when the Temple bustles with preparations for the day's ceremonies, there may be more people inside the Temple than in the square outside. From 2,000 to 4,000 Saints a day arrive from Mormon stakes (dioceses that support the Church, as a stake helps support a tent) all over the Mountain States to don ceremonial robes and take part in marriages, in baptisms of the living, and in vicarious baptisms of a Saint's ancestors, "who may have died without a true knowledge of the gospel," as the Saints put it.

Activity in and around the Temple makes quite an experience of a night spent in the Church-owned Hotel Utah Motor Lodge on Temple Square. From the motel window at 4 a.m. no cars or people can be seen on well-lighted South Temple Street. Then the rush begins. Mormon rites take time and therefore must be started early. By 4:30 a.m. every parking place on both sides of West Temple Street is taken as supervisory and service personnel arrive to prepare for the day's proceedings. At 6:30 the participating Saints begin to appear, each with a little overnight suitcase holding his Temple garments and clutching his Recommend, or permit, from his ward bishop to enter the Temple.

There is a certain elation in the way they walk, as though they were all eager to get where they are

Mormons believe that in 1827 an angel led Joseph Smith to Hill Cumorah, near Palmyra, New York, there to take the golden plates buried centuries before. From inscriptions on the plates, Smith compiled the *Book of Mormon*, a foundation of this faith. This 19th Century painting of the event was done by C.C.A. Christensen.

going. They are a middle-class crowd of men and women, well groomed, obviously successful, obviously in good health, obviously the kind of people who neither smoke nor drink, and probably abstain from tea and coffee too. They are bound for the little Moorish Temple Annex, where they will put on their ceremonial clothes and then go into the Temple by one of three underground passages. On the way they pass the Temple guard who checks their Recommends. Once in the spectacularly arranged Temple, they will be involved in ceremonies or in contemplation. The various events take place in the Celestial Room or the Creation Room, the World Room or the Sealing Room for the Living, where Mormon marriages are solemnized, or in a room where a baptismal font rests on the backs of 12 golden oxen. This font is an extremely busy place. About three and a half million people, living and dead, are baptized annually in the eight U.S. and five foreign Mormon Temples.

The worldwide administration of the Mormon Church is directed from offices near Temple Square by a chain of command much like that established by Joseph Smith more than a century ago—a President-Prophet, Twelve Apostles, and the seven-man First Council of the Seventy. The President makes decisions based on revelations that he receives from the Lord; the others enforce the decisions and conduct the business of the Church. Most of these ecclesiastical executives are modest and appealing older men who have had successful careers in business and in the professions. They have a fresh, well-scrubbed, alert look and their manner is cordial, courtly, informal and gently commanding. They have the same air of ability, integrity and dedication to civic good that stamps an able Rotarian.

These general officers have absolute control over Church members, as in Joseph Smith's day. From them, authority filters down to officers of the dioceselike stakes, whose boundaries are based on the limits of river valleys. The Salt Lake region has 13 stakes, the Oquirrh region just to the west has 10 stakes and the Cache Valley region to the north has 10 stakes. There are many stakes all along the Snake River and its branches in Idaho and many more in the salubrious Virgin River area of southern Utah. The 11 stakes in the Salt River Valley of Arizona reflect the recent growth of Phoenix, but the four stakes along the Little Colorado of northern Arizona date back to the 1860s. Each of these administrative stakes has a president and two counselors who run the overall affairs of the several wards, or parishes, in the stake, whose combined congregations may amount to several thousand people. Each ward is run by a bishop and two counselors, called to unpaid duty for indefinite terms by the stake president. When a Saint is called to be a bishop he is not likely to refuse to serve. It is a very great honor, and, anyhow, as we have noted, a Saint's whole life is his Church and he fits family and career into that mandatory frame.

The Mormon Church is said to take in as much as $125,000,000 each year. Much of this is spent on Church programs such as the operation of 16 hospitals, Brigham Young University with its 20,000 students, and Church-owned properties that give aid to 100,000 needy Saints annually. These properties include canneries, grain elevators, spaghetti, soap and milk plants, a pineapple plantation, peanut farms in Texas and a 360,000-acre cattle ranch with orange groves in Florida. Much money goes for the upkeep of historic sites, for the Tabernacle Choir, for 74 mission headquarters throughout the world, for building some 300 ward chapels each year, and for the training of youngsters, starting at age four, in the Mormon faith.

The general authorities do not publicize their financial affairs, but it might be a reasonable guess that the Church derives around $50 million of its annual income from its business enterprises. One of these, the quaintly ornate Zion's Co-operative

Mercantile Institution, is Salt Lake City's largest department store, with annual sales of more than $35 million. Its helter-skelter, old-fashioned air gives the impression that it has not changed much since Brigham Young opened it in 1869—though its methods are thoroughly up to date. The Church also controls the Utah-Idaho Sugar Company, which has sales of more than $70 million a year (the Mormons pioneered beet-sugar making in America in 1891); the Beneficial Life Insurance Company (life policies worth more than $700 million in force); the Deseret Book Company, which sells great numbers of the Book of Mormon every month; *The Deseret News* (daily circulation, nearly 100,000); radio and television stations all over the nation, including the international short-wave radio station WRUL in New York; and Zions Securities Corporation, which owns 30 acres of downtown Salt Lake City.

Such business enterprises are not, of course, the Church's only source of revenue. More than half of its total income derives from members' tithes, which are collected by some 6,000 ward bishops who can estimate a Saint's tithable income from personal observation. Additional money is donated in the form of fast-day gifts. Devout families give up two meals on one Sunday a month and pay their bishop what the two meals would have cost.

Not all Mormons are regular tithepayers, but the percentage of contributors is surely higher than that of most American Churches. One reason for the high percentage is the tremendous attraction of the Mormon Temples, which can be used by nondrinking, nonsmoking tithepayers only. A Saint who is lax in his tithing, teetotaling and other matters is called a Jack Mormon, and a Mormon joke has it that a sea gull that refused to eat crickets to help the pioneers in 1848 was a Jack Mormon. Such an erring Saint may go along for months without feeling a need to enter his Temple. But, sooner or later, he will want to get married—or, as the Mormons put it, "sealed for eternity"—or see a son or daughter sealed, or baptize an ancestor, or just yearn to enjoy the Temple's interior beauty and reassurance of immortality. To get a Recommend and enter his Temple, he must call on the bishop of his ward, declare himself ready to reform his behavior and pay up his tithe in full.

In recent years hundreds of thousands of Saints have had their ancestors vicariously baptized at the oxen font in the Temple so that they will have the pleasure of their ancestors' company in the Mormon hereafter. Church authorities have stimulated interest in this curious and unique process by making it easy for a Saint to find out who his ancestors are for centuries back. The Church has built up for him, at an annual cost of four million dollars, what may be the largest genealogical library on earth. Wherever Saints have lived, anywhere in the world, expert researchers gather official birth, marriage, death and census records, copy tombstone inscriptions and send them to the main library, in a former Montgomery Ward store in Salt Lake City, to be translated, catalogued and distributed on microfilm to 17 branch libraries. Mormons and Gentiles alike have made a serious hobby of searching for ancestors in these extensive microfilm records.

The average Mountain States Mormon looks like any other urban, middle-class Westerner, talks like him, acts like him, is equally patriotic, and thinks like him—up to a point. The difference lies in the Mormon's utter absorption in Church affairs, his devotion to the new brand of Christianity that Joseph Smith gave to his Saints in 1830. Lorin D. Wiggins, a Salt Lake City bishop who has 860 Mormons in his ward, has this absorption. He is a stocky, considerate, outgoing, enthusiastic man around 40 who holds the position of photographer for a Mormon-owned advertising agency (his color photos of Temple interiors have been widely published). He lives in a comfortable, tawny brick home southeast of the city with his wife, LouJean, a pretty brunette, and six children. One of these children, Alvin, is not a Wiggins. He is a Navajo Indian boy, a descendant, according to the Book of Mormon, of the Lamanite Israelites, and the Wigginses are putting him through school at their own expense, as part of the Church's foster-parent program to educate Indian children. Alvin spends his summers with his parents back on a Navajo reservation.

A typical week in the life of this family indicates the commitment to the Church expected of an active Mormon. On Monday Bishop Wiggins starts his week at 5:45 a.m. by helping three of his children in an hour of Church-sponsored music study. During breakfast, his ward secretary gives him a list of the parishioners whose birthdays fall on that date, and he spends from 7:30 to 8:00 a.m. phoning greetings to these people. He works on his photographs in town all day, has supper with LouJean and the children at 6, and hurries to the ward chapel after supper to spend four hours with his counselors drawing up a program for the following Sunday. Tuesday is a repetition of Monday, except that the photography is interrupted by interviews that Wiggins gives to young Saints who want advice about college, missionary work and marriage. It is broken also by problem Mormons who feel it is

their right to drop in on their bishop at any time. These Saints may have strayed from the Church's ways in the past, but they have changed of late and they want Wiggins to reach a decision about issuing their Recommends.

Wednesday is an easier day unless the bishop's birthday list is long. Both Lorin and LouJean look forward to the Wednesday Home Night, when, after supper, the children gather around their parents in the living room. Home Night symbolizes the place of the family as the focal point of Joseph Smith's Church. Wiggins may start the proceedings by reminding the members of his family to be happy and kind to one another. Then he leads a discussion on the meaning of the Mormon Bible lesson for the evening—"Am I a Pretender?" perhaps, or, "Two Words: What and Why." Even three-year-old Teddy is encouraged to give opinions and to pose questions about the Bible. The essence of Mormon education is to teach children to think almost from infancy and to instill in them a habit of responsibility and leadership. After the discussion, 14-year-old Linda may play a classical selection on the spinet piano and nine-year-old Janice may deliver a closing Home Night prayer that she has composed herself.

After work on Thursday, Wiggins is likely to drive to Ogden or Brigham City to attend a meeting with officials from nearby stakes. Fridays and Saturdays are free days—except for the birthday greetings, chats with Recommend seekers, or perhaps a stop at the chapel to check something, such as the plumbing in the "cry room," where noisy babies are parked during Sunday services. Of course Lorin and LouJean try to attend some of the weekend Mormon doings—talent shows at Temple Square, tributes to the President and Apostles, building dedications, historical ceremonies, Boy Scout circuses and so on.

The bishop needs his Friday-Saturday rest, and LouJean Wiggins needs it too. The wife of a bishop is every bit as busy all week as he is. Besides cooking and housekeeping for eight, LouJean calls on the poor as a Relief Society member, teaches crafts to the Little Homemakers, is active in the Young Women's Mutual Improvement Association and the Scout-like Beehive Girls, takes part in Church cultural programs, spends a few hours doing research at the Genealogical Society and a few more at the beauty parlor having her glossy black hair done. Mormon women are even more meticulous about their appearance than are men.

And so Sunday comes, the day of days. Bishop Wiggins rises and breakfasts in time to reach the chapel at 7. He and his two counselors and other volunteer officials prepare the day's agenda and shape up ward plans, such as who will cook, wash dishes, wait on table and entertain at a forthcoming fund-raising dinner. The bishop works also on the records of young male Saints seeking advancement in the Aaronic priesthood—12-year-olds eligible to be deacons, 14-year-olds ready to be teachers and 16-year-olds who want to be priests. At 8:15 a.m. all the males gather for an hour's priesthood service and at 9:30 Lorin and his welfare committee consider requests from members for financial help. Sunday school for children and adults is held from 10:30 to noon, after which Wiggins receives in his chapel office any ward member asking for guidance. Sometimes the bishop manages to get a bite of lunch before his two-hour round of Sunday sick calls. From 4:25 to 6 p.m. he takes part in a prayer meeting and a kind of communion service and then spends one more hour in welfare interviews. The Wigginses wind up their Mormon Sunday with an informal discussion of Church doctrine at a "fireside" gathering of young married couples. When Lorin and LouJean arrive home about 10 p.m. they are ready for a good night's sleep. Monday will be another busy Mormon day, starting at 5:45 a.m.

This Wiggins family week is exactly what Joseph Smith had in mind for his Saints when he founded his remarkable Church in upstate New York. It is a week of improving each shining hour by hard work, hard study, hard play and hard worship of God, the better to be happy and prosperous in this life and in the Mormon life everlasting, and to keep out of mischief all the while. The Prophet's intent could hardly have been more admirable. And yet it brought on his own tragic death at the age of 38, and those who made his intent their rule subsequently endured many years of severe persecution.

The persecution did not begin to taper off until the Saints banned polygamy in 1890, long after they had settled in the Mountain West. They are much too strong and too important now to be persecuted, but they are criticized for the same sort of reasons that Gentiles criticized them in the 1840s and forced them from Illinois. Some disapprove of the economic and political solidarity of the Saints. Some object to their placid insistence that they are right and everybody else is wrong where religion is concerned. Some are infuriated by the serene Mormon conviction that Joseph Smith actually did dig up the plates with the angel Moroni's help and actually did translate the reformed Egyptian into the Book of Mormon by looking through magic stones. These critics may accept the Bible and its parables literally, but they seem to feel that miracles should not be believed in if they occurred after the Saviour's time. In their view, the Saints show disrespect for Jesus Christ in having their own additional prophet of the Lord—a man with the banal name of Smith whose earthly career can be traced in the files of American newspapers.

Social drinkers in Utah reprove the Saints for their sobriety and accuse them of stalling progress by keeping out bars. Some are resentful that young Mormons are deferred from the draft when called into missionary service. Some claim that Mormon doctrine holds back Brigham Young University because, among other things, it teaches as incontestable fact ideas that Gentile scholars consider untrue—most historians and archeologists, for example, cannot accept the Book of Mormon thesis that American Indians are descended from Israelites.

Before Joseph Smith died he declared Negroes to be ineligible for the Mormon priesthood because, he said, they were descendants of Noah's son Ham, who by marrying the dark-skinned and cursed Egyptus perpetuated the seed of Cain. The Prophet may have interpreted Scripture in this way to make Mormonism popular with proslavery whites. Whatever his reason, the exclusion is a problem to Church officials in these days of agitation for civil rights—even though Negroes are scarce in Deseret. Some leaders are bothered too by charges within and without the Church that they oppose any kind of new thought on Church matters and that their intolerance produces squeezed minds. These leaders are charged with being too fond of statistics, particularly those having dollar signs in front of them, and with leaning heavily on materialism—fancier Temples, costly festivals, overelaborate programs such as the Mormon Tabernacle Choir—as the driving force in place of belief in a sublime idea that gave the Utah pioneers the strength to triumph over every obstacle.

If these criticisms are signs of weakness, the average close-knit Mormon family is blissfully unaware of it—and statistics from Temple Square show that by 1967 there were twice as many blissful Saints as in 1950. By all appearances anywhere in Deseret, what the Saints want and what they still get is the loving, zestful, industrious, romantic example of their spiritual father from upstate New York, Joseph Smith. They have his revelations from the Lord to guide them through every minute of every day. And finally, they have his promise of greater joy to come in the Mormon heaven, united at last with those ancestors who paved the way for their Mormon life on earth.

Navajo herd their sheep and goats through a stark sandy stretch of desert in Utah. Although there are occasional water holes and patches of greenery, much of the American desert is barren. As many as 50 of its sparse acres may be needed to feed one sheep.

The desert's harsh assets

The American desert, which is comprised of five smaller deserts, stretches into all the Mountain States except Montana. It is a relatively barren land with scant rainfall and dramatic contrasts between day and night temperatures. Only plants and animals physiologically oriented to the area can survive there. The desert offers regions of awesome beauty as well as great monotonous wastes; none of it would seem to be of much value to man.

Yet the desert is a highly important national asset. Here both the government and private industry conduct vital research. Irrigation projects have enabled cities, towns and farms to flourish. The desert has, as well, become a popular recreational center. The word "desert" comes from the Latin *desertum* meaning "abandoned," but certainly the American desert belies that root.

Man's deeds and products preserved in the wasteland

The American desert is extremely dry and, in the daytime, searingly hot. Because of the interaction of air currents and the terrain of the Western states, moisture-laden clouds from the Pacific Ocean rarely release their moisture over the desert; some sections have gone for many years without rain. And because there is little cloud cover over the desert, the sun beats down with baking intensity.

The combination of dryness and heat can be a great preservative, however. The Strategic Air Command, for example, has found the

American desert an ideal storage area for unneeded planes. Near Tucson, Arizona, SAC has created a 3,000-acre depot *(below)* for storing, refurbishing or eventually scrapping its bombers. There the multimillion-dollar aircraft can be left in the open with a minimum of maintenance because of the almost total absence of the two prime causes of corrosion, humidity and precipitation.

Just as it will preserve man-made objects, so will the desert preserve man's imprint. Tank tracks made by General George Patton's armored forces in Arizona during World War II are still clearly visible *(below, left)*. After the tanks made their marks, such rain as did fall seeped into the ground and dissolved subsurface minerals. These minerals, rising by capillary action, were resolidified when they reached the imprinted ground level, and the resulting bond of soil and minerals has withstood decades of erosion. The same process took place over many centuries in Africa's Sahara, where age-old caravan trails have been preserved by nature.

Immense but secret areas for vital research

Space and privacy are two vital prerequisites for certain types of research, and the American desert offers both. These desert assets enable government and industry discreetly to test machinery as diverse as rockets and automobiles. The Nike-Hercules missile lifting into a dawn sky in New Mexico *(top)* is being fired from the White Sands Missile Range, the largest all-land missile test center in the Western Hemisphere.

Established in 1945—it was there that the first atomic bomb was exploded—the range occupies some 4,000 square miles of the desert. Today, the various branches of the Armed Forces, the National Aeronautics and Space Administration and other government agencies are using the facilities at White Sands for the testing of space and other equipment for both military and scientific use. Other parts of the desert are being employed for a variety of government research projects including explorations into the peaceful uses of nuclear energy.

Big business is also experimenting in the desert. The Ford Motor Company, to gain privacy in the secretive automobile industry, has built a 4,000-acre testing grounds near Kingman, Arizona. There, cars are put through a variety of trials such as dust tests *(bottom)*, in which special devices stir up dust to check out the vehicles' sealing systems, and endurance tests, in which cars are run on tracks for many hours at high speeds. This influx of governmental and private projects bolsters the region's economy and is an important step toward eventual reclamation of the area.

The difficulty of human adjustment

Although seemingly remote and inaccessible, the American desert has for many years been used as a convenient backdrop by Hollywood filmmakers, who can reach it swiftly and find suitable settings there for anything from Biblical epics to routine Westerns. Desert shooting has its drawbacks, however, for the hot, parched surroundings can be hard on the cast. The unhappy looking extras at left, costumed for their roles in *The Greatest Story Ever Told*, sit at the foot of a massive butte in northern Arizona with lunch trays on their laps. Their discomfort is understandable; the ability of humans to adjust physiologically to the rigors of the desert is extremely limited. The plants and animals of the desert have evolved defenses to counter a constant need for water; the human body, though it can make several minor adjustments to extreme temperatures, cannot cope with a severe water loss for a prolonged period.

A man in the desert loses as much as a quart of fluid an hour. To survive, he must consume fluids voluminously. A movie actor, while on desert location, often drinks eight quarts of liquid a day, about four times the usual daily consumption.

Speeding on salt, skiing on sand

Increasingly, Americans are discovering that the desert provides exciting new opportunities for sport and recreation. Campers pitch tents in austere settings of rugged beauty; gliding enthusiasts wheel and turn aloft in eerie silence, riding their frail craft on the air currents that shimmer above the hot desert floor; men strapped in or on high-speed machines hurtle across Utah's Bonneville Salt Flats in quest of speed; skiers glissade down the bleached dunes of New Mexico, finding sand a quite acceptable substitute for snow.

Bonneville is a 200-square-mile phenomenon: a desert surface made up of an estimated billion tons of salt. This deposit was caused, and is added to annually, by runoff water from the mountains. The runoff, carrying salts dissolved from the rocks, raises the water table beneath the flats. The saline water is then high enough to be drawn to the surface by capillary action. When the moisture evaporates, the salt solidifies into a rock-hard surface. This solid smooth surface has made Bonneville the American mecca for drivers of ultra-high-speed land vehicles. Each fall, when the runoff has ceased and the flats have hardened, the drivers converge on a small area that is set aside as a race course. They bring with them a dazzling array of expensive machinery, ranging from super-powered motorcycles *(above, right)*, to jet-powered automobiles. It was in the jet vehicle *Spirit of America* that Craig Breedlove, following a straight black guide line painted on the white salt, set a land speed record of 600.601 miles per hour in 1965.

Thrill-seekers also make use of the desert dunes. Gliding down these wind-drifted mounds of sand, skiers can wear beach costumes and still enjoy all the excitement of the snow slope. The more adventurous skiers hang on to billowing parachutes *(right)* that serve as sails to pull them before the wind.

Air-conditioned cities of steel and glass

The cities, towns and farms that are sprouting all over the American desert are dramatic evidence of man's current success in reclaiming even the bleakest of wastelands. In the past, his meager accomplishments in the area might be symbolized by the farmhouse *(top)* sitting forlornly on a scrubby New Mexico prairie. In sharp contrast, cities like Las Vegas *(bottom)*, casting a neon glow into the night sky, represent the look of today and tomorrow.

Man no longer nibbles at the desert, he takes a healthy bite; armed with knowledge, experience and money, he builds air-conditioned cities of steel and glass. In 1950, Las Vegas had a population of less than 25,000; by 1967, the number of permanent residents had shot up to over 100,000. Other desert cities such as Tucson and Phoenix have had similar growths. The burgeoning metropolises are the most obvious examples of desert reclamation, but they are no more significant than the smaller communities and the numerous areas of newly arable land that are now contributing to the economy of the Mountain States. In times past, the major barrier to such development was, of course, the lack of adequate water supply. The driving of deep wells, the diverting of water from other areas and the construction of elaborate irrigation systems have helped clear this hurdle. Though the increased demand for water may pose problems for the future, the opening of new areas for settlement and expansion seems thus far to be well worth the effort.

8

Everybody's Wilderness

Autumn is a time of special splendor in the Mountain States, and the opening of the deer- and elk-hunting season is a stirring event on both sides of the Continental Divide from New Mexico and Arizona to Montana and Idaho. During the 24 hours before dawn of opening day, mountain highways are crowded with campers, station wagons, pickups and Jeeps as hunters from all over the nation hurry toward the higher hills. Many saddle horses are in the cavalcade, carried in trailers towed by the cars.

Some of the hunters are of the Peck's Bad Boy sort, littering the landscape with beer cans, leering at the waitresses in the cheeseburger joints, warming up their guns by shooting at road markers and cutting up generally. But one is inclined to overlook such behavior. For 11 long months the hunters have been dreaming of the autumn season, counterpart in their minds of adventurous days gone by when this exotic land was probed by Lewis and Clark, by Jim Bridger and Kit Carson, by Texas cowboys driving their Longhorns toward Wyoming and Montana, by uranium prospectors like Charlie

Steen and Vernon Pick. All through the humdrum year today's red-capped adventurers have been checking their guns and compasses and binoculars. They have spent many hours gathering maps and camping equipment and reading up on woodsmanship. They have been preparing to live like pioneers for a little while.

Now it is autumn and they are almost there. Soon they will leave civilization and ascend some back-country trail to a remote campground several thousand feet up in the high wilderness. A strong hint of winter is in the air. They risk freezing in a blizzard, getting lost in an early snowstorm, dying of a heart attack or injuries of the chase or being mistaken for a bear by some other hunter. But most of them will not come to any of these griefs. Whether they bag their deer or not, theirs will be the joy and excitement of satisfying a basic urge, the urge to put one's own resources to test in meeting the challenge of a trying environment.

Which brings us to the point. The Mountain States constitute one of the few regions left in the United States with the kind of wilderness and woodlands in which deer, elk and antelope can multiply at an appreciable rate. But what if too many hunters come, too many roads are pushed into the wilderness, too many of the Peck's Bad

Elk graze against a spectacular background of rugged peaks in Colorado's Rocky Mountain National Park. Rocky Mountain, one of 11 national parks in the Mountain States, preserves its natural environment in the best interests of the land, wildlife and man.

Returning from a bear hunt in the Rockies in 1905, outdoorsman President Theodore Roosevelt *(on light horse at right)* and his companions ride toward Glenwood Springs, Colorado. "My hunt has begun well," Roosevelt wrote during this trip, "and I killed a big bear, making a rather good shot at him." During earlier visits to the Far West, Roosevelt had developed a deep love for the Mountain States, which was to last throughout his life. He was an ardent conservationist and was greatly alarmed at the wasteful depletion of the nation's natural resources. As president, he was able to do something about it: under his administration a National Conservation Commission was established and the areas devoted to national forests increased from 43 million to 195 million acres.

Boys forget to drown their campfires? Then there will be little wilderness left for anybody—neither deer, nor elk, nor antelope, nor hunters, nor plain citizens who just want to relax in the mountain air away from the cities once in a while.

Hunting is just one thing Americans do on their federal lands, the usage of which has increased vastly since World War II. Up to 1941, users of federal lands in the West were relatively few—mainly miners, ranchers, lumbermen and summer visitors to the national parks. During the war, the region's federal real estate provided space for training soldiers in the techniques of modern war. It also supplied room for testing atomic bombs.

When the war ended, tens of thousands of ex-GIs returned to the West to live near some national forest, partly because the open space gave them a feeling of elbow room, of freedom from the increasing congestion of more populous regions. Others visited the forests and parks on summer camping excursions or came to ski in the winter on the same federal lands that they had known during their wartime training. Part of the rise of the Rocky Mountain skiing industry, which grew from almost nothing in 1945 to dimensions rivaling those of any other area in the world, can be traced to the determined efforts of ex-GI skiers to make use of the opportunity that the public lands presented to them.

As the skiers on the public lands have multiplied, so have the fishermen, hikers, amateur geologists, bird watchers, duck hunters, artifact collectors, wild-flower students, ghost-town fans and explorers in four-wheel-drive cars. Other enthusiasts pack by horseback into federal wilderness areas, those last strongholds of unspoiled nature, where anything motorized is forbidden—entrancing spots like Bridger National Forest in the Wind River Range of Wyoming and Snowmass Lake in the White River National Forest in Colorado. Some take float trips in rubber rafts down remote and almost inaccessible canyon stretches of the Yampa, the Green, the Colorado or Salmon Rivers.

These increased recreational uses of space in the Mountain States have been encouraged by national prosperity, improved highways, better cars, and the trend toward longer summer and winter vacations. If a man has three or four weeks of vacation coming to him instead of one or two, he may, instead of restricting himself to areas close to home, take his family on a 10,000-mile Western tour—perhaps with stops at Carson National Forest near Taos, New Mexico, at Grand Canyon in Arizona, at the ancient cliff dwellings of Mesa Verde National Park in southwestern Colorado, or at the canyonlands of eastern Utah and Glacier National Park in Montana. In 1940 attendance at Yellowstone and Rocky Mountain National Parks amounted to around half a million visitors each. These days, attendance at each is in the neighborhood of two million annually. As the parks have become crowded, the Forest Service has enlarged camping facilities in the national forests, which are far more extensive than the parks, and has pushed roads serving the new campsites deeper into the forests.

All this increased recreational use has had profound national effects, the most marked of which has been a great wave of conservationist sentiment, often focused on these federal lands of the West. Militant groups of nature lovers, notably the California-based Sierra Club, have been insisting that the lands be preserved so that future generations may be able to enjoy them as citizens do today. Conservationists have complained that lumber companies and sheep ranchers have violated the spirit of conservation by logging off irreplaceable stands of timber and by fencing in federal lands, thus interfering with wildlife. They have also been critical of certain government agencies, especially the Department of the Interior's Bureau of Reclamation. They charge that the bureau is damaging the pristine loveliness of parts of the region by erecting dams on sites close to national parks.

A case in point is the Central Arizona Project, a controversial feature of the $1.8 billion Colorado River Basin Project. As we have noted, the conservationists achieved a triumph in 1966 when the Department of the Interior felt compelled to revise its original plans for the Central Arizona Project. This project, as first constituted, had been backed by the vast majority of Arizona residents for what seemed very good reasons. The Arizonans contended that the volume of water available to them from local underground sources was insufficient to meet present, to say nothing of future, needs. The water table in Arizona was falling at an alarming rate—as much as eight feet a year. And so the Arizonans felt that their economic survival depended on having water pumped to them from the Colorado River, a supply to which they were entitled by a 1963 Supreme Court decision.

The Central Arizona Project had been designed to solve Arizona's critical water problem. It called for the building by the Bureau of Reclamation of two hydroelectric power dams on the Colorado River in the Grand Canyon area. The sale of the power created at the dams would have been used to finance the cost of bringing water to the burgeoning Phoenix and Tucson areas. But the dams would

The greatest single force in planning land usage of the vast and varied terrain of the Mountain States is the federal government, which owns almost half of the approximately 550 million acres encompassed by the eight states. National parks and monuments preserve unspoiled vistas and areas with scenic, historic or scientific importance. National forests are set aside for public recreation and for conservation and orderly use of the forest land. National wildlife refuges provide shelter for game animals and birds. Public lands are areas reserved for future recreational sites, for the expansion of existing communities or for military or industrial use.

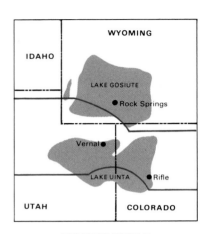

MAP OF AREA SHOWN IN
CROSS SECTION AT LEFT

A vital new source of oil

Buried under parts of the Mountain States is one of the nation's greatest untapped natural resources, two huge beds of oil shale known as the Green River Formation *(shown in cross section above)*. These shale beds cover about 16,500 square miles, extend as deep as 2,400 feet into the ground and may contain as much as 2.5 trillion barrels of oil. The history of this priceless deposit goes back some 40 million years, to the Eocene epoch. During this time two large lakes *(upper right)*, Gosiute and Uinta, apparently occupied much of today's Wyoming, Utah and Colorado. Surrounded by mountains on all sides, these lakes had no outlets and, like great stagnant pools, were covered with a scum of tiny organisms. As these organisms died they sank to the bottom with inorganic sediment and the mixture solidified into oil shale, a kind of rock containing solid bituminous material. Because the oil of the Green River Formation does not exist as a fluid like regular crude oil but is a solid locked in the shale, the rock must be mined and the oil extracted from it by a heating process.

have flooded considerable sections of Grand Canyon, removing from view—or so the conservationists charged—some of the loveliest scenery in the nation.

The conflict between avowed economic need and avowed esthetic need was classic. Arizona desperately needed additional water for expansion, said one side; a beloved national spectacle, the Grand Canyon, should be preserved for posterity, said the other. The idealism of the conservationists was not expected to triumph over Arizona's practical necessity. But idealism did win—plans for the two dams were shelved—and the long debate stirred still more interest among Americans in protecting the natural state of their magnificent public spaces. Late in 1966 Secretary of the Interior Stewart L. Udall remarked during a political rally in Colorado Springs that the nation's conservationist minority seemed to have become a majority.

The fight over the Colorado dams was scarcely over when the forces of long-term conservation and of immediate economic need began warming up for a new fight. The battlefield now was the 16,000 square miles of oil-bearing shale lying mainly in federal holdings in Colorado, Wyoming and Utah. The richest portion of the shale is beneath federal lands controlled by the Department of the Interior in northwestern Colorado. This beautiful section of the Roan Plateau between the Colorado and White Rivers was a favorite hunting ground of the White River Ute Indians before their removal to Utah after the Meeker Massacre of 1879. It is watered by Piceance, Parachute and Roan Creeks and is covered with Piñon and juniper, scrub oak and serviceberry, wild currant and sage. It remains a popular deer- and elk-hunting country.

But experts have estimated that the oil shale in the three states contains three times the world's known reserves of oil and 70 times the proved U.S. reserves. It appears that the time may not be far distant when oil can be extracted from the shales at commercially profitable costs, and oil-company men feel that a great new oil-shale industry should be established on these federal lands.

This new source, the petroleum people say, would make the United States completely independent of the Middle East and other foreign sources of oil, and would avert the problems attendant upon the exhaustion of presently developed domestic sources. Thousands of workers would be needed to run the new industry, which would be a huge economic blessing to the sparsely settled western slope of Colorado. But the oilmen maintain that they must have wide latitude—freedom to operate on federal property as they see fit—if they are to accept the financial risk of developing new industry. They have been petitioning the Department of the Interior to grant them long-term leases of the federal shale lands at royalty rates that they judge to be economically feasible. Also they have sought incentives to large-scale investment in the form of helpful tax allowances.

The conservationists have opposed such requests. They charge that the companies are attempting a land grab reminiscent of the Teapot Dome scandal of the 1920s, which raged over government oil leases in Wyoming. They estimate that the oil-shale industry and its new horde of workers would require vast amounts of water each year, and they ask where so much water will come from in a region whose water resources are already overstrained.

Another complication is the fact that every 15 barrels of oil extracted by a process known as pyrolysis above ground would leave 24,000 pounds of waste rock, a total of perhaps 2.4 billion tons of waste yearly if annual production reached three billion barrels. Such waste, the conservationists declare, would bury the Roan Plateau, one of Colorado's finest scenic and recreational areas, in layers of ash thousands of feet high. They also fear that if the oil should be melted out by a proposed method of underground nuclear blasts, water and fumes escaping from these explosions could poison both the air and the river water of northwestern Colorado.

In the midst of the debate, officials of the Department of the Interior proposed leasing to the oil companies a maximum of 30,000 acres of the richer shale lands as a starter to development, subject to a graduated royalty scale and an annual rental fee of 50 cents per acre. In restricting this preliminary development to a very small part of its shale lands, the department seemed to lean a bit toward the suggestions of some economists that such a stupendous resource might better serve the people of the nation if it were to be developed under stringent federal control.

The problems of developing the oil-shale lands— and the difficulties raised by such other pressures upon the open lands as the activities of hunters and the needs of industry and other water users—may not be resolved for years to come. But it is clear that the current national wave of interest in conservation has a most important bearing on the trend of Mountain States affairs, for tremendous numbers of Americans feel they have a proprietary interest in the region—and their interest cannot be ignored in the respective state capitals or in Washington.

This is not to say that all residents of the eight Mountain States are enthusiasts for the conservationist cause. The average Westerner feels his hackles rise when anyone—government official, conservationists, businessman or whoever—tells him what is best for his piece of country. Westerners must earn a living from their land, and many of them see no purpose in opposing a hydroelectric project that may bring industry and jobs to their region. And whatever the conservationists may say about beauty and encroachment upon open land, many Westerners see no point, to cite another example, in proposals to reduce the amount of federal acreage on which cattle may be grazed, since it is to the cattlemen's interests not to abuse their grazing privileges.

Still the region has its special idealisms, reflecting the peculiar makeup of the population. It has, for instance, a great many health seekers who feel that they owe their lives to the health-giving Western environment and who are therefore more acutely concerned than the average American about the evil effects of smog and stream pollution. It has, in addition, a great many people who are concerned with their intellectual as well as their physical environment. Large numbers of residents have come here from other parts of the country to retire, and many of them are ardent supporters of cultural attractions in their adopted communities. Western colleges and schools have a full share of educators who give copious amounts of their time to civic improvement. Other residents concerned with both the physical and the cultural setting include scientists working on nuclear and space programs, military leaders of wide experience, and specialists like those who direct research at the U.S. Geological Survey field center in Denver or at the New Mexico Museum's Laboratory of Anthropology in Santa Fe. Many such people find themselves in strong disagreement with Western businessmen who say that esthetics brings no money into their cash registers.

For esthetics sometimes does bring financial rewards. Cities like Boulder and Colorado Springs, both in Colorado, have lured business to their areas because employees prefer to work in cities that are attractive to live in and that support lively art, music and drama programs or that contain universities with stimulating graduate-study programs. Walter P. Paepcke, the Chicago packaging magnate, raised the mountain town of Aspen, Colorado, from a ghost camp to a world-famous resort partly by bringing to it festivals devoted to the arts and humanities. Some years back, Aspen residents claimed both a cultural and an economic victory when they brought about strict control over the erection of billboards there. Billboards, they argued, had the effect of lowering property values.

The assorted idealists have won a few victories. But in the Mountain States, as elsewhere, the conflict will continue between the desire of people to live in an uplifting environment and the demands of an incessantly growing economy. In 1940 the eight states had a population of a little more than four million. Twenty-five years later they had eight million, and by 1980 they may have more than 16 million. The Western economy is helping to fulfill the American dream of ever-higher personal income and living standards, even though such splendid results threaten to take a lot of splendor out of Western life. Industry and population growth have combined, for example, to bring about the pollution of most of the West's rivers. The city of Denver, which can be proud of its generally progressive record, only recently bothered to treat all its domestic sewage before letting it run into the tiny South Platte River, where it had caused trouble in a dozen towns in the lower South Platte Valley. Lake Tahoe, a formerly clear body of water on the state line between California and Nevada, is on its way to becoming a cesspool as officials of the two states debate means of sewage disposal. Utah's Great Salt Lake, once a superb water playground, is being shunned by sportsmen because so much filth flows to it from Salt Lake County. Even Utah's new Lake Powell, which stores Colorado River water behind Glen Canyon Dam, is unsightly in places

because the Department of the Interior cannot stop the dumping of garbage and litter into it from the thousands of motorboats using the lake. In Arizona the Oak Creek Canyon resort area north of Phoenix has witnessed a controversy over whether leaks into the creek from the septic tanks of summer residents make the water unsafe for recreation.

The Mountain West is not immune to the problem of dirty air, either, for all the talk of the delightful purity of the atmosphere. The isolated lumber-mill city of Missoula in the lovely Bitterroot Valley of Montana has been condemned as one of the smoggiest in the United States. In 1965 a bill to control air pollution in Montana was vetoed by Governor Tim Babcock on the ground that it was "punitive" to industry. Denver, a handsome city on a clear day, is shrouded often in effluvia from car exhausts, plant stacks, used-car incinerators and trash burners. Growth-induced smog is making trouble also for metropolitan Phoenix and its $250 million winter-resort industry. Dirty air from the copper smelters east of the Superstition Mountains reduces visibility and makes eyes smart as it floats low over Camelback Mountain and the fine homes and motels, the golf courses and kidney-shaped swimming pools of suburban Scottsdale and Paradise Valley, Sunnyslope and Glendale and Mesa. The Arizona legislature has not seen fit to antagonize the big copper corporations by establishing stringent statewide pollution controls.

Such problems and dilemmas have vast significance for the U.S. as a whole and will continue to do so for many years to come. As yet, however, they have had small effect on those special attributes that make Westerners so helplessly, so foolishly in love with their wide-open spaces, their salubrious and whimsical climate, their dizzying altitudes, their gray-green plains and red plateaus and purple canyons. Western men and women approve of progress, of realism, but they cling hard at the same time to romance and the old frontier spirit —the string tie, the big hat, the "Howdy, podner" and the rest. It would break their hearts to see their environment become dull and docile.

Their characteristic optimism may derive in part from their view that change comes slowly in a land that puts up so many obstacles to the schemes of men to tame it—obstacles such as the pull of gravity, the obduracy of rock and the scarcity of water. They feel there is as much to be dared, as many challenges to meet, as there were a century ago.

And they firmly believe that a century hence, the challenges of the Mountain States will stir the blood just as much as they do now.

Visitors at the observation center in Dinosaur National Monument watch a worker chip away rock to expose fossilized bones. The monument, a 326-square-mile area in Utah and Colorado, is on land where giant reptiles roamed 140 million years ago.

Guarding a natural heritage

The incomparable setting of the Mountain States, from sun-baked canyons to lush evergreen forests and jagged mountaintops, and the wildlife that abounds there comprise a priceless natural resource for everyone to use and enjoy. But with this gift of nature comes the responsibility to maintain it for both present and future generations. Some of the land is set aside as national parks, where every tree, plant, animal and rock formation is inviolate. Some of it is national forest land, where logging is controlled and new trees are planted to replace those cut down. Everywhere, constant vigilance is necessary to protect the land and its wildlife from careless visitors and such natural enemies as famine, disease and fire. All the while, experts use this vast outdoor laboratory to study the region's rich present and amazing past.

Sweeping low over a burning hillside in Wyoming's Shoshone National Forest, a Forest Service plane releases a spray of fire-retarding chemicals. During a recent season, some two million gallons of chemicals were used to assist fighters on the ground.

Varying patterns of timber checker an experimental forest *(right)* in Colorado's Arapaho National Forest, aiding rangers in their studies of new planting and cutting techniques to encourage the growth of young trees and increase the water runoff without causing erosion.

Science, men and mountain greenery

Among the most valuable public lands are the great forests—lush green tracts of spruce, fir and pine sprinkled with aspen and maple and hundreds of other kinds of trees. In the Mountain States more than 92 million acres of these woodlands are set aside as national forests and maintained by Department of Agriculture Forest Rangers. Along with keeping the areas clean and safe for the public and doing fire-prevention work, the rangers supervise the cutting of timber by private firms that have contracted for the privilege. Some forest land is also allotted to ranchers for sheep and cattle grazing; this, too, is directed by the rangers, who make certain that enough vegetation is retained to feed wildlife and to prevent land erosion.

Besides erosion, disease and insects, the forests' greatest threat is fire. In 1966 nearly 560,000 acres of fine timber in all parts of the Mountain States were destroyed by fires started by man or lightning.

The winter's beautiful white menace

Winter snow brings a fresh beauty to the Mountain States, and with it a season of new sports—and new hazards. From Big Mountain, Montana, to Mount Lemmon, Arizona, skiers by the thousands flock to nearly a hundred ski areas, 80 of them within the national forests. But with the heavy snow comes the danger of avalanche. Snow rangers highly trained in rescue work constantly patrol avalanche-prone slopes, closing them when necessary and then triggering slides with hand-placed explosives and artillery shells so skiing can continue. Nearly every year, however, skiers who ignore posted warnings—and occasionally even snow rangers testing the slopes—are swept to their deaths by cascading tons of snow and ice that may reach speeds of more than 100 miles an hour, ripping down trees, smashing houses and even burying highways and railroads.

Using a war-surplus howitzer, a Colorado avalanche-control team shoots down a dangerous snow formation near a highway in Loveland Pass, a major route west of Denver. In 1962 three avalanches within an hour trapped seven people in the pass, but all survived.

Trainees in a Forest Service avalanche rescue school practice probing the snow with poles to find possible victims. A rope keeps the men in a straight line as they move forward together, putting down their probes at each step so that every spot will be checked.

Wildlife management
for sport and science

Much of the wildlife of the Mountain States, from the piglike peccaries rooting through the brush of southern Arizona and New Mexico to the fierce grizzlies roaming the high slopes of the northern Rockies, lives in the national parks and forests. Here rangers work with state game and fish departments to direct scientific wildlife studies and to control the activities of sportsmen. In the national parks only fishing is allowed. In thousands of lakes and streams anglers cast for salmon, pike, bass and a half dozen varieties of trout. However, outside the parks, hunters have their choice of large or small game—but limits are set on all quarry. Conservation-minded authorities are determined that the unchecked slaughter of the past, which almost brought about the extinction of the bison and pronghorn, must not be permitted to happen again with other animals.

Workers gingerly weigh a drugged grizzly bear in Yellowstone
National Park as part of a research project to observe the behavior of
the animals. After the bear's size is recorded, a tiny radio transmitter
is tied around its neck so its ramblings can be traced.

Thousands of trout spill from an airborne fish tank as a plane of the
Wyoming Game and Fish Commission stocks a lake near Jackson
Hole. The commission replenishes the state's lakes and streams to
provide sport for the 150,000 fishermen who come there annually.

Tipping the scales for a "natural balance"

To preserve the abundant wildlife in the Mountain States, authorities often find it necessary to adjust the numbers of animals. In northern Yellowstone National Park, for example, herds of elk grown too large in number for the available winter forage are driven to other ranges or shipped to state parks, zoos, ranches and experimental labs. Outside the parks, other preserves, off limits to hunters, have been set up to provide sanctuary for animals that might not otherwise survive. Game refuges shelter buffalo, elk, deer, bighorn sheep, moose, antelope and many smaller animals. In addition, bird refuges provide safe resting and feeding areas for millions of migrating ducks and geese. The rangers guard the welfare of animals with the same zeal they bring to the preservation of the other components of the Mountain States' great natural heritage.

Herded by a helicopter, elk in feed-short northern Yellowstone National Park plod through the snow toward trapping areas, where some 1,300 of the animals will be caught and transferred to new land to keep the herd at the range's winter feeding capacity of 5,000.

172

Suggested tours

The seven maps on this and the following pages show sections of the Mountain States that are of particular interest to the tourist. No attempt has been made to show every road and town. Instead, scenic routes, historic sites and other special features are emphasized. The text accompanying each map describes the area. Opening dates and hours should be confirmed locally, since they may vary with the season. The areas covered are numbered on the small map below. A key to symbols used is also provided.

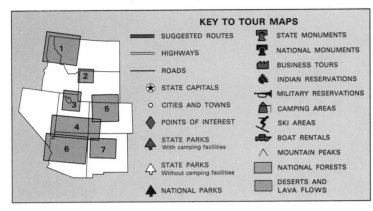

KEY TO TOUR MAPS

- ▬ SUGGESTED ROUTES
- ═ HIGHWAYS
- — ROADS
- ★ STATE CAPITALS
- ○ CITIES AND TOWNS
- ◆ POINTS OF INTEREST
- ▲ STATE PARKS With camping facilities
- △ STATE PARKS Without camping facilities
- ▲ NATIONAL PARKS
- ♨ STATE MONUMENTS
- ♨ NATIONAL MONUMENTS
- ⌂ BUSINESS TOURS
- ❦ INDIAN RESERVATIONS
- ⌐ MILITARY RESERVATIONS
- ⛺ CAMPING AREAS
- ⛷ SKI AREAS
- ⛵ BOAT RENTALS
- ⋀ MOUNTAIN PEAKS
- ▨ NATIONAL FORESTS
- ▨ DESERTS AND LAVA FLOWS

1. Northern Idaho and Montana

The northwest corner of the Mountain States is a heavily wooded region—much of it preserved in state parks and national forests—that supports a booming lumber industry and abounds in camping and boating facilities. Starting at Lewiston near the Washington-Idaho border, the tourist can watch huge trees turned into paper at Potlatch Forests, Inc. To the north is Cataldo Mission, built in the middle of the 19th Century. And farther north, Schweitzer Basin offers excellent skiing.

To the east lies Whitefish, Montana, a gateway to the Big Mountain ski area, and Glacier National Park. In the highlands of the park's million acres there are still some small glaciers, remnants of the rivers of ice that carved their way through the mountains eons ago. Just east of Whitefish is the Hungry Horse Dam, where elevators carry visitors far below the water line. Helena, the capital of Montana, is the seat of the Montana Historical Society, which operates a museum devoted to the history of the region and a gallery exhibiting the works of such Western artists as Frederic Remington. To the south of Helena at Butte the visitor can tour the huge open-pit Berkeley copper mine of the Anaconda Company. Farther south is Big Hole National Battlefield, the scene of a historic battle between the U.S. Army and Chief Joseph of the Nez Percé Indians in August of 1877.

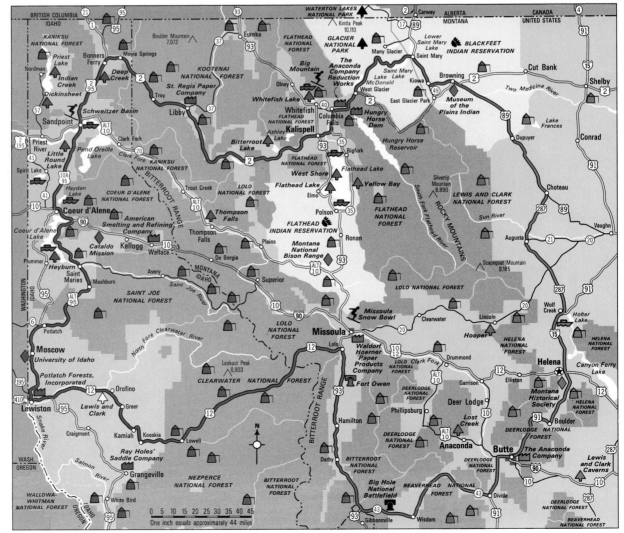

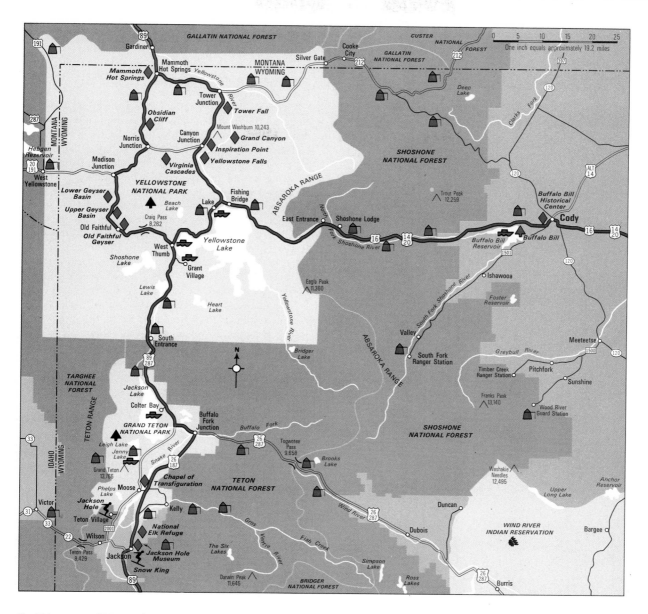

2. Western Wyoming

The rugged natural beauty and the unusual geological formations in the forests and mountains of western Wyoming provide an unsurpassed setting for two of the nation's most popular national parks, Yellowstone and Grand Teton. Yellowstone, the oldest and largest U.S. national park, abounds in geysers and hot springs of such size and variety that the early explorers who described them were called liars. Most of these attractions are within easy hiking distance of the 143-mile Grand Loop Road. At Mammoth Hot Springs, near the north entrance to the park, terraced springs rise in great tiers of limestone, laid down by the flowing hot mineral water and tinted by algae.

The Upper and Lower Geyser Basins contain most of the park's nearly 200 geysers, the largest concentration in the world. There steaming springs, bubbling mud pools and gushing geysers turn the landscape into a steaming cauldron once described as "the lid of Hades, and it ain't clamped down very tight either." Old Faithful, though not on schedule to the minute, can still be counted on to thrill spectators with its 100-to-185-foot spurts at intervals of from 35 to 95 minutes. Near Canyon Junction, Inspiration Point overlooks an impressive stretch of the Yellowstone River as it cuts its 25-mile-long gash between brightly tinted red-and-yellow rock walls as high as 1,200 feet.

Only a few miles south of Yellowstone, the jagged peaks and cool, green valleys of Grand Teton National Park offer a sharp contrast to this land of steamy beauty. Dominating the park is the Teton Range, perennially snow-capped mountains that rise sharply for more than a mile from the flat valley floor, itself at an altitude of about 6,000 feet. Like Yellowstone, Grand Teton provides a wealth of activities for hikers and campers, and there is even a school for mountain climbers. During the winter, horse-drawn sleds at the National Elk Refuge carry visitors to view the 7,000-to-9,000-animal herd.

East of the parks is the town of Cody, where the Buffalo Bill Historical Center displays Buffalo Bill's guns and personal effects, his boyhood home moved there from Iowa, and memorabilia from his popular Wild West Show. Cody's Whitney Gallery of Western Art, part of the center, contains paintings by the Western artists Frederic Remington and Charles Russell (*see page 99*).

175

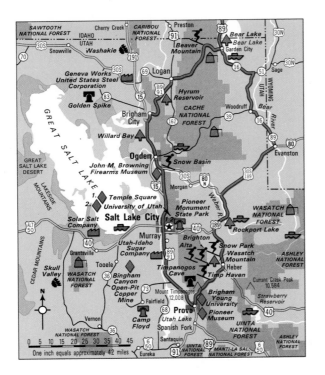

3. Central Utah

Central Utah offers a variety of interesting sites, all within driving distance of Salt Lake City, the state capital. Located on the southeast shore of the Great Salt Lake, the city is the world center of the Mormon religion. The famous Temple Square, with its six-spired Mormon Temple and its domed Tabernacle auditorium, is in the heart of the community. This city is also the home of the University of Utah, and near the campus is Pioneer Monument State Park, marking the spot from where Brigham Young first viewed Salt Lake valley.

North from Salt Lake City, near Ogden, is the John M. Browning Firearms Museum, which has a good weapons display. The Snow Basin, also near Ogden, is an excellent ski area. West of Brigham City, at Promontory, is the Golden Spike National Monument, commemorating the driving of the final spike in the nation's first transcontinental railway in 1869. Bear Lake, near the Idaho border, is a popular recreational area offering camping, fishing and swimming. Ski resorts such as Brighton and Alta lie to the south of Bear Lake. West of these resorts is the Bingham Canyon open-pit copper mine—the world's largest man-made excavation. The mine, two miles across and half a mile deep, is open to visitors.

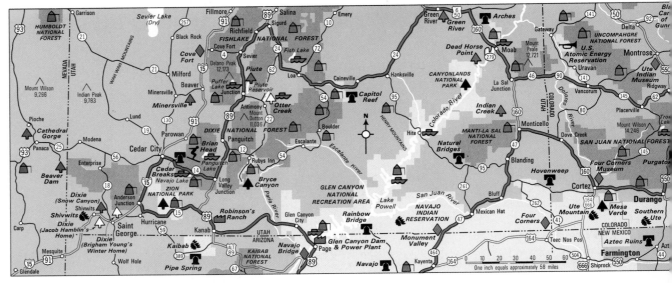

4. Southern Utah and environs

The landscape of southern Utah and of the surrounding portions of the other Mountain States is endowed with stark beauty. The arid land abounds in broad mesas and deep canyons tinted with an infinite variety of color.

In southwestern Utah, narrow roads wind through Zion National Park along great gorges lined with walls of rock that rise thousands of feet in layers of gray, yellow, brown, purple and scarlet, often topped with a band of glistening white. Some 35 miles east is Bryce Canyon, where erosion has left pinnacles of pink and white limestone described by the Paiute Indians as "red rocks standing like men in a bowl-shaped canyon." A short drive away near the border between Utah and Arizona colorful canyons branch out through Glen Canyon National Recreation Area. Here too, on the Colorado River, is Lake Powell, a man-made lake that will eventually stretch 186 miles northeast behind the Glen Canyon Dam.

To the east, in the southwestern corner of Colorado,

Mesa Verde contains the celebrated cliff dwellings built in the 11th to 14th Centuries by ancestors of the present Pueblo Indians. One site called Cliff Palace contains more than 200 rooms and probably housed about 400 people. North from Durango is the rich greenery of the San Juan National Forest. Nearly two million acres of forest provide an excellent setting for camping, and there is a spectacular background of 14,000-foot peaks, alpine lakes and waterfalls. In the winter, the slopes of the Purgatory ski area draw skiers from across the country.

The road winds westward across the Colorado Plateau to Moab, in Utah, near an entrance to one of the nation's newest national parks, Canyonlands. There rough but adequate dirt roads lead back into a huge region—parts of which are still unexplored—of multicolored canyons and grotesquely carved rock formations that were described by 19th Century geologist John Wesley Powell as "grandeur, glory and desolation . . . all merged into one."

5. Denver and the Central Rockies

Denver, the second largest city in the Mountain States according to 1967 estimates, not only offers the advantages of a major metropolitan center, with numerous parks and museums, but is also a good starting point for driving tours to many of the region's natural attractions and historic sites. In the city itself, *The Denver Post* offers a complete tour of its plant, from news room to engraving, printing and mailing divisions. At the Union stockyards visitors may watch livestock being auctioned off throughout the year, and in January they may attend the popular National Western Stock Show and Rodeo.

A few miles south lies the resort town of Colorado Springs, a pleasant community in the shadow of Pikes Peak. A cog railway and a tortuous but safe highway lead to the 14,110-foot summit for a magnificent view of the nearby mountains and distant plains. Deep in the mountains on Route 91 west of Colorado Springs is Leadville, where amid new houses the nearly century-old Healy House stands as a reminder of the opulent past when mining fortunes were easily made and spent in this town. A 20th Century boom is apparent in nearby Aspen, where winter snows bring skiers by the thousands, and art and music festivals make the town an ideal summer retreat.

Starting at Leadville and driving north via Routes 91, 6, 40 and 34, the tourist passes through dramatic mountain country, with skiing everywhere. This stretch culminates in Rocky Mountain National Park, whose peaks reach altitudes higher than 13,000 feet; warm coats are necessary there even in midsummer. Occasional deer and elk are visible in the upland meadows of the park. Route 66 just outside the park leads east to Platteville, where the State Historical Society has reconstructed Fort Vasquez, founded in 1836 as a fur trading post and later used as a military base during the Indian wars.

To the north is Cheyenne, capital of Wyoming and once known as "Hell on Wheels." The town revives its frontier spirit during the last week of July for Frontier Days, one of the country's most exciting rodeos. At Laramie, a few miles west, the University of Wyoming offers a geological museum with numerous local fossils, rocks and minerals, and a herbarium that houses plants indigenous to the Mountain States. Northwest of Laramie the road winds through the forests of Medicine Bow National Forest to Rawlins, an oil-and-cow town in the middle of a barren plateau. There the Carbon County Museum exhibits artifacts of Mountain States Indians of former years.

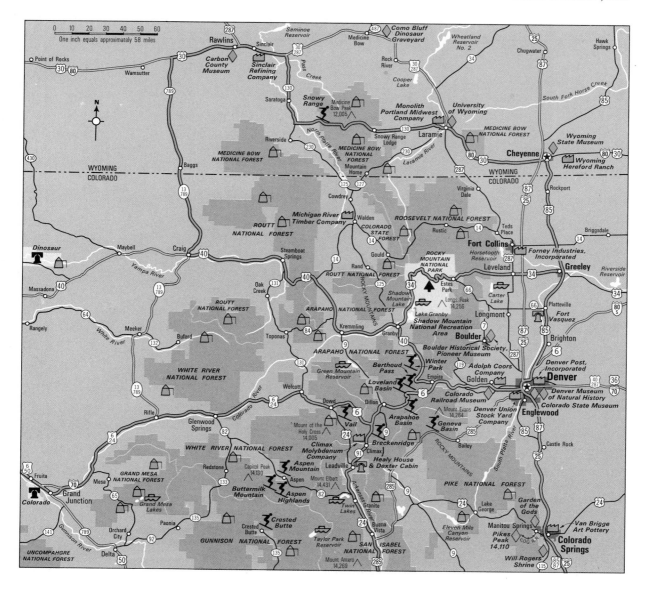

6. Lower Nevada and Arizona

At the northwest corner of this region lies Las Vegas, the nation's gambling center. Surrounded by desert on all sides, Las Vegas is a round-the-clock city of dice, cards, slot machines and roulette wheels. For those interested in the inner workings of the gambling industry, such casinos as the Mint in downtown Las Vegas offer tours, from the repair shops where the operation of slot machines is explained, to counting rooms where the day's earnings are tallied.

East of Las Vegas, on the Nevada-Arizona border, is gigantic Hoover Dam, one of the highest in the Western Hemisphere. Farther east is the spectacular mile-deep Grand Canyon. Accommodations ranging from modern hotels and motels to campgrounds are available, and bus tours, as well as mule and horseback trips along the canyon's rim, can be arranged for those who want to see this natural phenomenon up close.

South of the Grand Canyon, the town of Flagstaff contains the Museum of Northern Arizona where much of the art and culture of the region's early residents has been preserved. Just north of Flagstaff lies Sunset Crater that juts 1,000 feet above the surrounding lava fields, meadows and pine forests. It is thought that the crater was formed by a volcanic eruption, which occurred long before the white man arrived, and which buried many

Indian pueblos in the area. An easy drive to the south is Meteor Crater, which is about a mile in diameter, and is thought by some geologists to have been caused by a falling meteor some 50,000 years ago.

East along Route 40 is the Petrified Forest National Park. Here are great trees, believed to be 150 million years old, that were submerged by streams and rivers laden with minerals from the mountains. Slowly these minerals took the place of trees, duplicating them in stone. Southwest of the park at Roosevelt is the Tonto National Monument where the visitor can inspect two cliff dwellings built in the 14th Century by Pueblo Indians.

Near the Tonto National Monument in Miami is the Inspiration Consolidated Copper Company that offers a firsthand view of mining in Arizona. For those interested in the history and science of this booming industry, Phoenix, the capital of Arizona, offers two excellent museums, the Heard and the Arizona Mineral. Visitors to Phoenix can also tour Phoenix Newspapers, Inc., publishers of the state's largest daily paper.

North of Phoenix, in the Coconino National Forest, stands Montezuma Castle, one of the well-preserved prehistoric cliff dwellings. Nearby, at Tuzigoot National Monument, there are the remains of an ancient pueblo that was inhabited by Indians during the 13th Century.

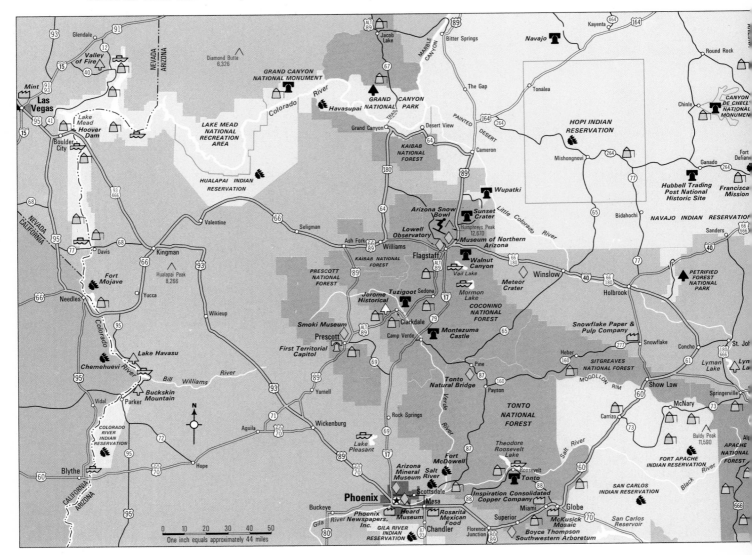

7. The heart of New Mexico

New Mexico offers the visitor a wealth of spectacular contrasts; from towering, snow-capped mountains to alabaster-white deserts; from ancient sites rich in Spanish-American history to space-age laboratories.

Entering from the west the visitor can see the crumbling ruins of an 18th Century church at Zuni Pueblo. Farther east lies El Morro National Monument, built around Inscription Rock. On this rock hundreds of explorers, among them Governor Oñate, the first colonizer of New Mexico, signed their names. And just past El Morro is the Perpetual Ice Cave, a volcanic sinkhole with crevices that are always packed with blue ice. East of the ice cave is Acoma Pueblo, one of the oldest continuously inhabited villages in the U.S., whose residents are renowned for their excellent pottery (see page 85).

Albuquerque, the home of the University of New Mexico, also contains the Church of San Felipe de Neri which, according to local records, has had services on every Sunday since Father Manuel Moreño opened the church in 1706. Albuquerque is rich in industry, and such companies as Eberline Instrument offer guided tours of their plants. South of Albuquerque, in Socorro, seat of the New Mexico Institute of Mining and Technology, is the Church of San Miguel, an excellent example of early Spanish-Indian mission architecture.

Traveling northeast from Socorro the visitor can inspect the Abo, Quarai and Gran Quivira ruins near the town of Mountainair.

Farther north, in Santa Fe, the tradition-steeped capital of New Mexico, the visitor can see one of the oldest houses in the U.S., purchase fine pottery from Indian artisans and tour the elegant Palace of the Governors, reputedly erected by the Spanish in 1609. The palace now houses the Museum of New Mexico with a fascinating collection of the art and culture of historic New Mexico. East of Santa Fe stands historic Fort Union where the great Apache chief Geronimo and outlaw Billy the Kid are said to have been imprisoned.

In the northeast corner of the area, near Taos, is the St. Francis of Assisi Mission, a fortresslike adobe building originally constructed about 1730, while nearby Taos Ski Valley is readily accessible to the sportsman. And at Taos Pueblo, the traveler can visit a mission erected in 1704 and perhaps witness the ritualistic Indian dances performed by descendants of the original pueblo dwellers. Southwest of this historic pueblo lies one of the nation's newer cities, Los Alamos, a frontier of nuclear-age activity. Daily the Los Alamos Scientific Laboratory presents programs dealing with the past, present and possible future of man's struggle to harness the atom.

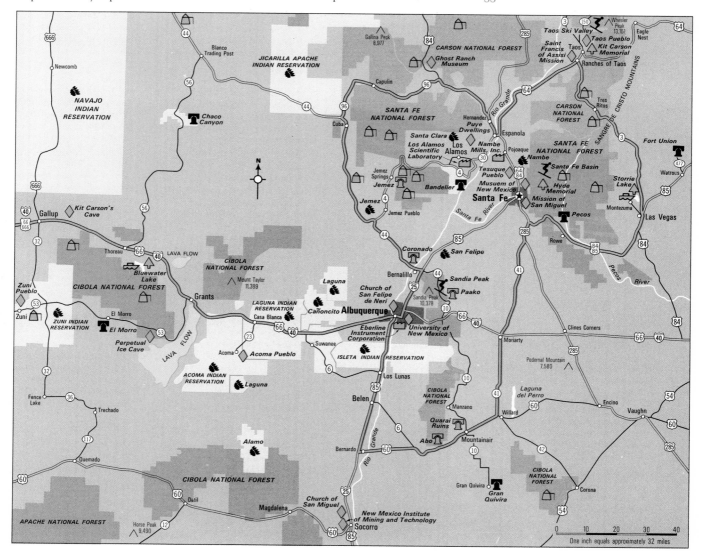

One inch equals approximately 32 miles

Museums and galleries

Arizona

Flagstaff
Museum of Northern Arizona, University of Northern Arizona. Regional anthropology, geology, biology. Mar 1-Dec 24: Mon-Sat 9-12, 1-5; Sun 1:30-5; June-Aug: Mon-Fri 9-5.

Phoenix
Arizona Mineral Museum, State Fairgrounds. Regional minerals and ores; fossil and rock collection. Mon-Fri 9-4:30; Sat 9-12.

The Heard Museum of Anthropology and Primitive Art, 22 E. Monte Vista Rd. Exhibits on primitive cultures of Africa, Asia, North America and Oceania. Tues-Sat 10-5; Sun 1-5.

Phoenix Art Museum, 1625 N. Central Ave. Fine general collection. Tues-Sat 10-5; Sun 1-5.

Tempe
Arizona State University Collection of American Art, Matthews Library. Most schools and periods of American painting. Mon-Sat 9-5; Sun 2-5.

Tombstone
Tombstone Courthouse Historical Monument, 219 Toughnut St. Memorabilia of the town "too tough to die" displayed in original courthouse. Daily 9-5.

Tucson
Arizona State Museum, University of Arizona. Extensive mineral and geological displays; Indian arts and crafts. Mon-Sat 9-5; Sun 2-5.

Yuma
Yuma Territorial Prison State Historical Museum, Prison Hill. Unusual presentation of early Arizona penal life. Daily 8-5:30.

Colorado

Boulder
University of Colorado Museum, Broadway. Natural history museum and art gallery. Mon-Sat 8-5; Sun, hols 2-5.

Colorado Springs
Cheyenne Mountain Zoological Park, Cheyenne Mountain. Natural history museum, zoo, aviary. Summer: daily 8-6; winter: daily 9-5.

Colorado Springs Fine Arts Center and Taylor Museum, 30 W. Dale St. General collection plus outstanding Spanish-American and Southwest Indian arts and crafts. Mon-Sat 9-5; Sun 1:30-5.

Denver
Colorado State Historical Museum, E. 14th Ave. Comprehensive state history collection. Mon-Fri 9-5; Sat, Sun, hols 10-5.

Denver Museum of Natural History, City Park. Excellent exhibits of prehistoric man and beast in natural surroundings. Summer: Mon-Sat 9-5; winter: Mon-Sat 10-4:30; all year: Sun, hols 12-5.

Evergreen
Hagans Clock Manor Museum, Highways 68 and 74. One of the finest clock and watch collections. June-Oct: Tues-Sun 10-4.

Golden
Colorado Railroad Museum, 17555 W. 44th Ave. Extensive exhibits on early Colorado railroad history. Daily 9-sunset.

Mesa Verde National Park, Mesa Verde National Park Museum. Archaeological displays; cliff dweller artifacts. June 20-Labor Day: Daily 7:45-7:30; Labor Day-June: daily 8-5.

Idaho

Boise
The Boise Gallery of Art, Julia Davis Park. General collection emphasizing Western artists. Daily 1-5.

Idaho State Museum, 610 N. Julia Davis Dr. History of Idaho and Pacific Northwest. Tues-Fri 9-5; Sat, Sun, hols 1-5.

Lapwai
Spalding Museum. Art and culture of Nez Percé Indians. Times vary.

Pocatello
Idaho State University Museum, University Library Building. Regional natural history collections. Summer: daily 8-9; winter: daily 8-5.

Montana

Browning
Museum of the Plains Indian. Indian relics, crafts, dioramas. Daily 9-5.

Butte
Montana College of Mineral Science and Technology, W.

Park St. Mineralogy and geology past and present. Daily 8-5.

Crow Agency
Custer Battlefield National Monument. Relics and dioramas associated with Custer and Little Big Horn. Summer: daily 8-5; winter: daily 9-5.

Great Falls
C. M. Russell Gallery, 1201 Fourth Ave. N. Painting and sculpture of Western artists in Russell's original studio. Sept-June: daily 2-4; June-Aug: Mon-Sat 10-4; Sun 1-4.

Helena
Montana Historical Society, Capitol Complex. Excellent collection of Western art and state historical items. May 1-Labor Day: daily 8-8; Labor Day-May 1: Mon-Fri 8-5; Sat, Sun 1-5.

Nevada

Carson City
Nevada State Museum, N. Carson St. Natural science museum and mint room with late 1800s equipment; replica of underground silver and gold mine. Mon-Fri 8:30-4:30; Sun, hols 10-4:30.

Las Vegas
Desert Research Institute Museum, Nevada Southern University, Maryland Parkway. Natural science museum of the Great Basin Region; Indian artifacts, mining items, aquarium. Mon-Fri 9-4:30; Sat, Sun 1-4:30.

Overton
Pueblo de Grande Lost City Museum of Archaeology, Nevada Highway 12. Artifacts from ancient Pueblo cultures. Daily 9-5.

New Mexico

Abiquiu
Ghost Ranch Museum. Natural history and forestry museums. Daily 8-5.

Albuquerque
Museum of Anthropology, University of New Mexico. Fine collections of indigenous cultures of Southwest. Tues-Sat 9-4.

Los Alamos
Los Alamos Scientific Laboratory Museum. Historical documents and devices associated with atomic age. Mon-Fri 8-12, 1-5; Sat 9-5; Sun 1-5.

Roswell
Roswell Museum and Art Center, 11th and Main Sts. Southwestern art; Robert H. Goddard rocket collection. Mon-Sat 10-12, 1-5; Sun, hols 1-5.

Sante Fe
Museum of Navajo Ceremonial Art, Camino Lejo. Archives, graphics, ceremonial objects. May 15-Sept 15: Mon-Sat 9-5; Sun, hols 2-5.

Museum of New Mexico, Central Town Square. In the square are the Palace of Governors (archaeology, ethnology, history of New Mexico); Fine Arts Museum (regional art of the Southwest); Museum of International Folk Art (1½ miles south of square) (folk art from around the world). May 15-Sept 15: Mon-Sat 9-5; Sun, hols 2-5.

Taos
Kit Carson Home and Museum, E. Kit Carson Ave. Personal articles of early American frontiersman; regional history displays. Summer: daily 7-6; winter: daily 8-12, 1-5.

Utah

Jensen
Dinosaur National Monument, Quarry Visitor Center. "In place" fossil exhibits; explanatory displays of varied fossils. June-Aug: daily 7-7; Sept-May: daily 8-5.

Logan
Utah State University, Man and His Bread Museum, 10th N. and 11th E. Traces growth and processing of grain to edible product; agricultural implements. Mon-Fri 8-5.

Salt Lake City
Pioneer Memorial Museum, 300 N. Main St. State pioneer articles; Indian artifacts. Mon-Sat 9-5; Apr-Sept: Sun 9-5.

University of Utah, Utah Museum of Fine Arts, Second S. and University Sts. Painting, sculpture, furniture. Mon-Fri 9-4; Sun 2-5.

Utah Pioneer Village, 2998 Conner St. Re-created pioneer town with period furnishings. Apr 1-Oct 31: Mon-Fri 9-5; Sun 1-5.

Vernal
Utah Museum of Natural History, 235 E. Main. State industry and natural history. May 15-Sept 30: daily 8-9; Oct 1-May 15: daily 9-6.

Wyoming

Big Horn
Bradford Brinton Memorial Ranch, Quarter Circle A Ranch. Early 20th Century working ranch, pioneer art and Indian relics. May 1-Sept 1: daily 8-6.

Cheyenne
Wyoming State Museum, Capitol Complex. Wyoming and Western history. Winter: daily 9-5; summer: daily 9-8.

Cody
Buffalo Bill Historical Center, Buffalo Bill Museum, 720 Sheridan Ave. Memorabilia of famed Indian scout; Plains Indian collection. May: daily 8-5; June 1-Sept 1: daily 7-10; Sept: daily 8-5.

Fort Laramie
Fort Laramie National Historic Site. Restored military outpost. Daily 9-5; summer evening programs.

Laramie
University of Wyoming Geological Museum, Geology Hall. Fossils, rocks, prehistoric displays. Mon-Fri 9-5.

Moose
Grand Teton National Park Museums and Visitor Centers. Exhibits on early fur trade, local geology and Western history. Hours vary with museums.

Yellowstone Park
Yellowstone National Park, Visitor Centers. Regional history and park natural history. All centers: June 1-Aug 31: daily 8-5; evening programs.

Local festivals and events

Arizona

Parada del Sol Rodeo, Scottsdale. All-Arabian horse show; parade. Feb.

Fiesta de los Vaqueros, Tucson. World's longest all-horse-drawn parade. Third week in Feb.

Annual National Indian Arts Exhibition, Scottsdale. Mar.

Rodeo of Rodeos, Phoenix. Best riders and ropers from U.S. and Canada. Mar.

Fiesta de Mayo, Nogales. Celebration of French defeat by outnumbered Mexican forces in 1862; bull fight, parade. Statewide. May 5.

Hopi Indian Dances, Hopi Indian Reservation. Ceremonial dances in such villages as Polacca, Shongopovi and Walip. Weekends, late Aug.

Historic Brewery Gulch Days, Bisbee. Contest in mining skills; celebration. Sept.

Mexican Independence Day, Statewide. Fiestas, especially big in Tucson and Phoenix. Sept. 16.

Colorado

National Western Stock Show, Denver. Nine days starting second Friday in Jan.

Winterskol Carnival, Aspen. Skiing and winter sports; entertainment. Three days, mid-Jan.

Arkansas River Boat Race, Salida to Cotopaxi. International competition for whitewater honors. Mid-June.

Pikes Peak Auto Hill Climb, Manitou Springs. Automobile race to summit and back. Late June.

Central City Opera and Drama Festival, Central City. Two major operas, last week June—July. Broadway play, Aug.

Pikes Peak or Bust Rodeo, Colorado Springs. Spencer Penrose Stadium. First week in Aug.

Navajo Trail Fiesta, Durango. Rodeo, square dancing, parade. First weekend in Aug.

Little Britches Rodeo, Littleton. World's largest junior rodeo; national championships. Mid-Aug.

Aspen Music Festival, Aspen. Nationally known artists and symphony orchestra performing in tent amphitheater and opera house. Annual, summer.

Idaho

Sun Valley Ski Club reunion Festival, Sun Valley. Skiing competitions by world renowned skiers. Mid-Jan.

Idaho Craft Show, Boise. Arts and crafts by Idaho citizens. June.

Snake River Stampede, Nampa. Rodeo. Mid-July.

Annual Loggers Celebration, Priest River. Logging contests and festivities. Third week in July.

Basque Festival, Boise. Annual celebration by largest Basque colony in North America. First week in Aug.

Western Idaho State Fair, Boise. Stock judging, rodeo, dances. Last week in Aug.

Eastern Idaho State Fair, Blackfoot. Indian exhibits, dances, horse races. Early Sept.

Montana

Vigilante Parade, Helena. Pageant of Montana History. First Friday in May.

Annual Bucking Horse Sale, Miles City. Rodeo cowboys ride wild bucking horses for sale to rodeos. Third weekend in May.

Virginia City Playhouse, Virginia City. 19th Century dramas nightly. June—Labor Day.

Wild Horse Stampede, Wolf Point. Rodeo, parade, local celebrations. Early July.

North American Indian Days, Browning. Blackfoot dances and ceremonial. Third week in July.

Last Chance Stampede, Helena. Rodeo and parade. First weekend in Aug.

Nevada

Helldorado, Las Vegas. Rodeos, parades, beard-growing contests and burro races. Re-enactment of Old West. Third weekend in May.

Reno Rodeo, Reno. One of best professional rodeos in West. Late June.

Basque Festival, Elko. Celebration based on sports and customs from Pyrenees. Contests include woodchopping, stone throwing, weight lifting; folk dances in native costume. First week in July.

Pony Express Days, Ely. Horse races and pari-mutuel betting. Western dress, street dances and barbecues. Last two weeks in Aug.

Nevada Rodeo, Zucca. Oldest rodeo in Nevada; features semi-professional riders. First week in Sept.

National Championship Air Races, Reno-Stead Airport, Reno. All sizes of propeller-driven planes plus aerobatic contests. Entrants are top pilots throughout country. Late Sept.

New Mexico

Teddy Roosevelt Rough Riders and Cowboys Reunion, Las Vegas. Oldest regular rodeo in Southwest. Mid-June.

New Mexico Arts and Crafts Fair, Albuquerque. Exhibits representing Spanish, Indian and other cultures. Late June.

Intertribal Indian Ceremonial, Gallup. Lyon Memorial Park. Largest Indian event in nation. Tribes from U.S. and Mexico perform ceremonial dances and present arts and crafts show. Four days starting second Thursday in Aug.

Fiesta, Santa Fe. Oldest community celebration in the U.S.; commemorates reconquest of New Mexico by Spanish Conquistadores in 18th Century. Labor Day weekend, beginning Friday.

Utah

Annual Utah Winter Carnival, Statewide. Winter sports competitions and entertainment. Feb.

Annual Friendship Cruise, Green River. All sized boats cruise Green and Colorado Rivers 180 miles to Moab. Late May.

Annual Shakespearean Drama Festival, Cedar City. Three plays presented in nightly rotation. Amateur cast. Elizabethan music played between acts. Early July.

Pioneer Days, Statewide. Commemoration of Mormon entry into Valley of the Great Salt Lake. Rodeos, parade. July 24.

Annual Timpanogos Hike, Aspen Grove. Thousands attempt hike to top of 12,000 ft. Mt. Timpanogos. Mid-July.

Annual Cache Valley Threshing Bee, College Ward (four miles west of Logan). Competition of late 1800s grain harvesting machinery. Early Sept.

Wyoming

All American Cutter Races, Jackson. National championships. Three days in late Feb.

Fine Arts Festival, Jackson. Music and arts festival. June—Aug.

Green River Rendezvous, Pinedale. Re-creation of early fur trapping; bartering and celebrations. Second Sunday in July.

Frontier Days, Cheyenne. Self-styled "Daddy of 'em all" Rodeo; parade and celebrations. Last week in July.

All-American Indian Days, Sheridan. Seventy Indian tribes participate in games, dancing, arts and crafts; election of Miss Indian America. First week in Aug.

Wildlife of the Mountain States

The Mountain States, with their wide variety of terrain, are the home of many forms of wildlife. The numerous isolated sections in this region, including 38 national wildlife refuges, contribute to the preservation of species such as the bison and the trumpeter swan. Examples of the wildlife of the eight states appear on these pages, with both their common and scientific names. A number of useful specialized reference books on wildlife are listed on page 188.

Mammals

Desert shrew

The insect-eating *Notiosorex crawfordi* is a small, silver-gray, rodentlike mammal. It is at home in both desert and rangeland, and can be found in the Southwest.

Yellow-bellied marmot

Often called a rock chuck, *Marmota flaviventris* is one of the largest rodents in the Mountain States. It has a characteristic piercing whistle, and burrows for safety.

White-tailed prairie dog

This prairie dog *(Cynomys gunnisoni)* lives in small colonies in highland meadows. Its diet of grasses, roots and barks is augmented by worms and beetles.

Kaibab squirrel

Sciurus aberti lives in ponderosa pine forests in the Grand Canyon of northern Arizona. It has a chestnut-brown back, deep gray sides and sports a white tail.

Western jumping mouse

Found in areas with abundant ground cover, this small mouse *(Zapus princeps)* has strong hind legs for leaping, kangaroo-style, and a long tail for balance.

Red fox

The red fox *(Vulpes fulva)* looks like a small collie and has a distinguishing white tail tip. An inhabitant of dry uplands, it favors a diet of rabbits and hares.

Gray wolf

Resembling a large shepherd dog, *Canus lupis* is a cunning, vicious —and much-hunted—carnivore that is retreating to more remote areas of the Mountain States.

Grizzly bear

Ursus horribilis is the largest carnivore in the Mountain States and can be very dangerous to man. Grizzlies usually live in isolated mountain areas of national parks.

Ringtail

This omniverous catlike mammal *(Bassariscus astutus)* ranges from Arizona to Utah under a variety of names—cat squirrel, American civet cat, mountain cat.

Coati

The long-snouted *Nasua narica* is comfortable on the ground, in trees and in water. Found in the Southwest, it is omnivorous but shows a preference for lizards.

Black-footed ferret

This rare mammal *(Mustela negripes)*, protected by law in New Mexico, has nocturnal habits. It is shaped like a weasel, and its coat is predominantly a buff yellow.

Mountain lion

A source of legends, *Felis concolor* has a number of aliases: cougar, puma, panther. A carnivore, it lives in mountains and woodlands and may weigh 200 pounds.

Moose

Pronghorn

Bison

Bighorn sheep

Alces alces is the largest member of the deer family in the United States, reaching 10 feet in length and weighing 1,400 pounds. The bulls' antlers are prized by hunters.

The pronghorn *(Antilocarpa americana)*, which uses its speed to outrun predators, is peculiar to North America. It is found throughout the Mountain States.

Once numbering in the millions, *Bison bison* was killed by man until in 1889 there were only 541 left. Now protected by law, the bison number more than 10,000.

The agile Bighorn *(Ovis canadensis)*, which may attain a weight of 320 pounds, lives in mountains, where it can escape enemies by leaping from crag to crag.

Fish and reptiles

Kokanee salmon

Rainbow trout

Rocky Mountain whitefish

Montana grayling

Onchorhynchus nerka kennerlyi is a small landlocked member of the salmon family. It is a bright silver-blue except during mating season, when it becomes spotted.

Also known as the steelhead, *Salmo gairdnerii* is a game fish that thrives in lakes, streams, rivers and creeks. Rainbows commonly weigh eight pounds.

Prosopium williamsoni is a game fish that prefers clear waters and lives in both cold, shallow streams and deep mountain lakes. It is dark blue with a silver belly.

An inhabitant of clear cold streams, *Thymallus signifer tricolor* is a brightly hued fish; its body is purplish-gray and silver, its head blue and bronze.

Green sunfish

Squawfish

Chuckwalla

Gila monster

This sunfish *(Leopmis cyanellus)* has a variety of common names, including blue bass and little red-eye. It prefers sluggish creeks and other small bodies of water.

Abundant in Montana and Idaho, the *Ptychocheilus oregonensis* may grow to a length of four feet. It is also known as the yellowbelly and the big-mouth.

The chuckwalla lizard *(Sauromalus obesus)* is a rock-dweller found in deserts. When disturbed, it will gulp air to bloat its body and wedge itself firmly into a crevice.

This lizard *(Heloderma suspectum)* is black with pink, orange or yellow. Although it is one of the two known venomous lizards, it is not considered dangerous.

Desert spiny lizard

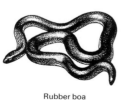

Rubber boa

Western ground snake

Sidewinder

Sceloporus magister is a light-colored lizard with a distinguishing black wedge-shaped mark on each side of its neck. It inhabits arid and semiarid regions.

The rubber boa *(Charina bottae)* is sometimes called the "two-headed snake," since its head and tail are shaped alike. Nonvenomous, it kills its prey by crushing them.

Sonora semiannulata, a small snake whose body markings vary according to locale, is a reptile found in deserts and semiarid regions. It feeds on insects.

This desert rattlesnake *(Crotalus cerastes)* is named for its odd tracks. Hunching along with only two points of its belly touching ground, it moves in S-shaped curves.

Birds

Trumpeter swan

Canada goose

Baldpate

Swainson's hawk

Found only in parts of Wyoming and Montana, this rare swan (*Cygnus buccinator*) has a distinguishing all-black bill. It is named for its loud, buglelike call.

The most common Mountain States goose, *Branta canadensis* has a characteristic white patch under its chin. It is the only goose that breeds in this region.

This duck (*Mareca americana*) is named for its shining white crown; it is distinguishable in flight by the white streaks on the front edges of its wings.

Buteo swainsoni has a hawk's broad wings and a broad, rounded tail. While gliding, it holds its wings above the horizontal, giving it a vulturelike appearance.

Bald eagle

Gambel's quail

California gull

Cactus wren

The rare and noble-looking *Haliaeetus leucocephalus* has a wingspread of up to seven feet and a snowy-white head and tail. It prefers to live near water.

This desert-dwelling quail (*Lophortyx gambeli*) can be found throughout the Southwest. Its russet crown and flanks give rise to its local name, "redhead."

One of the most common of the Western gulls, *Larus californicus* breeds on inland lakes. It is identifiable while in flight by its black underwing markings.

A rather large wren, *Heleodytes brunneicapillus couesi* inhabits the cactus-studded deserts of the Mountain States. It has a heavily spotted throat and breast.

Flowers and trees

Spanish bayonet yucca

Blue camas

Sego lily

Blue columbine

Yucca aloifolia has a base of daggerlike, bluish-green leaves; from this base, the stem rises as high as 15 feet. At the top is a cluster of cream-colored flowers.

Camassia quamash grows in wet meadows and bottomlands. Its flowers are bright blue, and its starchy bulbs have long been considered a delicacy by Indians.

The state flower of Utah, this lily grows throughout the Southwest. The bulbs of *Calochortus nuttallii* were an important part of the diet of early Mormon settlers.

This slender plant, also called the Rocky Mountain columbine, has large blue-and-white flowers. *Aquilegia coerulea* is the state flower of Colorado.

Prickly poppy

The orange-yellow *Argemone mexicana* flourishes in land that has been overgrazed by livestock. Its acid yellow juice has been used to treat skin diseases.

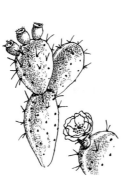

Prickly pear

A cactus that is found throughout Arizona, *Opuntia phaecantha* has a wine-colored, fleshy fruit that can be eaten by many desert animals.

Red heather

This small shrub, *Phyllodoce empetriformis*, has yellowish-green leaves and purplish-pink flowers that bloom in the summer. It usually grows on mountainsides.

Shootingstar

The shootingstar *(Dodecatheon pauciflorum)* is a perennial herb. It flourishes in the mountain meadows, and has a red stem and either rose or purple flowers.

Jacob's ladder

This plant is named for its leaf arrangement. *Polemonium pulcherrimum* grows in damp mountain areas and has a pale purple flower with a yellow "eye."

Indian paintbrush

The Indian paintbrush *(Castilleja miniata)* grows to a height of two to four feet in meadows and moist places. Its leaves have a bright orange or yellow color.

Rocky Mountain juniper

Juniperus scopulorum reaches a height of 40 feet; it has reddish-brown bark and bears bright blue fruit. Junipers are commonly seen scattered over dry, rocky ridges.

Tamarack

The tamarack *(Larix lyallii)* can be found along the north half of the Continental Divide. It can grow 50 feet high, but its slim trunk rarely exceeds 20 inches in diameter.

Blue spruce

Picea pungens has the small, thin, pointed needles typical of the spruce family. This cone-bearing tree may be 100 feet or more tall. It is used as a garden tree.

Piñon pine

Found throughout the Mountain States, this pine *(Pinus edulis)* bears seeds that are used as food by Indians and Mexicans. Its wood is valued for fuel and for fencing.

Ponderosa pine

Pinus ponderosa gets its name from its heavy wood, which is used in construction. Its trunk may grow as high as 230 feet and as thick as eight feet in diameter.

Quaking aspen

Found throughout the mountainous areas of this region, *Populus tremuloides* is a slender tree with pale bark. When the wind blows its leaves, they flutter or "quake."

Statistical information

State nickname, date of admission, capital

Arizona: Grand Canyon State; admitted 1912 (the 48th state); Phoenix.

Colorado: Centennial State; admitted 1876 (the 38th state); Denver.

Idaho: Gem State; admitted 1890 (the 43rd state); Boise.

Montana: Treasure State; admitted 1889 (the 41st state); Helena.

Nevada: Silver State; admitted 1864 (the 36th state); Carson City.

New Mexico: Land of Enchantment; admitted 1912 (the 47th state); Santa Fe.

Utah: Beehive State; admitted 1896 (the 45th state); Salt Lake City.

Wyoming: Equality State; admitted 1890 (the 44th state); Cheyenne.

Population

By state (U.S. Census, 1966 preliminary estimate):
Colorado: 1,977,000
Arizona: 1,618,000
New Mexico: 1,022,000
Utah: 1,008,000
Montana: 702,000
Idaho: 694,000
Nevada: 454,000
Wyoming: 329,000

By city (region's 10 largest cities are listed below, followed by their population according to the estimate of the *1967 Editor and Publisher Market Guide*):
Phoenix: 528,322
Denver: 505,002
Albuquerque: 261,546

Tucson: 244,187
Salt Lake City: 196,464
Las Vegas: 135,482
Pueblo: 109,691
Boise: 88,030
Colorado Springs: 87,852
Reno: 75,455

Land areas

Montana: 147,138 square miles.
New Mexico: 121,666 square miles.
Arizona: 113,909 square miles.
Nevada: 110,540 square miles.
Colorado: 104,247 square miles.
Wyoming: 97,914 square miles.
Utah: 84,914 square miles.
Idaho: 83,557 square miles.

Bodies of water

Principal lakes, including man-made ones

Great Salt Lake (Utah): 1,500 square miles; maximum depth 48 feet; natural.

Fort Peck (Montana): 383 square miles; maximum depth 220 feet; man-made.

Lake Mead (Nevada): 247 square miles; maximum depth 589 feet; man-made.

Yellowstone Lake (Wyoming): 137 square miles; maximum depth 300 feet; natural.

Bear Lake (Utah and Idaho): 136 square miles; maximum depth 30 feet; natural.

Pend Oreille (Idaho): 133 square miles; maximum depth 1,150 feet; natural.

Principal rivers (total lengths in miles)

Note: Only the states in the Mountain States region that these rivers flow through are named.

Rio Grande (Colorado, New Mexico): 1,885.

Arkansas (Colorado): 1,450.

Colorado (Utah, Colorado, Arizona): 1,360.

Snake (Wyoming, Idaho,): 1,038.

Pecos (New Mexico): 735.

Green River (Wyoming, Utah): 730.

Yellowstone (Wyoming, Montana): 671.

Gila (New Mexico, Arizona): 630.

North Platte (Colorado, Wyoming): 618.

Little Missouri (Wyoming): 560.

Humboldt (Nevada): 290.

Agricultural statistics (1964)

	Number of farms	Acreage (in millions)	Principal commodities
Arizona	6,477	40.6	Cattle, cotton lint, lettuce.
Colorado	29,797	38.3	Cattle, wheat, dairy products.
Idaho	29,661	15.3	Cattle, potatoes, wheat, dairy products.
Montana	27,020	65.8	Cattle, wheat, barley, dairy products.
Nevada	2,156	10.5	Cattle, dairy products, hay, sheep.
New Mexico	14,206	47.6	Cattle, cotton lint, dairy products.
Utah	15,759	13.0	Cattle, dairy products, turkeys.
Wyoming	9,038	36.2	Cattle, sheep, wool, sugar beets.

Minerals, petroleum and natural-gas production (1965)

	In millions of dollars	Principal minerals
Arizona	580.2	Copper, sand and gravel, molybdenum, cement.
Colorado	331.2	Petroleum, molybdenum, coal, sand and gravel.
Idaho	105.1	Silver, lead, zinc and phosphate rock.
Montana	229.4	Copper, petroleum, sand and gravel, phosphate rock.
Nevada	99.9	Copper, sand and gravel, iron ore.
New Mexico	773.3	Petroleum, potassium salts, natural gas, and copper.
Utah	431.4	Copper, petroleum, coal, molybdenum.
Wyoming	498.6	Petroleum, natural gas, iron ore, sodium salts.

Some U.S. superlatives

Colorado is the most mountainous state in the Union with 53 peaks over 14,000 feet and 300 peaks as high as 13,000 feet.

Lake Mead, created by a back-up of the Colorado River at Hoover Dam, is the nation's largest (by volume) man-made body of water.

Of the great American desert's nearly 500,000 square miles, about 75 per cent of the total is in the Mountain States.

Biggest open-pit mine in U.S. at Bingham Canyon, Arizona, belongs to Kennecott Copper Company.

About half the area of the Mountain States is federally owned, the highest percentage of any region in the U.S.

Pronunciation glossary

Albuquerque (AL bah kur kee). Largest city in New Mexico.
Berthoud (BURR thud). High pass in Colorado Rockies.
Boise (BOY zee). Largest city in Idaho.
Butte (BEAUT). Second largest city in Montana.
Coeur d'Alene (COOR dah lane). City, lake, and mountain range in Idaho.

Cheyenne (shy YANN). Capital of Wyoming.
Gila (HEE la). River in the Gila National Forest where the Gila cliff dwellings are preserved.
Gosiute (go SHOOT). One of the two lakes of the Eocene epoch in which shale oil beds were deposited.
Gros Ventre (grow VAHNT). Range in northwestern Wyoming

of Rocky Mountains.
Helena (HELL en nah). Capital of Montana.
Hovenweep (HOE ven weep). National monument of pre-Columbian ruins in southwestern Colorado.
Moab (MOE ab). City in Utah.
Mohave (mo HAH vee). County in Arizona containing parts of Grand Canyon and Hoover Dam.
Navajo (NAH vah hoe). Largest tribe of Indians in the U.S.

Oquirrh Mountains (OH kwer). Mountains in Utah rich in metals.
Phoenix (FEE nix). Largest city in Mountain States region.
Moroni (more OWN eye). The angel through whom God sent messages to his prophets.
Shoshone (show SHOW nee). River in Wyoming and Montana and tribe of Indians.
Taos (TAH os). Village in New Mexico.
Teton (TEE tun). Mountain range of the Rockies in Wyoming.

Credits and acknowledgments

Maps for front and back end papers by Jeppesen & Company, Denver, Colorado, and for pages 174 through 179 © by The H. M. Gousha Company, San Jose, California. Maps on pages 33, 37 and 77 by Lothar Roth.

The sources for the illustrations that appear in this book are shown below. Credits for the pictures from left to right are separated by commas, from top to bottom by dashes.
Cover—Josef Muench.
Front end papers—Drawings by John Rivera.
Chapter 1: 8—Fletcher Manley. 10 through 12—Map and drawings by Jerome Kuhl, map on page 10 adapted from U.S. Geological Survey, Department of the Interior. 14—Drawing by Rudolf Freund. 19—Frank Jensen. 20, 21—A. Y. Owen. 22, 23—A. Y. Owen, Bill Bridges. 24, 25—A. Y. Owen (2). 26, 27—A. Y. Owen, Marvin Newman. 28, 29—A. Y. Owen.
Chapter 2: 30—W. H. Jackson courtesy Denver Public Library Western Collection. 35—Denver Public Library Western Collection, Library State Historical Society of Colorado (3). 38—The Bettmann Archive (2). 39—Culver Pictures, Inc. 41—Denver Public Library Western Collection. 42—U.S. Geological Survey, courtesy The National Archives. 43—W. H. Jackson, courtesy Denver Public Library Western Collection. 44, 45—Library State Historical Society of Colorado, T. H. O'Sullivan (top) and W. H. Jackson, courtesy Denver Public Library Western Collection. 46, 47 —T. H. O'Sullivan, courtesy The James D. Horan Civil War and Western Americana Collection, W. H. Jackson, courtesy U.S. Geological Survey. 48—Haynes

Studios, Inc. (2). 49—W. H. Jackson, courtesy State Historical Society of Colorado.
Chapter 3: 50—Lawrence Schiller. 52—Map and drawing by Vic Kirishjian. 55—Drawings by Otto Van Eersel. 57—Drawing by Jerome Kuhl adapted from the Bureau of Reclamation, U.S. Department of the Interior. 58—Charts by James Alexander. 59—Drawing by Jerome Kuhl adapted from the U.S. Bureau of Reclamation, Department of the Interior. 61—A. Y. Owen. 62, 63—Monkmeyer Press Photo Service, Clyde Thomas. 64, 65—Lawrence Schiller. 66, 67—Joe Munroe. 68, 69—A. Y. Owen, Ralph Crane. 70, 71—Map and key by Jerome Kuhl. 72, 73—Ralph Crane, Bill Belknap from Rapho Guillumette.
Chapter 4: 74—Ken Heyman. 78, 79—Drawings by Otto Van Eersel. 80—Charts by James Alexander. 83 through 95 —Richard Noble.
Chapter 5: 96, 97—Ralph Crane. 99—The Thomas Gilcrease Institute of American History and Art, the Amon Carter Museum of Western Art. 103—Roger Appleton from Photo Researchers, Inc. 104 through 114—Maps by Gaetano di Palma. 104, 105 —Josef Muench, Ray Atkeson. 106—Bill Belknap from Rapho Guillumette. 107—John Lewis Stage. 108, 109—Ernst Haas, Tom Plofchan. 110—Carl Iwasaki. 111—Bob Walch. 112, 113—Eliot Elisofon. 114, 115 —Bob Walch, John Lewis Stage. 116, 117—John Lewis Stage (2).
Chapter 6: 118, 119—Ted Speigel from Rapho Guillumette. 121—Map by Lothar Roth adapted from Mining Guide, Industrial Atlas Corporation, 1967. 122—Denver Public Library Western Collection —Culver Pictures, Inc., Library State Historical Society of Colorado, W. H. Jackson for Denver Public Library Western Collection, Brown Brothers. 127 through 137—Evelyn Hofer.
Chapter 7: 138—Bill Bridges.

143—Culver Pictures, Inc. 147— John Lewis Stage. 148, 149— Carl Mydans, Howard Sochurek. 150, 151—Bill Bridges (2). 152, 153—John Launois from Black Star. 154, 155—James Drake for SPORTS ILLUSTRATED, Bill Bridges. 156, 157—Bill Bridges (2). 158 —Hansel Mieth and Otto Hagel. 160—Culver Pictures, Inc. 161 —Map by Lothar Roth adapted from U.S. Geological Survey and Land Management, Department of the Interior. 162—Drawing and map by Vic Kirishjian drawing adapted from Robert A. Reilly —U.S. Geological Survey. 165 —N. R. Farbman. 166, 167 —U.S. Forest Service (2). 168, 169—Carl Iwasaki, U.S. Forest Service. 170, 171—A. Y. Owen, Wayne Replogle. 172, 173—U.S. National Park Service. 182 through 185—Drawings by Rudolf Freund. Back end papers —Drawings by John Rivera.

The editors of this book wish to thank the following persons and institutions for their assistance: Tom Bahti, Tucson; Stanley Bartos, Bureau of Indian Affairs, Fort Wingate, New Mexico; Daniel B. Beard, Regional Director, U.S. Park Service, Santa Fe; Arthur B. Campbell, Branch Chief, U.S. Geological Survey, Denver; Helen Carlton, Evanston Public Library, Nevada; Walter Van Tilburg Clark, Reno; C. Gregory Crampton, Professor of History, University of Utah, Salt Lake City; David Crandall, Regional Director, Bureau of Reclamation, Salt Lake City; Arthur Cronquist, Senior Curator, New York Botanical Gardens, New York City; William C. Culbertson, U.S. Geological Survey, Denver; Dan Cushman, Great Falls; James Davis, Western History Collection, Denver Public Library; Palmer DeLong, Project Manager, Central Utah Project, Bureau of Reclamation, Provo; Frederick J. Dockstader, Director of the Museum of the American Indian, New York City; Mr. and Mrs. George Ely, Billings, Montana; Frank Forrester, Information Officer, U.S. Geological Survey,

Washington, D.C.; Jack Goodman, New York Times, Salt Lake City; James Harpster, Information Officer, Bureau of Reclamation, Denver; Grant Heath, Church Information Service (Mormon), Salt Lake City; Joseph Hessel, U.S. Forest Service, Denver; Kip Hinton, U.S. Forest Service, Denver; James W. Hulse, Professor of History, University of Nevada, Reno; Governor Robert E. Lewis, Zuni Pueblo; Martin A. Link, Director of Navajo Tribal Museum, Window Rock; Martin Litton, Sunset Magazine, Menlo Park, California; Corinne Locker, Association on American Indian Affairs, Inc., Santa Fe; Governor John A. Love of Colorado; Glen Lovejoy, Lake George, Colorado; Robert J. Magirl, United Pueblo Agency, Bureau of Indian Affairs, Albuquerque; Marvin E. Magnuson, U.S. Weather Bureau, Salt Lake City; Robert K. Measeles, Bureau of Indian Affairs, Albuquerque; James E. Miller, Chairman of Meteorology and Oceanography Department, New York University, New York City; Kay Pierson, State Historical Society of Colorado, Denver; Steven M. Poe, Bureau of Reclamation, Denver; Harold J. Prostka, U.S. Geological Survey, Denver; Joe C. Ray, Secretary of Acoma Pueblo; Mr. and Mrs. John Robertson, Twin Falls, Idaho; Mr. and Mrs. Henry Ruggeri, Moab, Utah; W. L. Rusho, Bureau of Reclamation, Salt Lake City; Governor Abel Sanchez of San Ildefonso Pueblo; Governor Syme Sanchez of Acoma Pueblo; J. D. Seery, Bureau of Reclamation, Montrose, Colorado; Henry Shipley, Salt River Project, Phoenix; Ben H. Slothower, Kennecott Copper Corporation, Salt Lake City; Harry Smedes, U.S. Geological Survey, Denver; J. Morgan Smith, U.S. Forest Service, Albuquerque; Mr. and Mrs. David Vhay, Reno; Joseph Watson, Bureau of Indian Affairs, Window Rock; William T. Williams, Bureau of Reclamation, Boulder City; Joseph A. Wraight, Chief Geographer, U.S. Coast and Geodetic Survey, Washington, D.C.

Bibliography

*Available also in paperback.
†Available only in paperback.

General and historical reading

Athearn, Robert G., *High Country Empire.* McGraw-Hill, 1960.

Beck, Warren, *New Mexico, A History of Four Centuries.* University of Oklahoma Press, 1962.

Billington, Ray A., *Westward Expansion.* Macmillan, 1960.

Bourne, Edward Gaylord, *Spain in America, 1450-1580.* Harper, 1904.

Cleland, Robert Glass, *This Reckless Breed of Men: The Trappers and Fur Traders of the Southwest.* Alfred A. Knopf, 1950.

De Voto, Bernard A., *Across the Wide Missouri.* Houghton Mifflin, 1947.
Editor, *Journals of Lewis and Clark.* Houghton Mifflin, 1953.

Hawgood, John A., *America's Western Frontiers.* Alfred A. Knopf, 1967.

Hollon, W. Eugene, *The Southwest Old and New.* Alfred A. Knopf, 1960.

Horgan, Paul, *Conquistadors in North American History.* Farrar Straus, 1963.

Hulse, James W., *The Nevada Adventure: A History.* University of Nevada Press, 1966.

Larson, T. A., *History of Wyoming.* University of Nebraska Press, 1965.

Paullin, Charles O., *Atlas of Historical Geography of the United States.* Carnegie Institution of Washington and American Geographical Society of New York, 1932.

Sprague, Marshall, *Great Gates: The Story of the Rocky Mountain Passes.* Little, Brown, 1964.

Van Every, Dale, *The Final Challenge: The American Frontier 1804-1845.* William Morrow, 1964.

Webb, Walter Prescott, *The Great Plains.* Ginn and Co., 1959.

Special topics

Atherton, Lewis, *The Cattle Kings.* Indiana University Press, 1961.

Bailey, L. R., *The Long Walk: A History of the Navajo Wars, 1846-1868.* Westernlore Press, 1964.

Barrows, Harold K., *Floods: Their Hydrology and Control.* McGraw-Hill, 1948.

Bartlett, Richard, *Great Surveys of the American West.* University of Oklahoma, 1962.

Brodie, Fawn M., *No Man Knows My History: The Life of Joseph Smith.* Alfred A. Knopf, 1963.

Caughey, John, *Gold is the Cornerstone.* University of California Press, 1948.

Clawson, Marion, and Burnell Held, *The Federal Lands.* Johns Hopkins Press, 1957.

Clawson, Marion, *Uncle Sam's Acres.* Dodd, Mead & Co., 1951.

Dale, E. E., *The Indians of the Southwest.* University of Oklahoma Press, 1949.

Dellenbaugh, Frederick, *A Canyon Voyage.* Yale University Press, rev. 1962.

Dobie, J. Frank, *The Longhorns.* Little, Brown, 1941.

Fletcher, Robert, *Free Grass to Fences: The Montana Cattle Range Story.* University Publishers, 1960.

Halacy, Daniel S., Jr., *The Water Crisis.* E. P. Dutton, 1966.

Hodge, Frederick Webb, *Handbook of American Indians North of Mexico,* 2 vols. Pageant Books, 1960.

Hollon, W. Eugene, *The Lost Pathfinder, Zebulon Montgomery Pike.* University of Oklahoma, 1949.

Horgan, Paul, *Great River: The Rio Grande in North American History.* Holt, Rinehart & Winston, rev. 1960.

Hundley, Norris, *Dividing the Waters: A Century of Controversy Between the United States and Mexico.* University of California Press, 1966.

Hyde, G. E., *Indians of the High Plains.* University of Oklahoma, 1966.

Kluckhorn, Clyde, and Dorothea Leighton, *The Navajo.* Harvard University Press, 1946.

Linn, William Alexander, *The Story of the Mormons.* Russell & Russell, 1963.

Mann, Dean E., *The Politics of Water in Arizona.* University of Arizona Press, 1963.

Meinzer, Oscar E., ed., *Hydrology.* McGraw-Hill, 1942.

Mullen, Robert, *The Latter-day Saints.* Doubleday, 1966.

Nadeau, Remi A., *The Water Seekers.* Doubleday, 1950.

Oppenheimer, Harold L., *Cowboy Arithmetic.* Interstate, 1962.

Powell, John Wesley, *Exploration of the Colorado River and its Canyons.* Dover, 1961.

Sonnichsen, Charles Leland, *Cowboys and Cattle Kings.* University of Oklahoma Press, 1950.

Sprague, Marshall, *Massacre: The Tragedy at White River.* Little, Brown, 1957.
Money Mountain. Little, Brown, 1953.

Stegner, Wallace, *The Gathering of Zion.* McGraw-Hill, 1964.

Thomas, Harold, *The Conservation of Ground Water.* McGraw-Hill, 1951.

Turner, Wallace, *The Mormon Establishment.* Houghton Mifflin, 1966.

Underhill, Ruth, *The Navajos.* University of Oklahoma Press, 1956.

Whalen, William J., *The Latter-day Saints in the Modern Day World.* John Day, 1964.

Williams, Albert, *The Water and the Power: the Development of the Fiver Great Rivers of the West.* Duell, Sloan & Pearce, 1951.

Wissler, Clark, *Indians of the United States.* Doubleday, 1966.

Wolle, Muriel S., *The Bonanza Trail.* Indiana University Press, 1953.

Natural setting and wildlife

America's Wonderlands. National Geographic Society, rev. 1966.

Armstrong, Margaret, *Field Book of Western Wild Flowers.* G. P. Putnam's Sons, 1915.

Atwood, Wallace W., *The Rocky Mountains.* Vanguard Press, 1945.

Beal, Merrill D., "Grand Canyon: The Story Behind the Scenery."† K.C. Publications, 1967.

Craighead, John J., and others, *A Field Guide to Rocky Mountain Wildflowers.* Houghton Mifflin, 1963.

Corle, Edwin, *The Gila, River of the Southwest.* Peter Smith, 1966.

Cunningham, Floyd F., *1001 Questions Answered About Water Resources.* Dodd, Mead & Co., 1967.

Fenneman, Nevin M., *Physiography of Western United States.* McGraw-Hill, 1931.

Fergusson, Harvey, *Rio Grande.* Morrow, 1955.

Finch, Vernor C., Glenn Trewartha and M. H. Shearer, *The Earth and Its Resources.* McGraw-Hill, 1948.

Frome, Michael, *Whose Woods These Are: The Story of the National Forests.* Doubleday, 1962.

Helfman, Elizabeth S., *Rivers and Watersheds in America's Future.* David McKay, 1965.

Holbrook, Stewart, *The Columbia River.* Holt, Rinehart & Winston,* 1965.

Hollon, W. Eugene, *The Great American Desert.* Oxford University Press, 1966.

Hundley, Norris Jr., *Dividing the Waters.* University of California Press, 1966.

Jaeger, Edmund C., *Desert Wild Flowers.* Stanford University Press, 1941.

King, Philip B., *The Evolution of North America.* Princeton University Press, 1959.

Leydet, François, *Time and the River Flowing: Grand Canyon.* Sierra Club, 1966.

Palmer, Ralph S., *The Mammal Guide.* Doubleday, 1954.

Peterson, Roger T., *A Field Guide to Western Birds.* Houghton Mifflin, rev. 1961.

Porter, Eliot, *The Place No One Knew: Glen Canyon on the Colorado.* Sierra Club, 1963.

Pough, Richard H., *Audubon Western Bird Guide.* Doubleday, 1957.

Powell, John Wesley, *Report on the Lands of the Arid Region of the United States,* ed. by Wallace Stegner. The Belknap Press of Harvard University Press, 1962.

Stebbins, Robert C., *A Field Guide to Western Reptiles and Amphibians.* Houghton Mifflin, 1966.

Guidebooks

Arizona Writers' Project, *Arizona: The Grand Canyon State.* Hastings House, 1956.

Colorado Writers' Project, *Colorado: A Guide to the Highest State.* Hastings House, 1941.

Fodor, Eugene, Robert C. Fisher and Barnett D. Laschever, eds., *Fodor Shell Travel Guides U.S.A.: Rockies and Plains.* David McKay, 1966.

Idaho Writers' Project, *Idaho.* Oxford University Press, 1950.

Montana Writers' Project, *Montana.* Viking, 1939.

Nevada Writers' Project, *Nevada: A Guide to the Silver State.* Binfords & Mort, 1940.

New Mexico Writers' Project, *New Mexico: A Guide to the Colorful State.* Hastings House, 1962.

Utah Writers' Project, *Utah.* Hastings House, 1954.

Wyoming Writers' Project, *Wyoming: A Guide to its History, Highways, and People.* Oxford University Press, 1941.

Index

Numerals in italics indicate an illustration of the subject mentioned.

The Mountain States: the works of man

Total area of the Mountain States is 863,887 square miles, constituting almost one fourth of the entire U.S. The region, however, is sparsely populated, with an average of fewer than 10 people per square mile; four of the states rank among the nation's 10 least populated.

The economy of the region is largely supported by the exploitation of such natural resources as timber, petroleum and minerals. The last is the most valuable of all. During the past century, the eight states have mined some $34 billion worth of metals, predominantly copper and silver. The region produces 70 per cent of the nation's uranium and most

of its molybdenum—minerals of enormous importance in the space age. Man has also made good use of the limited water in the area with huge hydroelectric plants and elaborate irrigation systems. In all of the eight states, cattle ranching has become the prime agricultural enterprise; some six million head of cattle are marketed there annually.

Historical monuments in the Mountain States usually commemorate the once-dominant Indian culture or the white settlers who supplanted it with their own. Cliff dwellings in Mesa Verde, Colorado, are the 1,000-year-old remnants of a vanished tribe. The white man's relics include mining-era ghost towns and frontier forts.

Scale of map: one inch to 128 miles

HUMBOLDT

PERSHING

WASHOE

Lovelock

Reno

CHURCHILL

Fallon

Carson City

ORMSBY

N

DOUGLAS

LYON

MINERAL